Ever,

9

Minutes

A Memoir

Christina Vitagliano

Printed in the United States of America by Bob John Chicken Federation LLC
April 2021

Composition and Editing by Polished Print - Stacey Kucharik.
Cover Illustration by Corey Marier

Copyright Song Lyrics:
Time To Change
Words and Music by Chris Welch, Billy Meshel and Raymond Bloodworth
Copyright (c) 1961 Sony/ATV Harmony
Copyright Renewed
All Rights Administered by Sony/ATV Music Publishing LLC, 424 Church Street, Suite 1200,
Nashville, TN 37219 International Copyright Secured   All Rights Reserved
Reprinted by Permission of Hal Leonard LLC

Unanswered Prayers
Words and Music by Pat Alger, Larry Bastian and Garth Brooks
Copyright (c) 1990 UNIVERSAL - POLYGRAM INTERNATIONAL PUBLISHING, INC., MAJOR BOB
MUSIC,
INC. and MID-SUMMER MUSIC, INC.
All Rights Reserved   Used by Permission
Reprinted by Permission of Hal Leonard LLC

Can't Keep It In
Words and Music by Cat Stevens
Copyright (c) 1972 Salafa Limited
Copyright Renewed
All Rights Administered by BMG Rights Management (US) LLC
All Rights Reserved   Used by Permission
Reprinted by permission of Hal Leonard LLC

Library of Congress Control Number: 2021908825

Publisher's Cataloging-in-Publication data

Names: Vitagliano, author.
Title: Every 9 Minutes: A Memoir, Christina Vitagliano.
Description: Las Vegas, NV. Christina Vitagliano, 2021.
Identifiers: ISBN 9781736971000 (pbk.) | 9781736971017 (ebook) | LCCN 2018954212
Subjects: Child Abuse - Memoir. |
Classification: LCC PS3613.C26545 B43 2018 | DCC 813.6--dc23

Dedication

To my husband, Patrick.

Your fearless and intense curiosity, led by near-extinct passionate devotion, broke through an emotional wall that I truly believed was unbreakable...thank you. You've taught me how to love. If it were not for you, I'd never dared to share my story.

To Debbie, Suzanne, and Heather. As a kid and to this day, our friendship will always be indescribably priceless to me. Thank you for being in my life. I love you.

For my honest and courageous group of friends, Shenna, Lana, Bobbi, Michelle, and Ken. I am infinitely grateful to all of you for enduring my *word-torture,* as you helped me edit a 211,000-word memoir, down to what I hope is readable.

This book is a memoir. It reflects my present recollections of experiences over time. Some names and characteristics have been changed, some events have been compressed, and some dialogue has been recreated. This is a book of memory, and memory has its own story to tell. But I have done my best to make it tell a truthful story.

Every 9 minutes

Child Protective Services substantiates,

or finds evidence for, a claim of child

sexual assault.

Chapter 1

"Christina, does your daddy ever hurt you?"

The man was way up in the air, sitting behind a desk as high as the sky, wearing a black cape and holding a hammer. I could feel myself fidgeting.

Mommy didn't tell me about these kinds of questions. Was I supposed to tell the truth? Was I supposed to say that my new daddy touched me in bad places? Or was I supposed to say what Mommy, the old lawyer guy in the suit, and Daddy had told me to say before we went to see the judge? Answering his questions was hard.

We'd gotten all dressed up, and the day had started out happy and fun. Mommy had said today was my special day, so I'd gotten to wear the outfit I wore for Easter, a pretty white ruffled dress, pink tights, and shiny black shoes.

When we'd first gotten to this place they called "court," we entered a room and sat at a large oval table with hard, bumpy leather chairs that made my legs cold. The walls were wood, with dark wooden shelves piled high with books.

I sat next to Mommy, and she'd said the lawyer guy was Mr. Morrison. He was like a giant compared to Mommy and Daddy. Mommy said Mr. Morrison was there to help us.

Once we'd settled at the table, Mommy smiled at me. Then she'd turned to Daddy and brushed a crumb off his shoulder. He nodded, smiled at her, and then smiled at me too. Daddy was all dressed up in his church suit, with his hair combed nice and neat. Mommy said he had salt-and-pepper hair, but I never saw him shaking any salt or pepper into it. Nana says Daddy looks like Jackie Gleason, whoever that is.

Mommy was dressed pretty in a dark-blue skirt and a white ruffled shirt that looked like Cool Whip, and her hair was done up for The Big Day. Mommy had gone to the hairdresser to have yellow frosting streaks put in her black hair and then wrapped it all the way up on top of her head. Mommy called it a beehive, but I didn't think there were any bees in it.

Mommy had told me this was the room we'd use to practice what to say to the judge.

Mr. Morrison had sat next to me and said, "We're going to help you answer questions the judge will ask. It's like practicing the answers, okay?"

"Okay," I answered.

Mr. Morrison had sucked on a pipe like Popeye's, but it didn't toot. He'd said they would ask questions like: Do you get along with your new brothers? Do you get enough to eat? What happens when you fight with your brothers? Does Mommy or Daddy yell at you? Do you miss living with Nana and Papa? And others that I forgot as soon as he said them.

Mommy had turned to me and said, "Christina, when we meet the judge, I want you to tell him all the good things about your new daddy, okay? That will make everyone happy."

I wanted to keep Mommy happy because she was always crying and yelling when we lived at Nana's.

"Okay, Mommy, I will," I said.

But now we weren't in the practice room. This was the real courtroom. And the man in the cape, the one they called the judge, didn't make this seem easy at all. Instead, it was scary. But I wanted to take care of this myself and not make anyone upset. If I answered all the questions right, my new last name would be the same as everyone else's. Mommy said I had to be adopted by Daddy because it would make us an official family, and everyone would be happy. She said some people might call him my stepdaddy, but I should always call him my daddy.

My new family would be me, Mommy, and my new daddy, who had three little boys, now my three brothers. Mommy and I used to live with Nana and Papa. Mommy said my old daddy— whom I can't remember—went away when I was just a baby. He was "a no-good," Mommy said, and he didn't want a baby in the house, so he left. She said other bad things about him too, but I didn't know what any of them meant.

Daddy's real name is Al. Mommy married Al on December 15, 1968, and us kids got to go to the wedding too. Daddy was also married before, but the lady he'd been married to died when Andy was born, and he was left to bring up three little boys all by himself, just like the guy from *My Three Sons* on TV. So now I had three new brothers, Danny, Zac, and Andy. Danny and Zac were both four years old, and Andy was three. Mommy called them Irish triplets.

If I got all these questions right, Mommy said our lives would be normal. She said people like normal families.

But something just didn't seem right about lying to that man in the black cape. Mommy taught me lying was wrong, but she also said my last name needed to change because it would cause problems in school. Everyone would pick on me because my name wasn't the same as my brothers'. My last name, DiMaggio, was hard to spell, but my new last name, French, was simple, so that was good enough for me. Christina Alina French.

I didn't think daddies were supposed to come into little girls' rooms at night and do things to them they couldn't do during the day when it was light out and other people were around. I didn't know if it was a rule, but it felt wrong inside.

I gazed around the room. Mr. Morrison was sitting in between Mommy and Daddy, and Mommy was smiling like today was the best day ever. Mr. Morrison was leaning back in his chair, sucking on his pipe, making smoky rings. They were all staring at me. Waiting.

Then Mr. Morrison spoke. "Christina, do you know when your birthday is?"

That one was easy.

"Yes, September 24, 1964. I'm four years old!"

I held up four fingers to show everyone.

"My, you're a big girl, and smart too!" Mr. Morrison said. He looked up at the judge and nodded.

The Judge cleared his throat like something big was caught in there.

Then he asked me again, "Christina, does your daddy ever hurt or touch you in private places?"

I looked out the window, swinging my legs back and forth, and then glanced back at those smoky rings.

I reminded myself that Mommy said if I told the judge we were happy, everything would be fine.

"Christina, answer the nice judge," Mommy said.

I remembered that Mommy said polite little girls call important men "sir."

I turned back to that scary judge and chose to lie.

"No, sir, Daddy is nice. He doesn't ever hurt me."

And Mommy was wrong, because things weren't fine after that.

Never, ever again.

***

It was a rainy Saturday in June. We had finished breakfast and were watching cartoons when Danny jumped up right in the middle of *Hong Kong Phooey*.

"I'm going to go clean the basement. Cartoons are for kids. I should be doing man stuff because I'm the oldest and I can do it all by myself," he said, leaving the room.

"Not me. I'm staying right here. *Captain Caveman* is on next!" Zac said.

Andy and I didn't bother to respond; we just kept watching the cartoon.

Danny was bigger than the rest of us, with a big round face and dark hair combed neatly and stuck to his head. He looked sort of like Captain Kangaroo, but bossy and mean. Danny scared me because he always made angry faces and he only got happy when he did bad things. Danny was a big jerk.

We watched the rest of *Hong Kong Phooey* and all of *Captain Caveman* before Danny came back.

"Hey, Mom, come see what a great job I did!" Danny exclaimed.

Danny didn't say "Mommy." He said only babies like me say "Mommy."

Danny and I were both born in 1964. His birthday was in January and mine was in September, so he wasn't really that much older than me.

Mommy and I followed Danny to the basement. Danny was right. The basement was Spic and Span clean! Everything had vanished, including my toys!

"Mommy, where are my toys that we brought from Nana's?" I asked.

"Danny, the basement is very clean, but where are Christina's toys?" Mommy asked.

He put his hands on his hips and motioned toward the back.

"Over there, so nobody trips on them."

We walked toward the back of the basement to find my toys pushed into the corner, smashed into a million pieces. He'd even stomped on my Romper Stompers and made them flat and punched a big hole in my Bozo the Clown blow-up punching doll. Someone should punch Danny! I started to cry.

"Mommy, why did he do that?"

"Danny, why did you break all of Christina's toys?" Mommy asked.

"Because they took up too much room, and someone was gonna get hurt."

Danny continued, "And besides, I'm the oldest, so I can decide how things get done."

I didn't understand. Mommy looked like she wanted to get mad at Danny, but then she didn't say anything at all. She just made us both go back upstairs.

Mommy later explained that before we moved in, it had just been Daddy and the boys in this house. And she said that Danny might've been upset because he didn't have as many toys.

"Daddy had three children in his family before we got here," Mommy stated. "Christina, remember, you were the only child living with Mommy, so you had more toys because Mommy just had to buy for you. Daddy had to spread all his money between Danny, Zac, and Andy."

This made me feel bad, and I understood. But I would never break somebody else's toys . . . and I still wanted to punch Danny in the face.

Later that night when I was in bed, I heard Mommy telling Daddy about what Danny had done. Mommy said it was wrong. Daddy said I shouldn't have so many toys anyway, so no sense in making a fuss. Mommy and Daddy started to argue. I decided not to ask Mommy too many questions about why Danny was so mean to me. I didn't want Mommy and Daddy fighting. I wished Daddy had a girl child, so I would have a sister to be my friend.

1969 — five years old

Chapter 2

Kindergarten started in a few weeks! I wasn't scared at all, plus Mommy said I would meet other girls too.

The people who lived on the third floor of our house were moving today, and Daddy said we'd get to watch!

"Hey, Dad, I'm going to help the movers. I can supervise because I'm the oldest," Danny said.

"What else is new," I whispered to Zac and Andy playing in the sand next to me.

They giggled.

"Christina, get outta the way so you don't get hurt," Dad said.

I ran against the house so I could still watch the movers. Daddy nodded okay.

I wasn't sure what happened next. Everything got kind of blurry. People were running all over the place. Daddy was carrying me around the yard, yelling about getting to the hospital, and there was blood all over me. Mommy was screaming.

"Al, the ambulance is taking too long to get here!" Mommy shouted.

Daddy wanted to drive, but our car had a flat tire. Daddy was yelling swear words while he put me into the car with the flat tire and made it go.

The next thing I remember, I was lying on a metal table. Things were blurry. I could hear Mommy, Daddy, and the doctor talking about me, but I couldn't really understand what they were saying.

"Mommy, what happened to me?" I asked.

"Everything's going to be okay, Christina, you just got a little cut on your head," she answered.

But my dress was covered in blood. I'd had little cuts before. Little cuts get Band-Aids. Little cuts didn't ruin my dresses and put me in the hospital.

This "little cut" scared me. The doctor looked at me and asked me if I'd like a lollipop. I did like cherry lollipops, but how was candy going to make me better?

"Yes, sir, I would like a red one, please."

I asked again, "What happened, Mommy?"

"The moving men took the window out of the third floor because the mattress wouldn't fit up the stairway. When they put the window back, it didn't go in all the way, and it fell out, bounced off of the clothesline, then crashed onto your head. If you'd been looking straight up, you wouldn't be here right now," Mommy explained with a sniffle.

Where else would I be?

The doctor kept talking to Mommy and Daddy.

"As you can see, we shaved the top front portion of her head and then stitched the cut up with over one hundred stiches," he said, pointing above me to the top of my head.

I couldn't feel anything up there.

"We'll run a few tests to make sure everything is okay. She can go home, but just to be safe, stay inside for a couple of weeks."

After that, he said I could do almost anything the other kids did because he was going to protect the cut with something new he called "an experiment." Then he took a big can and sprayed the experiment on my head.

"This will dry like thin, clear plastic. People won't even see that it's there."

"So, I can go to school?" I asked.

"Yes, you can go to school in a couple of weeks, and everything will be just fine," he replied.

Everything will be just fine. I'd heard that before.

I sat up, and the doctor held a mirror to my head so I could see myself. It was horrible! How was I supposed to make new friends with a bald plastic-coated head?

Danny, Zac, and Andy had been waiting at home with my other grandmother, Daddy's mother. Her name was Ethel. Ethel didn't like me. She told everyone I wasn't Daddy's real kid. Ethel always called me "she" or "her," never my real name. Sometimes, when talking to my Daddy, Ethel called me "that new kid of yours." I called her Grandma because I had to, but inside my head, I called her Ethel. Grandmothers were supposed to be nice, and she was not nice at all, so she was mean old Ethel.

Zac and Andy kept looking at my head and making gross noises. Danny was way too adult to make any comment at all.

Ethel said, "If *she* hadn't been in the way in the first place, the whole thing wouldn't have happened."

I wanted to smack Ethel.

Ethel and Grandpa lived upstairs from us. Ethel was skinny, and her hair was white and loose. She looked mean, like that witch that put little kids into big ovens. Ethel looked nothing like my Nana.

Daddy's house, like Nana and Papa's, was in Providence too, but Daddy's house was in a yucky neighborhood compared to Nana and Papa's. Mommy said the area we lived in now with Daddy was called Whiffville. All the houses in Whiffville looked the same, all stacked high next to each other.

Our house was right next to the highway, and it was always noisy. Sometimes the noise came from the speeding cars, and other times, it was from people fighting in the streets. Mommy said Daddy lived close to Ethel because she took care of the boys while he was at work. That was before Mommy and Daddy got married, but I wondered why we lived here now.

Ethel didn't like Mommy. One night I heard Mommy tell Daddy, "Your mother hates me. She's always telling me how to raise the boys. I'm a mother too. I don't need her help, and I'd appreciate it if you would say something."

Ethel didn't want anybody to be married to Daddy. I heard her tell Daddy that she should be raising the boys and not have to worry about a wife that couldn't do the job right, never mind "some little girl" that wasn't even his.

She was wrong. I was not "some little girl," and he didn't have to take care of me. I could take care of myself. If I was just "some little girl," then I'd be tattling on everything that Daddy did to me and making lots of problems for our family. I didn't like this place. I missed Nana and Papa.

***

I had missed the first few weeks of school because my head was still healing, but finally Mommy said I was ready. I was so excited to be joining Danny and Zac, who had already started kindergarten.

"Remember, Christina, you have nothing to worry about. I called your teacher and explained all about your accident," Mommy said.

Zac was still putting on his socks as he ran out of his room, saying, "The teacher even told the class what happened, and I told them they better not make fun of you. All the boys want to see your cut. They think it's cool, but I think it's gross!" Zac exclaimed, acting tough.

Zac was nice, but cuts grossed him out, and the sight of blood made his face turn white like he was playing dead. Zac said it made him want to puke.

Danny walked out of the bedroom, pulling on his shirt sleeve, looking agitated.

"I don't like these clothes. I think I should get some dress-up suits because that's what big men wear."

He was such a weirdo!

If Danny wasn't picking on me, he was ignoring me. Today was an ignore-Christina day. I liked the days he ignored me.

I thought I'd be scared to be at school with my hurt head, but the day went by fast, and it was fun. The teacher read us a story about Dick and Jane, and we got a snack before we went home.

When the day was over, Mommy came to our classroom. The teacher asked Mommy to stay so she could go over a few things. We got to wait in the car. I hoped everything was okay because I liked school. I didn't want to have to stay home because of the cut on my head. I wanted to be a normal kid just like everyone else.

It seemed like forever before she came back.

"Is everything okay, Mommy?"

"Yes, Christina. The teacher just gave me some work for you to do at home. She said you shouldn't have any problems."

After dinner, Mommy sent us into the living room to play. I heard Mommy whispering to Daddy. I was afraid that Mommy hadn't told me everything the teacher said to her, so I tried to listen.

"The teacher is concerned about Danny."

Wow! I was worrying for nothing.

But I kept listening because I was nosy.

"His teacher said he has a problem getting along with the other children. She said we should consider getting him some help."

I wasn't sure what sort of help she meant, but it made Daddy mad.

"My son doesn't need any help! That teacher needs help for not realizing that my son is smarter than the rest of the kids. They probably just bore him!"

Mommy yelled back, but I blocked my ears and stopped listening because I hated fighting.

Danny sure made a lot of problems in this family. If someone could help Danny be nicer, why wouldn't Daddy let them?

I had a hard time falling asleep because I couldn't stop thinking about Mommy, Daddy, Danny, and all the yelling.

I dreamed about everybody yelling and screaming at each other. Mommy, Daddy, Nana, Papa, Grandpa, and Ethel were in a circle, and I was sitting in the middle of all of them. I just wanted to get out. Everybody kept yelling, and then someone grabbed me. It didn't hurt, but it didn't feel right either.

Uh-oh! I was so mixed up in my dream, I'd forgotten all about Daddy. The grabbing wasn't in my dream; it was Daddy, and it was real! *How do I make this stop! Why didn't I wake up when he came in?* He didn't know I was awake. I didn't move an inch.

Okay, Christina, relax, you've been through this before. Just get him away from you without making trouble. Count to ten. No, that will take too long. Count to three. Okay, onnne, twooo, threee—open!

I opened my eyes just enough to see him, like squinting. I didn't know why I expected to see something different, because he was there almost every night. Sometimes he did different stuff, but he always looked the same. I lay there all stiff, squinting up at him in his fuzzy red bathrobe, open, showing his fat belly. He wasn't wearing any clothes underneath, and from where I was, he looked like a blobby, ugly giant. One of his hands was between my legs, and then he put his fat finger right inside me while holding my leg still with his other hand. It hurt. His was so big and strong that I couldn't move.

Why hadn't I heard him coming? It'd been so many months of this that I'd taught myself to be aware. I'd listen for the shuffling of his slippers sweeping the floor as he entered my room and then get the whiff of Aqua Velva. Sometimes the smell woke me before the slippers. I used to hear the creaking on the floor right inside my bedroom door, but now he stepped over that. Sometimes I heard the dog barking next door, and I hoped that he was coming to get my daddy, but that never happened. When I squinted my eyes, all I saw was that fuzzy red robe and crusty knees. At the sight of his knees, it was time to be strong. I wanted to ask him why he was doing this to me, but I was too scared. I squeezed my hands together, super tight, and started thinking hard.

Daddies weren't supposed to do this. If I asked him why he was doing a bad thing to me, he might tell Mommy a lie, because I'd heard him lie about Danny. Then I'd end up in the home for bad children. Whenever we drove by the haunted-looking "home for bad children" in Cranston, Mommy called it Sockanosset and said we should never misbehave because we could end up there. I just wanted to be a normal kid.

I kept still, squinting, and then I made some noises like I was having a bad dream and started to cough. Sometimes that made Daddy leave. I felt his hand jerk away from me. I kept coughing in my sleep and rolled over onto my stomach, curled up tight in my blanket. He stood over me for a few seconds, tall and big, like a mean monster. When he saw that I was still asleep, the monster in the red bathrobe turned and walked out of the room. I could feel my heart bouncing out of my chest.

Why didn't Mommy ever wake up? Didn't Mommy know Daddy was missing?

✳✳✳

Mommy was going to have a baby. I'd been praying for a girl because three brothers are a lot, and a sister could be my friend.

I heard the milkman tell Mommy that if she ate broccoli, she would have a boy, so I didn't let Mommy eat broccoli the whole time she was pregnant.

Finally, the day arrived for Mommy to have the baby. I was excited because I was sure she would bring home a sister and I got to stay with Nana and Papa while Mommy was in the hospital.

Nana and Papa lived way on the other side of Providence. Mommy called it the East Side. The East Side was pretty, with big trees and green yards. I was happy when I was at Nana and Papa's because I never had to worry about anyone hurting me.

Papa was recovering from a car accident, and he only had one leg now and couldn't hear anymore. The doctors had given Papa a new leg made of wood with a few screws in it, so the knee bent, and Papa's socks and shoes fit right on the wooden foot too. Nana helped Papa practice walking on his new wooden leg, but mostly, he stayed in bed.

Papa spoke Italian and some English, but sometimes his English didn't make sense because Papa made everything shorter than it was supposed to be. At Easter, he said, "Happy East." His funny words made me laugh.

Papa and I had fun playing tea party with a little tea set I kept at Nana's. Papa might have lost one leg, and he couldn't hear anymore, but he was still my papa, and I loved him.

Daddy said he would call us as soon as Mommy had the baby. I told Daddy not to call unless Mommy had a girl. Daddy said we would love whatever God gave us, and he would call no matter what Mommy had. I knew Daddy was right, but I still prayed for a girl.

Finally, the phone rang. I heard Nana tell Daddy, "Congratulations!" I was so excited until Nana told me Mommy had a boy. I now had a new brother named Mikey.

Now I had four brothers!

"Why couldn't it be a girl baby?" I cried to Nana.

"Christina, the baby is healthy, and that's the most important thing."

I was sobbing, my nose running and tears coming down my cheeks.

"I prayed every night, and Mommy didn't eat any broccoli."

Nana laughed.

"God does things for certain reasons. Everything will turn out for the best."

I had no idea what that meant, but I got to sleep with Nana in her bed that night.

Once we were in her bed under the covers, Nana asked, "Is something else wrong?"

"No, Nana," I said, thinking that one more brother was enough to be wrong.

"Christina, why aren't you cuddling up close to me like you used to? You have your blankets wrapped around you so tight, are you sure there's nothing wrong?"

Oh, that kind of wrong!

I was scared to answer, but Nana wanted to know.

"Nothing else is wrong, Nana. I'm just sad about another boy in the house."

"Do you sleep this way all the time?"

"Yes."

"Are you afraid to be alone in your bedroom at the new house?"

Oh, no! I didn't want to lie to Nana. I didn't like the way it felt when I lied, but I didn't want Mommy to be unhappy with me.

I was getting good at stopping Daddy because I'd learned to stay awake. When he came into my room, I faked sleeping and held my covers real tight to my neck. Sometimes he went away, but sometimes I'd fall asleep and I would wake up too late. But I was getting much better at staying awake. He didn't know that I knew, because he never said anything to me about it. I was taking care of this myself without causing any problems, and when I got big, I would move out on my own, away from Daddy. If I told Nana, she might put what she called "an Italian Curse" on him, and then Mommy would be mad.

"No, Nana, I'm not afraid to be alone. I'm a big girl. I'm just upset about a boy baby."

What if Mommy did have a girl baby? And what if Daddy hurt her too, and I couldn't take care of her? Nana was right. God did do things for a reason.

1970 — seven years old

Chapter 3

We were moving to a new house in Hillsgrove, Rhode Island! Mommy and Daddy were taking us to see it today. I couldn't wait.

I felt like I'd been ready for hours. Mommy was getting Andy and Mikey ready. Mikey was a cute little ball with lots of black hair that ate, cried, and pooped.

"Mommy, I want to wear my red pants. No, I mean my green ones. No, how 'bout my jeans instead."

"Andy, can you let me finish getting Mikey dressed first?" Mommy snapped.

I could tell Mommy was angry with Andy today by the sound of her voice. Andy whined a lot and changed his mind every five minutes, but he wasn't a troublemaker.

It had become a routine. Mommy yelled, and Andy cried. Andy had too much energy and didn't mean to be bad, but sometimes he did it on purpose. I know baby Mikey kept Mommy up at night. Now she was tired and got aggravated faster.

Finally, we were on our way. Daddy said Hillsgrove was about fifteen minutes away. Everyone was talking at once. The radio was playing "I'll Be There" by The Jackson Five. Zac was singing loud, acting like one of the Fives.

"Our new house has four bedrooms," Mommy said, smiling.

"I should have my own room because I'm the oldest," Danny said.

Danny should have his own room—outside!

"Dad, me, and Andy are going to build a big fort in our new yard. Or maybe a treehouse!" Zac said, yelling over the car radio.

Mommy was talking about the colors she wanted on the walls. Daddy was talking about ripping down walls, Mikey was sleeping, and I was just glad we were moving away from the house where the bad stuff had happened.

"Our new house is right around the next block," Daddy said, pointing out the window.

We turned off the main road into a pretty neighborhood. Each house had its own style and a front yard with lots of green grass. Some yards had big trees that looked like they would be fun to climb. We rounded the next corner onto our street, Gavel Avenue, and saw a pretty house with a white picket fence, the kind you see on *Leave It to Beaver*. The house was just as I had imagined. But it was stuck next door to an icky, haunted-looking house. Yuck! We parked on the road, between the two houses. Hey, some old lady was coming out of our new home!

"Mommy, why is someone in our new house?"

"No, Christina, that's not our house. The other one is."

The other one? What was wrong with my parents? People weren't supposed to live in houses like that! That was a house for ghosts—and maybe Ethel.

Daddy stated, "We only paid $5,000 for this house."

That didn't make sense to me.

"But I have two dollars in my piggy bank, and I just started saving. If I had $5,000, I'd buy a castle, not a haunted house," I said.

"You'll understand when you get bigger, Christina. We're going to fix the house up and make it just the way we want it. Plus, you kids will have bedrooms up on the second floor," Daddy said convincingly.

"Okay," I answered apprehensively.

Then Daddy added, "We'll even let you pick out the color to paint your room. And when the house is ready to move in to, we'll get a puppy."

A puppy! Oh boy, now I was sold!

By the time Daddy started construction on the house, it was summertime. We still lived in Providence during the construction but knowing that we'd be moving soon made me happy.

One day, Mommy and I were making sandwiches for the guys working on the house. It was hardly ever only the two of us, so this was special. Mommy had turned the TV sound up loud so we could hear her favorite soap opera, *Another World*. Most of the time, Mommy just called it her "story."

"Are you happy you'll get to pick the colors for your room?" Mommy asked.

"Yes, Mommy. I'm excited to move! I don't like this house. It's too small." I didn't tell her the real reasons about Ethel not being nice or the bad things about Daddy.

"Mommy, how come my first daddy didn't want to live with us anymore?"

"Your old daddy didn't like babies," Mommy explained.

"Why, Mommy?" I asked.

"He said babies were messy and too much work. Your daddy didn't like girls," Mommy said.

Then Mommy told me there was no reason to ever talk about my old daddy, because he wasn't a nice person. She said my new daddy loved me and wanted to take good care of us, and there wasn't any reason to remember anyone terrible to us.

"Never say anything in front of your new daddy about your old daddy, because that would make him feel bad," she explained.

"Okay, Mommy, I won't."

But if my new daddy loved me and wanted to take care of me so much, how come he did awful things to me? I didn't think all daddies did things like that. And even if they did, I didn't like it. I didn't want anyone taking care of me, and if I ever met my old daddy, I'd let him know he wouldn't have to worry about taking care of me. I could do it myself.

Everyone worked very hard, and by the end of summer, we moved into our new house and we got a puppy. We named him Bandit because he looked like he was wearing a bank robber's mask. I wanted Bandit to live in our new house with us, but Daddy said he had to have his own house outside. So, Bandit lived in a small dirt area in the backyard on a short chain attached to a doghouse. We each took turns feeding him. I'd thought a puppy would be able to sleep in bed with me, but I was wrong. I didn't think Daddy would want the puppy in my bed. Maybe that was why Daddy put him on a chain outside? That made me sad.

If we hadn't taken pictures during construction, you'd never know that our house used to look haunted. I'd picked bright yellow and green for my walls and helped paint them too.

I taped a sign to my door: "Boys Keep Out!"

The boys put "Girls Keep Out!" signs on theirs, but that was okay with me.

I loved my new room. Mommy hung up two narrow wall paintings of big, brown-eyed little girls wearing ballerina outfits. They looked pretty.

This house felt safer than our old one because my room was on a different floor from Daddy's and my new room had a door. Maybe he wouldn't bother me anymore.

We had to go to bed at eight o'clock on the night before our first day of school. I was going to be in second grade in a new school because we'd moved, and I was scared that everyone might have made friends in first grade.

I woke out of a sound sleep and sat up quickly, still in bed but wide awake. Why was my breathing so heavy? Did I have a bad dream? My door was closed. Except for my smiley-face night light plugged into the dresser wall, my room was dark. I might have been brave enough to close my door, but I wasn't brave enough to sleep in the pitch dark. Besides, this way I could still check for monsters under the bed before going to sleep. I sat still for a few minutes, waiting for my heartbeat to slow, then I laid back down, covers tight to my neck, and scrunched up close to the edge of the bed, looking toward the doorway. I slept this way every night now.

I thought I heard a noise. Was it my imagination? No, just someone going into the bathroom. The bathroom was across from my bedroom, and I could tell when someone went in because the bathroom door creaked. Probably Andy. He had to pee every five minutes. I heard the bathroom door creak open, then waited for the floor to creak as Andy walked back to his room, but the floor didn't creak. Sometimes he sleepwalked and did funny things. One night, Andy had sleepwalked downstairs and peed in the hallway because that was where our old bathroom used to be.

From my bed, I could see hallway movement through the little gap under my door. I saw a shadow moving. It looked like it was coming toward my room! I wanted to scream but was afraid. I could see feet under my door. They stopped, and nothing happened for a few seconds—just silence. I was so scared. Then my bedroom doorknob started turning slowly. Every tiny turn seemed like slow, awful, scary sounds. *This monster is going to get me! I'm going to die, but I'm just lying here, too scared to move!*

As the door swung open, my room became a scene from one of Andy's scary ghost stories. Now I knew why Mommy got mad when we played campground outside and told scary stories in the dark.

It was a monster, all right. The one in the red bathrobe. The one I called my daddy. As he came toward me, I held my breath and lay as still as possible. Why didn't anyone ever come to help? He just stood there at the side of my bed. His crusty knees were inches from my face. They looked like the back of a baseball mitt. I was trying to think as fast as I could. Then his

He didn't stop watching as he spoke, "No."

"Why?" I asked.

"I don't need a reason. I'm your father."

I'd expected a lecture on why he thought I was too young, but the no-explanation thing was annoying.

"Mom?"

"Your father has decided, Christina. He has his reasons."

Did she know why and wasn't telling me? I didn't understand!

"It's just a matinee movie, with a bunch of other kids too. Can't you at least give me a reason, Dad?"

He turned to me, red-faced and now shouting, "I said no, and that's final! You put yourself in this situation. It's your mess. End it immediately and go to your room!"

I walked away, speechless and feeling the tears run down my face.

Why did he have to do that in front of my brothers? I hate him! He said no because he doesn't want me to be with ANY other boys, ever. And why doesn't Mom stick up for me anymore? I put up with him so she can have a happy family.

I stomped up the stairs to my room.

I should speak up and tell everyone the gross things he does to me. Then maybe someone would take him away!

Or maybe they would take *me* away and stick me in an orphanage, with a bunch of orphan kids, all because I couldn't put up with him anymore? I didn't want to live in an orphanage.

Be strong, Christina. Be strong.

I just kept repeating those words to myself.

I sat on my bed and thought about what to write in my diary.

I'd begun by writing silly stuff like what we had for dinner, my favorite TV shows, and fun stuff with my friends. Sometimes I added fights with Mom or my brothers. I wrote about when Danny didn't feed Bandit and how Danny likes being mean. He told everyone he'd fed Bandit his dinner. But when Zac and I were emptying the clean dishes from the dishwasher, we found Bandit's clean food bowl. Zac called him out for lying and accused him of trying to starve our dog. Danny yelled at Zac and said he was a jerk because he didn't know he loved Bandit so much he used his bare hands to feed him. Later that night, when we were playing in the yard, I saw Dad walk Bandit's bowl over to him so he could eat. If Dad knew Danny lied, why didn't he ever do anything about it?

Then I remembered what Rachel had said about this book being for me, so I started writing about Dad in my own way, in case anyone found it.

So far, it wasn't much, just words like "*it* happened again last night" or "*he* visited again." Maybe I'd get better at writing more someday, because Rachel said expressing myself would make me feel better inside. Whatever that meant.

Dear Diary,

Taylor Brown asked me out!! A boy! And he doesn't want to play baseball, he wants to go to the movies! BUT Dad won't let me go!!! He didn't even give me a reason! He's so unfair. Mom is becoming just like him. I may have chickened out anyway, but it would have been cool if my parents had given me a reason instead of being jerks! I'm not a little kid anymore. I handle more than most girls my age! Duh!!! I can't wait to be older so I can take care of myself.

Christina

1975 – eleven years old

Chapter 5

"You shouldn't have drunk all that Pepsi!" Dad yelled. "Now you gotta hold it till we stop again!"

"But I can't hold it, we have to stop!" Andy cried.

"Since you needed this so bad ten minutes ago, you can use it now too!" Dad said, as a Pepsi bottle went airborne from the front seat to the back and bounced right off Andy's rock-hard head. This made Andy cry louder, making Dad madder.

Now Andy was crying all scrunched down in the back corner of the car, holding himself because he didn't want to pee in a bottle.

"I don't know how to pee in a bottle!"

"Well, pee in the bottle, or pee in your pants. It's your choice!"

The rest of us were giggling.

"That's enough! Andy, you pee in that bottle, or hold it till we get to Arizona!" Mom screeched. Her voice could wake the dead.

I didn't know what my parents were thinking when they decided to cram us into a big Chevy Suburban, luggage and all, and assume everyone would get along.

"Andy, please stop crying," Zac said softly.

Andy stopped his whining and sniffling while Zac and Danny made a human wall so no one would see him pee. There was silence until we heard Andy start peeing, and then for some reason, that made everyone laugh again.

From that point on, Andy had a private plastic backseat bathroom. Every truck driver from there to California knew that Andy was responsible for filling that bottle, because he proudly made that known at each stop.

Over the next five weeks we would drive across the country and back, seeing sights and visiting relatives in California. We planned on stopping at the Grand Canyon, so Mom and Dad had convinced our school principles to extend our

Christmas break, as this trip would be an educational experience for all of us. So far, they were right!

Dad had gotten everyone up at two in the morning so we would drive through New York City before rush hour traffic. Even though we only got to see it from our car, New York City was mesmerizing, with zillions of lights and giant buildings everywhere. Dad had said we were lucky to be going through when it was dark because we wouldn't see all of the burglars. The city didn't seem bad to me. In fact, I thought it was magical. We went over the George Washington Bridge and saw signs that told suicidal people where to call for help.

Once over the bridge and into New Jersey, an awful smell filled the car. Zac thought Andy had farted, but Mom said it was just that area in New Jersey. I'd read that Bruce Springsteen lived in New Jersey. Maybe that was why he'd called his album *Born To Run*?

Dad wanted to try to drive straight through to Arizona. He said he and Mom would take turns driving so each one could get some sleep. I loved this trip because Dad couldn't do bad things to me while we were all in the same car.

With the nonstop driving, we made it all the way to Arizona in three days.

"It sure doesn't feel like Christmastime!" Danny piped.

"It's only a week till Christmas, and we're in shorts and T-shirts!" I exclaimed.

It was strange listening to Christmas carols on the radio as we passed palm trees and desert scenery. Driving through Phoenix, we noticed that a few people had painted their driveways white to look like snow; others had built snowmen out of tumbleweed. They looked nothing like real snowmen, and you could see right through them!

Dad said we were driving toward the Grand Canyon, Death Valley, and Las Vegas.

"Las Vegas is in Nevada, Dad. That's where they have hookers!" Zac said proudly.

Mom looked shocked. "Where in the world did you hear that? Do you even know what hookers are?"

Zac, proud that he knew more about Las Vegas than the rest of us, said,

"Yep. I saw them on the TV show, *Vegas*. Dan Tanner uses them to get information. It must be illegal to hang out on the streets at night, because when they tell Mr. Tanner the secrets, he says he won't put them in jail. I'll show them to you when we get there. They're super easy to pick out. They dress in clothes like Barbie dolls wear, use lots of makeup, and chew gum."

The rest of us looked at Mom and Dad for confirmation of Zac's story. Hadn't they heard Zac? They were looking at each other as if they'd both gone deaf.

After a few seconds, Dad spoke.

"Well, I don't think we're gonna go through the city, but if we have time, maybe we'll take a drive so you can show us."

"I will," Zac said, looking satisfied.

We arrived at the Grand Canyon just before sunset. It was the most fantastic thing I had ever seen. We ate roasted chicken and potato salad at a picnic table overlooking an endless, glistening backlit view of massive mountains made of butter-smooth carved rocks. The scene transitioned through varying shades of red as if Mother Nature herself, with the sun as her leading role, had created a perfect, slow-motion movie just for us as complementary dinner entertainment.

I moved from the table and finished my dinner on the warm ground to feel closer to the canyon. The sun made it look as if it was on fire. But not a scary fire: a gentle, beautiful fire. It felt like a nice, warm, safe hug from someone I knew and could trust. *Maybe this is where God lives?* Perhaps these weren't birds flying around us but angels, sent from God to look over all that visited the canyon.

I wonder if God knows I'm here. I wonder if he knows it's me, Christina, the little girl who prays to him each night before I lie down, asking him to help me stay awake so I can stop Dad from doing bad things to me. I thought God had listened, because now I could go to bed and sleep and stay awake at the same time, like sleeping with one eye open. Sometimes I felt like I didn't sleep at all, but I'd keep it up till I was old enough to move away. I knew God had millions of people to look after, so I felt fortunate that he'd given me this gift to stay awake most nights to try and keep Dad from hurting me. And those nights when I woke up too late, I didn't blame God for not helping me, because I was sure there were lots of other little kids who also needed his help. I was trying to get stronger and stronger every day so God wouldn't have to worry about me anymore. Then he'd have time for the kids who weren't as strong.

I made the sign of the cross on my chest, picked up my plate and the other dinner items, and threw them in the trash. I walked back to Mom, Dad, and the boys just as Mom was saying, "Time to go."

As we drove away, everyone waved good-bye to the Grand Canyon.

Shortly after, Mom began singing some *Viva Las Vegas* song and Zac had half his body sticking out of the car window, excited that he was going to see something from TV.

But by the time we approached Las Vegas, it was pitch-black outside.

"Do you see any yet?" Andy asked Zac.

Mikey, who was riding up front with Mom and Dad, asked, "What are they looking for, Mommy?"

Mom seemed confused, like she didn't know how to answer his question.

Dad answered, "Bad ladies, Mikey."

This got Zac's attention, and he pulled his body back into the car.

"How do you know hookers are bad, Dad?"

"Well, you were kinda right about Dan Tanner saying it was illegal for those ladies to stay on the street at night, but not because they can't stay on the street."

"Why then, Dad?" Zac asked, and now had everyone's undivided attention.

Mom was still looking at Dad in amazement.

"Well, ya know when two people are married, and they hug and kiss each other?"

"Yeah," we answered, although confused why that had anything to do with it.

"Well, dads have jobs that take them far away."

"Okay."

"Well, sometimes, when the dads are away, they get lonely, and they don't have anyone to kiss and hug."

"So, why don't they call their wives to make them feel better?" Zac asked.

"Because sometimes hearing a voice just isn't enough. That's what hookers do, but hookers sell their hugs and kisses for money, and that's illegal."

"Aren't husbands supposed to kiss their wives only? Wouldn't their wives be mad if they found out?" Zac asked.

"Yes, their wives would be mad if they found out. That's why it costs them money to have other ladies do that. The men give the street ladies money, and the ladies kiss them and don't ever tell anyone."

Zac was still concerned.

"Those are bad men, aren't they, Dad? Husbands that kiss anyone besides their wives are bad."

"Yes, Zac, they are bad men."

If it was bad to kiss and hug other ladies, then what he did to me must be extra bad.

I wanted to scream at the top of my lungs and tell everyone that my dad was a horrible husband. But, because it was important to Mom that this family be happy, I kept my mouth shut. The more I learned about life, the more I despised him.

We didn't actually drive through Las Vegas; we passed by it, so it looked like any other city from a distance. I don't think anyone was that upset, especially Zac.

We were all about the same age, yet so different. Zac was kind and believed everyone was good at heart, and if they weren't, then someone found out and fixed it. Andy was tough on the outside and mouthy, but he was a softy when it came down to it. Danny reminded me of Eddie Haskell from *Leave It to Beaver*. All the adults thought he was sincere, but the kids knew he was terrible. It was as if he'd been born with an evil bug in his head, and as the bug grew, he got worse. Mikey was still a baby, but so far, he was okay. I wondered what we'd all be like when we grew up. All I knew was that I wanted to be able to take care of myself. I didn't want to have to rely on anyone else. I wanted to learn to survive in all situations. I didn't want to be anyone else's responsibility.

Our next stop was Oakland, California, to visit Aunt Olivia and Uncle George. Dad said it was right near San Francisco and the Golden Gate Bridge. Most bridges scared me, but the Golden Gate Bridge, even though it was painted the color of Cheetos, looked magnificently strong.

Along the ride, there was chatter about Christmas, now only three days away, mixed in with excited talk of our upcoming Disneyland adventure.

"There it is, Al, the third house on the right." Mom pointed, and her eyes were sparkling with excitement.

"Okay, I see it," he said.

The house was pretty on the outside, like the Brady Bunch house, surrounded by beautiful shrubs and fruit trees.

Once inside the foyer, everyone welcomed each other. From where we were standing, I could see three rooms, all on different levels. The living room, decorated in all white except for a beautiful oak piano, was sunken three steps down from the foyer level. The kitchen, up three steps from the foyer, had expensive-looking marble countertops, with copper pots and pans hanging from the ceiling on giant hooks. The dining room, designed completely differently and on the same level as the foyer, featured an ornately carved wood dining room set. This house was like something out of a magazine. Even with all of us gathered in the living room, you couldn't even tell people lived here.

Aunt Olivia and Uncle George had come to visit us in Rhode Island, but this was my first time meeting our cousins: Ella, Jenny, and Kenny. Aunt Olivia, nicely tanned and physically fit, looked like she was from California. Uncle George was an average-looking guy, tall and rugged, with dark hair.

Ella and Jenny were about five years older than us and seemed wicked cool. Both girls wore funky hip-hugger bell-bottom pants. Jenny had straight, silky brown hair and big brown eyes, very earthy and pretty, even with no makeup. She wore a tie-dyed T-shirt with a huge peace symbol on the front. Ella was taller, with curly dark-brown hair and glasses and looked a bit more daring. You could tell they were sisters, but at the same time, they looked different. Ella wore a frilly white top with no bra. That was the new thing. The TV news said girls didn't want to wear bras anymore because that was their right.

"Hi, I'm Kenny. I'm thirteen. How old are you?" their younger brother said.

"Hi, Kenny. I'm eleven," I replied.

Kenny had dark hair and was sort of geeky. He was what Mom called husky and wore thick black horn-rimmed glasses and had curly brown hair like Willie Ames from *Eight is Enough.*

"Christina, you'll be staying with Jenny and me in my room. Jenny gave her room to your mom and dad. Follow me, I'll show you," Ella said.

"Wow, your room is super cool," I said.

Ella had beads hanging where a closet door was supposed to be and a huge *One Flew Over the Cuckoo's Nest* movie poster hanging above her headboard. She'd made a collage filled with words and photos that she'd hung on another wall. Right in the middle was a quote from Jane Fonda that said "You spend all your life trying to do something they put other people in asylums for." I had no idea what that meant.

Jenny said, "Ella's a nutcase."

But I still felt privileged staying in her room.

Mom and Aunt Olivia called us down to dinner.

Dinner consisted of some fancy recipe Aunt Olivia made, called chicken and an orange or something like that. Everything was so elaborate; it was like living in a movie.

"Paige, I started seeing a therapist once a week. It's included in a new program I've joined called EST. It makes me feel great and weightless. You should go too," Aunt Olivia said to Mom.

Aunt Olivia said it would make all of Mom's problems go away. Mom seemed very interested.

If this EST thing can make all your problems disappear, then why doesn't everyone go? Why can't I go?

"Aunt Olivia, is EST for kids too?" I asked.

She laughed.

"EST isn't a game, honey. EST is a special class for adults. It will help your mom deal with problems that go back as far as childhood."

"Can I go too?"

"Oh, Christina, you're funny. Why would you need to go to therapy?"

I think I've dug myself into a hole.

"I guess I don't have any reason. I just thought it would be fun."

"EST isn't fun, honey. EST is like medicine for the brain and heart. You're not sick, are you?"

"Oh, no. I'm not sick, Aunt Olivia. I just wanted to learn more."

"I see. Well, unfortunately, EST only deals with adults. And besides, it's costly."

"Oh, okay. I didn't know it was expensive. I don't even have a job yet."

This made the adults laugh, and everyone went back to normal, except me. My heart was racing a mile a minute.

The alarm went off at six o'clock for a day trip to the redwoods. At that hour of the day, the redwood forest didn't seem exciting to me, and from the looks of it, it wasn't to Ella or Jenny either.

The sign read "Now approaching The Redwood National Forest. Please keep lights on at all times."

"Do you think it's dark in the forest?" Kenny asked as we came over the top of a hill and saw the biggest, fattest, tallest trees we had ever seen.

Everyone made the ooh-ahh fireworks sound. And Aunt Olivia was right: cars *could* drive right through these trees and still have plenty of room on each side.

We drove, in awe, for miles before we arrived at the parking area of the forest.

Once the car was parked, everyone apprehensively exited, as if we'd mistakenly driven into the Land of Oz.

Uncle George spoke a whisper above the echoes of the car doors closing. "Okay, kids, please stick together, and follow the map into the forest."

Uncle George was a take-charge kind of guy.

"Everyone pick a buddy to stay with because the paths are narrow, and even though we're all together, it's good to be safe," Mom suggested.

No one argued. Within minutes, we paired up, lined up, and were ready to venture into the unknown. Kenny and I were buddies. Dad and Uncle George led the line, followed by the eight kids, two by two, like Noah's ark, with Mom and Aunt Olivia keeping tabs at the end.

Uncle George made us all laugh when he yelled, "Forward march!"

And so, the trip began, everyone a bit less scared and a lot more curious. We actually got to walk right through a tunnel carved into a tree.

"That's a giant sequoia," Uncle George stated.

We took turns reading the signs, probably not pronouncing all the names correctly. Before long, everyone sounded like a bunch of smarty-pants, recognizing tree names by the look and shape.

The last tree on the path was the tallest in the forest. The sign read "The Tall Tree." Not a very original name. Under that, it read "A Coast Redwood or a Sequoia Sempervirens." Okay, so it was much easier to call it The Tall Tree. It was over six hundred years old and measured 367.8 feet tall. We couldn't even see the top. When leaving the area, I felt different inside, knowing I had just experienced something some folks never got a chance to see.

By the time we got back to Aunt Olivia's house, we were like zombies shuffling up the stairs, quiet and slow. Only the sound of dragging feet and Andy's hiccups could be heard.

I had the bedroom to myself for a while because the girls had gone to a school dance. As I lay there in the darkness, I thought about what I could do to make my room special. I was a little scared being in a strange room by myself, but thanks to all the exercise we'd had today, I couldn't fight off the urge to fall asleep.

I awoke to someone shaking me. My heart started racing immediately.

Oh, no. Not Dad here too! It can't be!

And then I heard a little voice, and I knew it wasn't Dad.

"Christina . . . Christina . . . wake up."

Who in the world is waking me up in the middle of the night?

"Christina, wake up. It's Kenny."

"Kenny, it's late. What do you want?"

"I want to ask you some questions."

"Now?"

"Yeah, it's important, and I can't sleep."

I just stared at him. What could be so important?

"Do you like me?"

"Of course I like you. Why would you ask a stupid question like that?"

"No, I mean, really like me?"

"Really like you? What do you mean, really like you?"

And then I saw it in his eyes.

Oh, that *kind of like.*

"Kenny, you're my cousin. Cousins aren't supposed to like each other like that. It's not allowed."

"I know, but I can't help it. I want to kiss you."

I was about to say no, but he didn't give me a chance. He leaned over the bed and stuck his lips on my face. And before I could say anything, there was a loud voice at the door.

"WHAT ARE YOU DOING IN THIS ROOM? YOU BELONG IN BED!"

It was Dad, and he was furious! Kenny ran out of the room so fast I expected to see dust trailing behind.

"Christina, what were you two doing?"

"Nothing, Dad. I just woke up. Kenny came in and woke me up to ask me some questions. He just got here right before you did. Honest!"

"Did he do anything to you?"

Boy, he's got a lot of nerve asking me a question like that! And what is he doing up at this hour, anyway? Just wandering the halls, I suppose. For all I knew, Kenny saved me tonight.

"No, I'm okay."

"Okay, we'll talk about this in the morning. Go to sleep now."

We'll talk about this in the morning? Great, it's not over. What does he mean, go to sleep? Does he actually think I'm going to just nod off like nothing ever happened?

I woke in the morning to find Mom and Aunt Olivia sitting on my bed. Okay . . . it hadn't been just a dream.

"Are you okay, Christina?" Mom asked.

"Yeah, Mom. Why?"

"Your father told us about last night. Aunt Olivia and I would like to know what happened. Can you tell us?"

"Only if Kenny isn't going to get in any trouble."

Aunt Olivia answered that question. "Kenny won't get in any trouble, honey. We just want to help you both understand."

"Okay, Aunt Olivia. Kenny came into my room last night when I was sleeping. He woke me up to tell me some things."

"What did he tell you?" Mom asked.

I was so scared my knuckles were turning white from holding my hands together so tightly.

"He said he liked me. I told him I liked him too."

Mom spoke again. "He thought that was so important that he had to wake you in the middle of the night?"

"I guess so. Kenny said he couldn't sleep until he told me. I don't know why."

"What else did he say?" Aunt Olivia asked.

When Aunt Olivia asked questions, she seemed concerned. Not like Mom, who seemed mad, like she wanted Kenny punished or something. I felt like it was okay to tell Aunt Olivia the truth.

"Well, he said he liked me and wanted to kiss me. I didn't know what to do. I told him that cousins shouldn't kiss. Nana told me that boy relatives shouldn't kiss girl relatives unless it's a special occasion, like to say happy birthday or something."

Mom and Aunt Olivia looked at each other. I tried hard to stop them, but tears started falling out of my eyes as if I had no control.

"That's right, isn't it, Mom?"

"Well, yes, that's right, although I'm not sure Nana explained it right."

"I didn't want him to kiss me, Mom, but I didn't know what to do. If I screamed, then he would have gotten in trouble. I didn't want to get Kenny in trouble. He wasn't trying to hurt me."

By this time, I was really crying. I didn't know whether to tell the whole story about how Dad came in or just sit there because I was confused. Aunt Olivia decided to give it a try.

"Kenny is a couple of years older than you, right?"

"Yes," I replied, tears still streaming down my face.

"Well, when boys get to Kenny's age, their bodies and feelings begin to change. These are feelings even they don't understand. They're called hormones. And they make some boys do things that sometimes they shouldn't. Kenny shouldn't have come into your room, and he shouldn't have kissed you. Not only because you're his cousin but also because you didn't want him to. People should never touch you if you don't want them to touch you."

"Do you understand that? Does it make sense to you, Christina?" Mom asked.

It made a lot more sense than she would ever know. The question was, did *she* understand? Did she know about Dad but love him more than me? If so, did she think or believe those rules applied to dads?

At this point, I wasn't sure if it was courage, insanity, or plain curiosity that allowed the next question to travel from my brain and exit through my vocal cords.

"How come Dad was up so late, Mom?"

I don't know what I expected her to say. I think it was an opportunity for me to see if she would admit that she knew Dad was gone from her bed and that he shouldn't have been.

"Dad told me he was checking on you and the boys. He didn't mean to blow up at Kenny. He just cares about you so much that he got angry when he saw what might've been happening."

Her answer made my heart ache like it'd been sliced open, and now all hope of good was dripping out and into my stomach like acid leaking from a battery. It was making me nauseous.

I could tell by the look in Mom's eyes that she believed what she'd said, although the look in Aunt Olivia's eyes wasn't quite the same. She looked a little confused but didn't say anything.

"Oh."

That was all I could say. Anything else was pointless.

Mom would never believe me over him because she didn't want to. Mom loved Dad. What Dad did to me at night would have to stay a secret. Only I could know how bad he was.

"Aunt Olivia, Kenny's not in trouble, is he?"

"No, he's not in trouble."

"Okay. Can I go take a shower now?"

"Yes, you can. And let's put this all behind us now. Okay?" Mom said.

"Okay, Mom."

I walked out toward the bathroom, feeling very alone. Nothing more was ever said about that incident. And as Aunt Olivia had promised, Kenny didn't get punished, although we weren't pals like we had been earlier in the trip.

1975 — eleven years old

Chapter 6

Christmas in California was different, but it was still Christmas.

"I got an Evel Knievel with the motorcycle." Mikey was happy and yelling. "Now we can jump ramps!"

Mikey got a Stretch Armstrong toy too. He was a superhero made of rubber that stretched as far as you could pull him.

The rest of us got a few little gifts because our big Christmas present was going to Disneyland tomorrow. By the time we'd finished dinner and washed the dishes, most people had gone off to their bedrooms, the couch, or the living room floor to relax before our big journey to Disneyland.

During the ride to Disney, Mom preached to us about the importance of staying together inside the park, but we only half listened. The closer we got to Disneyland, Anaheim, California—the home of Mickey Mouse—the signs got more frequent, until finally, we turned into the parking lot and were at Disneyland.

Everyone was excited, talking over each other and asking questions. Dad whistled loudly, immediately putting a stop to the chaos, and pointed out the window.

"That little train is gonna take us from the car to the entrance of the park. Yes, you can ride on all the rides, either alone or with one of us. And yeah, Walt Disney's head is freakin' frozen, but nobody gets to see him. And everyone is to stay together! If anyone gets out of our sight, we're all going the fuck home, you hear me?"

I swear the TV people created Archie Bunker from my father.

We were sitting perfectly still from Dad's whistle and answered in unison, "Yes."

Mom and Dad weren't mad, they were just super serious.

We entered the park as if assembled for a fire drill. We were all behaving like angels, except Mom. Mom was acting silly and dancing down the middle of Main Street, singing "I Love a Parade."

Every sight was more amazing than the last. Colors were bright, railings were shiny, birds were chirping, and there were trees and bushes shaped like Donald Duck and Cinderella. As if that wasn't enough, there were men dressed in white pants and striped shirts on the sidewalk, singing "The Candy Man." Disneyland was the best thing ever, and we hadn't even gone on any rides yet! It was like Tinkerbell had sprinkled fairy dust all over us to make us feel special. *This is the happiest place on earth!*

We rode on a boat that took us through a jungle with alligators and elephants, narrated by a hilarious tour guide with a gun! He made fun of Dad's shirt, calling him Don Ho, whoever that was. It made Mom laugh hysterically.

The scariest ride was a roller coaster called The Matterhorn. It was a massive mountain shaped like a pile of melting chocolate chips. The car zoomed in and out of holes in the mountain, and as we came around each corner, we could hear everyone else screaming behind us. Except Mom—she was still laughing.

By the end of the day, we were bushed.

Throughout the day Mom and Dad had remarked about the entire park being spotless. I had never been to an amusement park like this unless you counted Rocky Point Park in Rhode Island, but that was dirty and didn't compare. Disneyland was magical! We'd been there for hours, and none of us had even had a disagreement, much less a fight, so that proved its magic.

We arrived home the day before we were to go back to school. I spent the afternoon catching up on homework, and then Mom let us stay up late to watch Carol Burnett, but by the end of the show, we could barely keep our eyes open.

It had been so long since I'd been in my room, it felt as if I was entering for the first time. *Where are my clothes again?* For the past five weeks, they had been in the car or mixed in with the boys' clothes in the suitcases. It felt good to open a drawer filled with my clothes. I wrote in my diary, filling up five pages about the trip. I skipped the part about Kenny because I couldn't bring myself to write it down, but I did note I hadn't seen the monster once during our trip, and it'd felt almost like being a normal girl. Maybe it was finally over.

But I was still scared to close my eyes at night.

Maybe Mikey would come and save me again. Mikey sometimes wet the bed. This had Mom worried, but to me, it was a blessing. Whenever Mikey wet the bed, he came tiptoeing to my room to wake me up. I didn't know why Mikey had chosen me. Maybe it was because he had tried to wake up the boys without any luck. I didn't think a bomb could wake them. Whatever the reason, I was grateful. Dad hadn't thought Mikey's bedwetting was a big issue until Mikey started sleeping with me. Then Dad decided that something had to be done about it immediately. Mom took his concern as love for Mikey. I was sure he loved Mikey, but I knew better.

The first night it happened, my body was sleeping but my brain was still awake when I'd heard a noise. I'd tensed up and prepared myself. Then I felt a touch and heard someone speaking. *Oh, my God*, I'd thought. *He's going to start talking to me!* But I recognized that little voice.

"Twistweena, Twistweena, wake up!"

It was Mikey. No one else said my name like that.

"Can I sleep with you? My bed's wet."

What a pleasant surprise. Not that Mikey's bed was wet, but that I now had a baby bodyguard, and as it happened, I did get a visit that night.

I was just falling asleep again when I heard the unquestionable footsteps. Even though I knew Dad couldn't do anything to me with Mikey in bed, my heart had still raced. I'd pulled my blankets up close to my neck and held on tight.

He was at my doorway.

I knew every creak on that floor and where each one was. And I knew the next step would be into my room. He'd begun advancing, as he hadn't seen Mikey yet. Mikey was sleeping on the window side of my bed. I'd wanted to stay on the door side just in case something like this happened. Then he was right in front of me. I could see his fat, scaly knees pointing toward my face while his disgusting red bathrobe waved open, slowly, in all the wrong places, from the walk into my room.

Is he actually going to do something with Mikey here? Doesn't he care? Is he that sick or that brave? No, I'm sure he's that sick.

He was kneeling down when Mikey moved. I was scared to death.

Is this it? Am I really in for it now?

Lying still, trying my best not to shake or cry, I didn't think I was going to make it. Just when I was about to snap, I'd heard the belt being tied on the bathrobe. Seconds later, the knees turned toward the door and walked out. I'd turned over, kissed Mikey on the cheek, and thanked God for looking out for me again.

The vacation had thrown me out of sync. I had developed a routine, and I'd learned not to be scared and taught myself to get through each night unharmed. But that night, it seemed new all over again. Maybe because I hadn't been in this bed for a while? Or was it because I had been safe while away, and I'd let my guard down? I needed to grow strong again. I had a feeling inside my chest, a pressure that forced me to take big gulps of air like someone had been holding me underwater and I'd barely escaped. I needed to get myself under control.

***

School was finally out for the summer. And in the fall, I'd be seventh grader in junior high.

After we'd gotten back from our trip, Mom and Dad decided they liked Arizona so much that they put our house up for sale. This scared me because it would mean a fourth new school and all new friends. Most of my friends had been to only one school since kindergarten.

I prayed that our house wouldn't sell and Mom and Dad would change their minds and decide to stay. We had a great house, and Dad seemed to be doing well with his carpeting store and other carpenter-type jobs. What made Arizona so much better?

Why was it whenever a kid didn't want to do something, the parents said it was for their own good? I thought it was for the parents' own good. Who were they trying to kid?

Now every Saturday morning, Mom screamed at us about cleaning everything to get ready for Sunday, when strangers would wander through our house, picking it apart and telling us what they didn't like about it. They called it open house day. Each open house session was followed by Mom screaming and taking her disappointment of not having any offers out on us. This house-for-sale thing was nerve-racking.

By the time summer was over and school was about to start, the house still hadn't sold. Sunday dinner concluded, followed by an afternoon parade of intrusive potential home-buying strangers.

"Christina, Dad and I want to have a talk with you out by the pool," Mom said, all casual, as if this happened every Sunday afternoon.

"Am I in trouble or something?"

"No, you're not in trouble. I just think it's time you, Dad, and I had a little chat."

A little chat? What did that mean? Did she finally figure it out? Am I going to be put away in some foster home? What exactly is a "little chat"?

I instinctively became a bundle of nerves.

"Okay."

I was petrified.

When I got outside, I quickly learned that this "chat" also included Danny!

What was he doing there? Did he know too? Or did they tell him because he's the oldest and supposed to know everything? Couldn't be.

"Why is Danny here too?" I dared to ask.

Mom said this talk was for both of us.

"Oh, okay," I answered, now completely baffled.

Danny and I sat on the grass while Mom and Dad sat in lounge chairs, feet extended. Mom crossed her legs, got comfortable, and lit a Salem Menthol 100 cigarette. Dad had already started on his Lucky Strike. One of Mom's favorite things was sending us to the store to buy cigarettes. I hated the smell of cigarettes.

Mom placed her ashtray on the ground right next to her chair. Dad, on the other hand, had the awful habit of using everything *but* an ashtray for his ashes. Today, he was using a glass that had a bit of Mom's Tab soda left in it. I thought that was disgusting, especially when it was my turn to do the dishes. His plate would be a mix of liquid food juice, burnt cigarette nubs, and ashes. It looked like the last few bites of six-day-old garbage lasagna.

Danny looked as confused as I was, so at least I knew this wasn't about some stupid lie he made up to get me in trouble.

Mom spoke first.

"We asked the two of you out here today because we feel there are some things that you are now old enough to know. We thought it would be a good idea to tell you before you reached junior high and heard it from your friends."

Mom continued to speak.

"Do either of you two know where babies come from?"

Holy cow! This is what she has to talk to us about! This is nuts! It has to be the most embarrassing thing that anyone could ever talk to their parents about, and these two want me to do it in front of my brother?

I was so shocked, I didn't reply.

Danny answered, "The mom's stomach."

"Yes, but do you know how it gets there?"

I ventured out this time. "Yeah, that's what happens when two people have sex. The girl gets pregnant and has a baby." I'd learned that from Patty. She said she knew everything about sex.

"Yeah," Danny agreed.

For once in my life, I was actually happy that Danny was sitting there. I didn't think I could have handled this alone after all. Now it was Dad's turn.

"Yeah, but do you know *how* two people have sex?"

Neither one of us answered, fearing a right *or* a wrong answer. We were both smart enough to keep our mouths shut. Dad went on to explain, but not before he put me on the spot personally and asked again.

"So, Christina . . . you're saying you don't know, right?"

Why was he asking me again? Was this a test? Is he really wondering "Do you know that I come into your room at night and stick my private parts inside you? Do you know that's sex?" *Is he scared and testing me, or is he completely and utterly shameless?* Either way, I really, *really* hated him.

It was a question I could not answer.

I still couldn't believe I was sitting poolside talking about sex with my parents. One parent lived in a fantasy world of make-believe, and the other did things to my body and then had the nerve to sit and publicly educate me on those very things! The questions seemed like a sick practical joke being forced upon me by the devil himself.

Is this really happening?

"Christina, did you hear me?"

Yes, I guess it is.

"No, I don't know how sex *actually* happens."

There, I hoped the monster was happy now.

But he wasn't. He rubbed it in even further. He answered, looking right into my eyes, "Sex is when the man takes his 'thing,' his penis, which has become hard from excitement of knowing that he's going to have sex, and puts it into a girl's vagina. After a while, the man ejaculates into the woman. Then his semen, or 'cum,' swims into her till it hits the one seed it's looking for and mates with that seed to form a baby. Nine months from that night, the baby is born."

Well, this is pretty embarrassing. I think he's actually enjoying this.

"Do either of you have any questions?"

"Does a woman have a baby every time she has sex?" Danny asked.

"No, a woman can't get pregnant until she gets her first period. Before that, she is not a woman yet."

So, that answered my question. Since I hadn't gotten my first period, in my messed-up, secret world, I was safe. But when I got my period, I wouldn't be safe anymore. Maybe that would be when my father, her husband, a man that others knew as happy-go-lucky-Al, would finally stop!

Then a cold, artic, ice-like chill ran through my body as another thought crossed my mind. *What if he doesn't stop? What then, Christina? What THEN?*

Mom continued the answer.

"But you never know when a woman can get pregnant. That's why young men and women have to be very careful. You should not have sex until you are in love, and sometimes even that might be too soon. A man doesn't have to be inside a woman for her to get pregnant. It can happen if some of the semen spills on her, or on a toilet seat, so be careful, Christina."

A toilet seat? That I didn't understand, but I didn't ask either, because getting pregnant from a toilet seat was quite literally the least of my issues.

"We've decided to tell you this before you enter junior high because we know you might hear all kinds of things that aren't true. This doesn't mean that we think it's okay for you to have sex. You're both far too young. Do you hear me?"

"Yes," we both replied.

"Christina, you understand everything we just told you, right? You know that boys shouldn't be touching you in private places. Right?" Mom asked.

That made me so mad that I wanted to stick that Salem 100 right up her ass. Maybe that would wake her up! One, because she didn't trust that I was smart enough to know that boys shouldn't touch me, and two, because she wasn't smart enough to know that Dad had been doing things like that long before this crazy, fucked-up conversation.

The thought made me snap at her, "Of course I know that!"

"We just don't wanna hear any stories about you with boys, do you understand me?" Dad said sternly. Too sternly.

My hate for him that afternoon, although I didn't think it was possible, intensified a thousand times over.

"Yes, I understand that! You two have nothing to worry about," I spoke right back at him.

"Are we done now, Mom?" Danny asked.

"Yes, we're done. Do you have any questions?"

"No," we both answered.

Danny got up and shook Dad's hand. It seemed creepy and weird. I got up and ran to my room as fast as I could.

Later, sitting at my bedroom window, I watched the sunset until that big ball of fire turned into the night.

Dear Diary,

Why do you think they did that tonight? Did Dad convince Mom that we should talk about sex? I think so. Maybe they were concerned, but I don't think that was all of it. I think my friends' parents would have explained it differently to them, and their dads wouldn't have looked the same. Dad got this look in his eyes when he was talking about the subject. It made my stomach feel sick and awful. Something inside told me that he was enjoying it in a way that he shouldn't. Perverted. The boys in school use that word for other boys that spend too much time thinking about the girls in those Playboy magazines. That's what I think he is...PERVERTED! There's something really wrong with him, and Mom won't see it. I don't think my real dad was all those bad things that Mom said he was, or at least I hope not, because I would sure like to meet him someday.

Christina

***

"What do you mean the house has sold?" I cried.

Mom was singing and jumping around, yelling, "We're moving to Arizona. We're moving to Arizona!"

"But I just made new friends. I'm just getting used to this school. I like it here!"

"Don't worry, you'll make new friends in Arizona. It'll be fun."

"But I like it here. Why do we have to move?"

"There's more work opportunity for Dad. You'll like it, trust me."

Trust her? The last time I trusted her with my life, I ended up with a fat, perverted, abusive father.

But I didn't argue, I simply walked upstairs to my room.

Why didn't I ever speak up? Why couldn't I just tell her about Dad? Maybe if I did, Mom and I could live here by ourselves. But I was terrified she wouldn't believe me because she loved him more than me. I feared if I told her, she'd confront him and he'd deny everything, and then my nights would be even worse. I knew what he did to me was wrong, but now, I could make myself wake up and then fake-sleep through it, protecting myself as best I could.

I wanted to grow up, be smart, and take care of myself. I wanted to be normal and in control of my life, not in some orphanage or mental hospital where no one believed me. I'd made it through eight years of this. Only six more years till I was eighteen and old enough to move out.

Dear Diary,

Today was my last day at Williams Jr. High. Patty and Denise made me smiley-face cupcakes to try to cheer me up, but it was still sad saying goodbye to everyone. I wish we weren't moving. I am so afraid that I won't meet any new friends. I'll miss my friends here in Rhode Island, but I certainly won't miss this house. We had a lot of fun here, but I will never forget the evil inside this house.

Christina

Once we were in Arizona, the plan was to stay with Aunt Marie in Phoenix while Mom and Dad searched for a house. It had been six weeks, and so far, Arizona was hot, dry, and lonely.

"Mom?" I yelled down the hall, peeking out the bedroom door.

"What, Christina?"

"Can you come here for a minute?" I said through the crack in the door opening.

I let her in and quickly closed the door behind her. Before she could say anything to me, I took my pants from the floor and pointed them toward her face.

"Look," I said, standing there, heart racing fast and furious.

I didn't know what I expected her to do. Maybe I hoped she'd make it all go away.

"What do I do now, Mom?"

My mother smiled, looking happy and proud, like *she* had just accomplished something great.

She opened her arms wide and went in for a big hug as she said, "Congratulations, honey, you're a woman now!"

Congratulations?

That nauseating sex talk by the pool came rushing back into my brain. Now I was an official woman. *Now* I could get pregnant. *Now* my life was one big panic button.

Chapter 7

We moved into 3640 Pauline road, making us official residents of Phoenix, Arizona, meaning, no more seasons, no green trees, and no more friends.

Our new house was nothing like our home in Rhode Island. This house was a brand-new single-story home, painted in dull tan, with a garage on one end, all the bedrooms on the other, and a big open living room and kitchen in the center. My bedroom was right across from my parents' bedroom, with only the bathroom as separation. I prayed every night for him to stop, but so far, no luck.

The rooms were so close we'd be able to hear each other's heartbeats. Maybe my prayers would be answered, and Mom would finally hear him roaming around.

It wasn't just the house that was new. The entire neighborhood was brand-new too. Our house sat on the circle end of a lollipop-shaped street called a cul-de-sac. Most of the houses looked the same. Mom called them cookie-cutter houses. Some backyards had in-ground pools, and some had fancy stones in the front area. Our yard was void of everything except dry, ugly dirt.

Because Aunt Marie lived on the other side of Phoenix, we had to enroll in yet another junior high, making this my third school while still in seventh grade.

We waited for the school bus for twenty minutes. It was cold, the kind of cold that makes your eyes tear, but it wouldn't last long, because temperatures in Arizona swung rapidly from one extreme to the other. There were days when we'd leave for school in winter coats, but by the end of the day, it'd be above ninety degrees.

We'd always lived close enough to walk to school, but now we rode a bus to Goldway Middle School. I didn't like riding the bus; it felt very lonely. Zac and Andy were a year behind me, so they went to another school. There was no one to talk to during the ride except Danny, but he was an obnoxious, hurtful blob.

As I climbed up the steps and onto the bus, the chattering noise I'd heard when the bus door opened had gone silent. The lack of sound made me queasy. I looked down a long, endless aisle of blink-less, curious eyes staring at me as if I'd come to spread an infectious disease. You could've heard a pin drop.

I walked down the aisle till I couldn't take it anymore and landed somewhere in the middle, all by myself. Danny had found a seat up front. He probably was going to tell the bus driver he already knew how to drive a bus.

The bus started rolling, and the kids went back to talking to one another like I didn't even exist. I sat in silence.

One unexpectedly cool thing about this bus was the radio. I didn't ride the bus back home in Rhode Island, but I knew those school buses definitely weren't equipped with stereos. The music helped ease my nerves, helping me to feel like I wasn't quite all alone. I sat and softly humming along to "Blinded by the Light," then the words to the Amour Hot Dog commercial jingle, "Fat kids, skinny kids, kids that climb on rocks . . . ." Then the DJ introduced a new song called "A New Kid in Town," by the Eagles. I felt my face turn red and hot like it was on fire. I wondered whether everyone was staring at me while listening to this. God. I wanted to go back home to Rhode Island.

Goldway Middle School was old, with several different buildings. So far, my classes were easy, and my history class was covering New England, so that gave me a bit of an advantage. The history teacher made me introduce myself to everyone.

I stood up. "Hello. My name is Christina. I'm from Rhode Island."

One kid asked, "Is Rhode Island an island?"

The teacher answered for me.

"No, but most of it borders the ocean, and it's the smallest state in the entire country."

These kids seemed grades behind New England kids.

My last class of the day was called Shop II. I'd been looking forward to it because I thought learning how to make something would be fun. I walked in and out of several buildings before I found the shop building.

As I entered the class, I realized it was going to be very different from any of my other classes. For one, there weren't any desks; instead, stools surrounded high butcher-block tables. Upon each table were various assortments of sharp, jagged-edged tools. But what was even stranger were the kids.

These kids were different than the kids in my other classes. Something was *off* about them. A few wore glasses so thick they looked like the giant eyes cartoon characters got when surprised. Some were in wheelchairs, and others appeared to be fine, but something inside told me they weren't. And one of them was yelling and pointing at me as I walked in.

He couldn't be talking to me, could he? Please, God. Don't let him be talking to me!

He reminded me of Jerry Lewis, only with blonde hair. I didn't remember what movie it was, but it was one where he was working in a department store. Did he watch the movie, thinking to himself, *I want to look just like that?* His clothes didn't even match. Powder-blue polyester pants and a checkered yellow-and-orange shirt complete with a white plastic pocket protector from some place called Crazy Ed's. And what was with that red hair? The top stuck so close to his scalp that it looked like it was still wet. And he was hollering my way—

"New girl! Hey, new girl. C'mere!"

Oh boy, he is *talking to me. God, I must be in the wrong room. Please tell me I'm in the wrong classroom.*

I looked at my schedule and then at the board and confirmed it. Shop II, Room 302. I was in the right classroom, but there had to be some mistake. Where was the teacher?

"New girl, did you hear me? I said c'mere!" He was still yelling.

I looked around and saw that everyone was waiting for me to answer him. I turned and walked toward him because it seemed better than standing in the center of the room, looking like a complete idiot. Besides, he was the only one who had made an effort to speak to me all day.

"Hi. I'm Christina," I said as I sat on the stool next to him.

"Hi, I'm Travis. My dad teaches this class. It's so much fun. We're going to make key chains next. I'll help you if you can't do it."

What is happening to my life? Is this a joke? What do I do? There's no teacher in this room!

Had I been tossed onto Santa's Island of Misfit Toys?

"Where's the teacher?" There. I'd spoken.

"He had to bring some kid to the office. He was acting like a stupid jerk, then he threw up all over himself."

"Oh." Well, that was more than I needed to know.

Thankfully, the teacher walked into the room.

My God! He was right. That was his dad! He didn't look quite as dorky, but there was no mistaking they were related.

"For those of you who were here before class started, I apologize for the interruption. And I see we have a new student. Would you care to stand up and introduce yourself?"

I didn't want to stand up and speak, but I knew I should, so I stood to answer.

"Hi, my name is Christina French."

"Class, say hello to Christina."

"Hello, Christina," they answered in giggles and snorts.

"My name is Mr. Travis. Could I see you at my desk for a minute, Christina?"

As I walked toward the desk, Travis snickered.

"Isn't it funny? Our first names and last names are the same. Isn't that cool? We're both Travis Travis."

This entire class is ridiculous! And what kind of parent would name their kid Travis Travis? And he's a Junior, so they passed that down intentionally!

"Yes, Mr. Travis?"

He spoke softly, "I suppose you're wondering why you're in this type of class?"

Oh, thank God. They know it's a mistake!

"Yes. . . ."

"Unfortunately, the other elective classes are full. It was either this or a study class, but you already have a study, and we don't allow two. I checked to see if we could move some of your classes around, but there was just nothing I could do. This class is for kids with different types of disabilities, both mental and physical. Do you think you can handle this?"

Finally, someone had an explanation for this madness, and honestly, this was the only class where anyone had made an effort to make me feel welcome.

"Yes, Mr. Travis."

"Okay, good. You'll find that most of the kids in this class are nicer than kids in other classes, although not always well-behaved. You may go back to your seat now."

That day's class began with Mr. Travis having us select designs to make key chains. I learned that Phoenix schoolteachers were allowed to hit the students with a wooden paddle if they misbehaved. I watched one boy throw a two-by-four at another because he'd called his mother fat. Mr. Travis beat him so hard the wooden paddle broke right over his butt. That afternoon I decided that silence was the best way to get through Goldway Middle School, though as weird as it might seem, Shop II was my favorite class. Sure, the kids were a bit off, but they were honest, and they made me feel welcome.

Maybe it was because, in different ways, we were all broken. Them, mentally or physically, and me, emotionally. I could feel their pain of wanting to be accepted by the normal people. I not just accepted them, I genuinely liked them.

Danny and I walked home from the bus stop together while he rambled on about everything that he already knew and how much the teachers liked him. When we got home, Zac and Andy had already arrived and changed into their play clothes. Danny bragged to Mom about how great everyone thought he was. That dude needed to mellow out.

"How was the school day for you, Christina?" Mom asked.

"Okay," was all I said, walking to my room.

By the time I undressed and composed myself, Zac, Andy, and Mikey had already gone out somewhere to play.

Dear Diary,

I really don't like it here. This place makes me feel awful. I want to go home, even if it means having to deal with that house again. At least my friends were there.

Christina

"Mom, I'm going for a walk, okay?" I yelled as I walked out the door.

"Okay but be careful!" she yelled back.

Our street was very quiet because only neighborhood residents or visiting guests had a need to travel on it. Pauline Road wasn't very long. It ended at a cement sidewalk, built as a boundary between our neighborhood and the desert.

Back home in Rhode Island, we'd played in the woods. Lots of places to hide and things to climb on. Here, in the desert, there was nowhere to hide and nothing to climb. It was just a whole lot of sand-colored nothingness, as if this was the end of the earth. It was like God had arrived at the desert and just stopped creating things. And then stupid people came and built here anyway.

Someone was cooking on a backyard barbecue, because the entire neighborhood smelled like hamburgers. I walked, eyes focusing on the sidewalk, careful not to step on any of the cracks for fear that I might break my mother's back, even though I knew it was just a game. I was concentrating so hard.

"Hi, I'm Liam."

I looked up, startled to see a boy standing there.

"Oh, hey, I'm Christina."

He seemed about my age, and except for a biggish nose, he was rather cute, with shiny, straight blonde hair and blue eyes.

"Do you live here too, or are you just visiting?" he asked.

"I live there, in the house at the end of the circle." I pointed.

"I live right here." Liam pointed to the house right behind where we were standing.

"I'm twelve. How old are you?" I asked.

"Thirteen."

"How come I don't see you at our school bus stop?" I asked.

"I don't go to regular school. My mom said the kids out here are a bad influence. I go to a private school for boys."

"I'm not bad, I'm nice," I said, kind of confused.

He laughed. "I don't think my mom meant everyone in public school, but a lot of them."

"Oh," I said, accepting that because I agreed with his mom.

"Are you going home now?" Liam asked.

"Yeah. It's almost dinnertime."

"Do you want to come out after dinner? We can play marbles."

"Sure, but I don't know how to play marbles."

"I'll teach you. It's fun. I'll come to your house after, okay?"

"About six thirty, okay?" I said, happy that I'd just found a friend.

"Okay. See ya later." And he went back inside.

I arrived back home much happier than I'd left. I told Mom that I'd met someone who lived right up the street. She was delighted too. At dinner, we all talked about our day. Dad told Mom about his new job as a tile man. He said the company was going to keep him real busy. Zac and Andy told us about how they'd gotten to shoot bows and arrows in gym class today. Mikey brought his school project to the dinner table, a mold of his hand in plaster with a ribbon stuck to the back so Mom could hang it up. It was pretty cool, and he'd even gotten to carve his name in it.

Liam knocked on the door as we were finishing dinner. Mom invited him in and introduced him to everyone. He was very polite.

"Mom, Liam is going to teach me how to play marbles. Is it okay if we go outside?"

"Yes, but please be home by seven thirty."

"Okay, Mom," I replied.

Zac and Andy chimed in, "Can we go too?"

"Yes, boys, you can go too." And they scampered off, following close behind.

Liam let us use his marbles as we learned the game. The boys liked it because playing marbles involved using a "shooter," but instead of using guns, we used our thumbs. We had a blast, and I liked Liam a lot, and not just because he was the first friend I had made so far.

As I got ready for bed, I realized, for the first time since we'd arrived in this flat, tan place, things might not be so bad after all. It was probably because I had a new friend, and that friend was a boy. My stomach got all tingly inside when I was with Liam.

Dear Diary,

Today I met a boy, and now he's my friend. His name is Liam. He's new here too. And CUTE! Liam said we'll have lots of fun this summer. I can't wait for school to get out. He's even going to teach me how to ride a skateboard! Well . . . back to school tomorrow . . . and my weirdo shop class . . . oh boy!

Christina

I drifted off to sleep wondering if Liam got that funny feeling in his stomach when he was around me.

I awoke at some time in the middle of the night to whispering voices in the distance.

Lying there facing the wall, it took me a couple of minutes to realize that it wasn't my imagination. I must have rolled over toward the wall in my sleep. Usually, I tried to sleep facing the outside of my bed, and I'd arranged my room myself, putting my bed against a wall so I would only have to worry about one side. I thought it might help me sleep better. As it turned out, I slept pretty much the same anyway.

What was that noise? Who was whispering? Maybe it was Mom and Dad talking in their bedroom.

I listened really hard. It wasn't Mom. Both voices were male.

Did Dad have someone visiting? Or was it robbers?

My heart began to thump. I was scared and didn't move an inch, and I could hear the voices getting closer.

Thump. Thump. *Oh, no. Are those voices going to hurt me?* Thump. Thump.

I rolled over slowly like I did when Dad came into my room, faking sleep and squinting really small so I could still see and they wouldn't know. I could see my doorway and the rest of my room. There was no one there.

Was I imagining it?

I lay still for a couple of minutes, almost too scared to breathe, too frightened to scream.

The voices started again, but they sounded muffled.

Maybe I was dreaming of one of those dreams where you're getting attacked and try to scream, but nothing comes out!

But I wasn't trying to scream. I was too scared.

The bathroom door opened. I knew that creak. The voices, now in the bathroom, were a bit clearer, because the walls in the house were paper thin.

I was still squinting, but I couldn't see outside my bedroom door. I could hear feet squashing the carpet and voices coming toward me.

The voices stopped as two people entered my room. The hall light was shining into my room and making them into life-sized silhouettes. The first one was big and tall, hiding the second one behind him. As they rounded the corner toward my bed, the faces came into view, and I wasn't scared anymore—now I was terrified!

The silhouettes were naked, and I knew them! It was my brother Danny and my father, both completely naked! My brother was big and fat and gross, just like *him*. Their naked bodies were so disgusting!

What were they going to do? This had never happened before. I didn't know if I could handle this.

"Is she always asleep?" Danny whispered.

I could hear the evil in his voice, like Charles Manson from the *Helter Skelter* movie. I was so scared, my bones chilled.

"Yeah. If your sister starts to wake up, then I leave. She never knows what happens, so you have nothing to worry about," Dad answered, as if they were having a typical conversation between two people.

Fuck him! I always knew what happened. It was just that I didn't want to be an orphan, and I was scared to death my own mother wouldn't believe me because she loved him more than me!

"You gotta get hard again. Like you were in the bathroom," Dad stated, like he was teaching something as ordinary as inflating a tire.

Part of me wanted to cry out loud and run away, and another part wanted to jump out of this bed and kill both of them. But I continued to lay there, doing neither. *What's wrong with me? Concentrate, Christina, concentrate.*

I was so afraid I was going to die. Those two men were too big.

They just stood there, rubbing themselves while talking about touching me.

"Do you always do this before you touch her?"

"No. Sometimes, while I'm kneeling over her, I do it till I get off, and sometimes I use my tongue." And he stuck it out and wiggled it for Danny to see.

Stop! Make it end! I may throw up.

"Does the bed creak?" Danny asked, fearing they might get caught.

Deep down inside, I thought they were big fat cowards.

"Not really. Mom never hears anyway; she only wakes up when I get back to the bedroom. I just tell her I was watching TV. She snores too loud to hear anything."

Why was I allowing these two disgusting monsters to terrify me?

My heart was pounding so loud and fast I thought it would burst right out of my body. The thumping of the beat hurt my eardrums so badly that I couldn't hear myself think. I must have been shaking. Why hadn't they noticed I was shaking? *Don't let them scare you, Christina. Be stronger than them.*

"Are you ready yet?" Dad asked him.

"Yeah, I'm ready," he replied as he climbed onto my bed.

PLEASE, GOD, PLEASE. Help me be okay.

Then everything went black.

The alarm woke me up for school at six o'clock. The birds were chirping, and the sun was shining. It seemed like a typical, sunny desert day, but I felt strange. As I began to fully awaken, the night before played back in my head like a movie in slow motion—every horrible, agonizing moment. But I couldn't remember what happened *after* they'd climbed onto my bed.

It was real. I knew it. But why couldn't I remember? I remembered praying to God, and then everything went black. Maybe it wasn't real. Perhaps it was just a dream? Yes, that was it! It was just a dream. Nothing that bad could be real.

I untangled my covers, which were in an unusual mess.

Definitely an awful dream! I never moved in my sleep. I twisted my body, getting up to avoid a wet spot in the bed, consciously choosing to ignore it because I wanted to believe that the night before was not real.

I got out of bed, collected my school clothes, and headed for the shower.

The shower felt great, and I started to feel like myself again. I stayed in the shower twice as long as usual because feeling extra clean seemed important today. I washed everything hard and twice. I got out of the shower a bit refreshed and began to powder myself.

What happened to my leg?

Oh no, everything was getting foggy again. I felt faint and leaned against the bathroom wall and slid down the wall onto the tile floor. I sat on the floor while my entire body shook, trying to hold back from bawling out loud. The red bruise on my inner thigh was awful.

How did I get this? His leg? His hand? Danny's leg?

I didn't think I wanted to know how it'd happened. But now I knew. It wasn't a dream. This was my life. And now, with my father and my brother, we'd reached a new level of evilness. I sat lifeless on the floor, tears running down my face, wishing they could wash away the hurt from inside. I thought about my real dad, wondering if he'd really left for the reasons Mom said.

Why didn't my real dad ever try to find me?

Mom said he wasn't the type of guy that cared, but even if he did, she said she wouldn't let him near me anyway.

God, please help me be strong. I can't wait to be old enough to leave. Please make him stop. Please just make him stop.

"Christina, hurry up! I have to pee!" Zac knocked at the door.

I snapped back to reality, cleared my throat, dried my eyes, and replied, "Okay, Zac. I'll be out in a minute."

1977 – twelve years old

Chapter 8

I still didn't understand why people lived in the desert. I was tired of hearing "But it's a *dry* heat." As far as I was concerned, at 120 degrees, hot is hot!

But summer did allow for plenty of babysitting time, and soon I'd have earned enough for my own skateboard.

Dear Diary,

Tonight was the longest night of babysitting ever! I didn't get home until 3:30 a.m.! I kept awake by watching Elvis's (he's so hot) movie called Kissin' Cousins, but all I could think about was Liam. I wonder if he was thinking about me too?

Me and Liam have a blast together! Except when Danny's around. Danny's super mean to me when we're with Liam. He tries to get me to leave. Probably because he's got no friends, but mostly he loves being rotten to me. I hate Danny so much now.

He acts as if he has some superpower now, because he knows no matter what he does, he won't get in trouble because Dad always takes care of Danny.

It's like evil protects evil or something.

PS: Babysitting late nights are the best, no one visits my room on those nights. I love my job!

Christina

"Moving? What do you mean we're moving?" I asked.

"Yes, we're moving to Rhode Island," Mom answered.

"But why? We just got here. I'm just getting used to *this* place, and I have a job. And my old friends have probably forgotten all about me."

"Dad's not making enough money here because of the illegal aliens. They work for less than five dollars an hour, and the union workers aren't getting the hours they need, so we're going home to Rhode Island. It'll be better there."

"But why can't Dad get a job with a different company? Why do we have to move again? It's not fair!" I said, still crying but a little more understanding.

And with that remark came the all-too-familiar screeching sound of out-of-tune bagpipes.

"Fair? I'll give you fair! Your father and I sold our house so *you* kids could have a better life! Not us. You! I gave up *my* life when I had *you*! Then I married a man with three little boys that weren't mine and raised them too. That's giving! I'm a saint! You're selfish! Maybe you should sit down and think about what your mother has done for you! Do you hear me?"

"Yes, Mom. I understand," I replied, and quietly retired to my room.

> *Dear Diary,*
> *I can't believe we are moving—again!! And my mother is nuts! All she does is yell and tell me I'm selfish. What's wrong with her? I put up with HIM, FOR HER! Because she LOVES HIM.*
> *I don't understand anything anymore. I just want time to pass so I am old enough to move out.*
> *Reading makes me feel better. I'm almost done with Judy Blume's* Forever. *I wish I could meet Ms. Blume so I could thank her for writing* Are You There, God? It's Me, Margaret. *I liked it because I talk to God too. I don't know if there is really anyone up there, but it feels good to think there might be someone watching over me to make sure I am okay.*
> *I think it's working, because with all the bad stuff that Dad's done, I'm still okay. Some kids at the school said they did bad things because their parents were awful, so why not be bad too? Wow, then I should probably be a murderer or something.*
> *Some kids in school are so wasted, they never know what day it is. I don't even want to think of what would happen to me if I lost control. I'd never risk that, because I don't think I'd survive.*
> *Christina*

I woke up to my mother's voice, screaming, again.

"These kids have no damn consideration! I suppose I am to pack myself?"

We were packing this morning? If she'd woken us up and asked, I'd have been happy to help. Now I was afraid to get up! She'd gotten so mean.

Something was definitely wrong with her. Maybe her brain was in backward. That was why she thought that Dad was a great guy.

She was still screaming. Uh-oh.

"Christina, are you going to help your mother, or are you going to continue to be fucking inconsiderate?"

Something told me if I answered honestly, I'd end up in the hospital. Besides, I'd do anything to make her stop that screeching. If I died and went to hell, the acoustics would consist of the perpetual ear-bleeding blast of my mother's screaming voice.

"I'm up, Mom. I'll be right out to help, okay?"

"You should've been up hours ago! I do everything for you, and you don't appreciate shit!"

I sat upright on my bed. My stomach felt like an unbalanced, brick-filled washing machine.

Why is she screaming? Maybe the boys did something wrong, and she's just taking it out on everyone?

I managed to leave my bedroom and peek into the boys' room without being noticed. Zac was sitting on his bed with tears running down his cheeks, but from laughing, not crying. Then I looked at Andy and began laughing too. Apparently, they'd been listening to Mom yell, but unlike me, they didn't let it eat them up inside.

Andy, dressed as Mom, was imitating and translating his version for Zac. He had a handkerchief on his head like Aunt Jemima from the syrup bottle, his T-shirt tied up in a halter-type knot and pajama bottoms rolled up like shorts and had confiscated a pair of Mom's slippers. That sight alone was hilarious, but it didn't end there. Andy had Mom's expressions down pat, and he was quietly mouthing her words, shaking his hips, and evilly pointing his index finger toward Zac as he fake-yelled about what an inconsiderate kid Zac was. He was so funny!

"You boys should kiss the ground I walk on for what I've done for you. I'm a saint for this! What other woman would marry a guy that has three little boys? No, let me correct that: three babies still in diapers! No other woman, that's who! Me, only me! I'm a saint, a fuckin' saint! And you kids don't show one ounce of consideration!"

Zac and I were rolling now! I could never understand why she thought we were bad kids. I'd seen Beaver Cleaver do worse things than we did, and Mrs. Cleaver never called him an inconsiderate shit.

I quietly went back to my room, popped my head out of the doorway, and then, careful not to set her off on a rant, politely asked, "Mom, where would you like us to begin?"

My heart was pounding loud.

Why was I so scared of her? I never intended to make her scream. I went out of my way to try to avoid it from ever happening, but somehow, something always set her off.

She answered directly, but the yelling stopped, thank God.

"I'd like you to vacuum, dust the living room, and clean your room, please. Do you think you can do that for me?"

She was still on the edge of an explosion, so I answered quickly and quietly, then scurried off with the Lemon Pledge, dust rag in hand.

"Okay."

"Where are your brothers?"

"They're in their room, folding and putting away laundry," I yelled, hoping they'd hear the hint.

Dear Diary,

Our house sold in three days! We're moving back to Rhode Island. Mom is yelling constantly and getting crazier by the minute! They say we'll be "home" in two weeks. Home? We've never lived anywhere long enough to call it home. This sucks.

Yesterday she called me a pig for hanging with Liam. She said twelve-year-old daughters that hang around with boys are pigs. That made me cry. All we ever do is skateboard and hang out, but it would be cool to kiss Liam. I think we're both too chicken, though.

Lots of girls at school kiss boys, even French-kiss with their tongues (eww), but I've never even touched a boy. I put up with her disgusting husband every night and keep my mouth shut—for her! He's the pig. I am NOT a pig.

Christina

Dear Diary,

Tonight's our last night in Arizona. I got to see Liam after dinner. We went skateboarding, and then when it was time to go. He told me he dreamt that Rhode Island burned down, and we had to

*stay. It made me blush, and I explained the state isn't really that small.
He said he would miss me. I said I would miss him too, and then . . .
whammo! It finally happened! Liam kissed me!! It only lasted a
second, but it made my insides feel warm and happy! Then he got on
his skateboard and zoomed away as quick as it had happened. And
just like that, Liam was gone. Forever.*

Christina

We were back in Hillsgrove, Rhode Island, temporarily
living in a home owned by a cousin of Dad's we'd never met, until
we found a permanent home. It was a small, old, musty-smelling
Hansel-and-Gretel fairy-tale-style home in a clustered
neighborhood. But it was clear on the other side of town in a
completely different school district from where our old friends
lived, making it junior high number four for me. Totally sucked!

The next few days were a whirlwind. Between registering
for a new junior high and shopping for school clothes, there
wasn't much time left. It was midnight, and I was in bed, wide
awake, thinking about my first day at Rookwood Junior High. My
bedroom smelled like mothballs and old people.

By 2:30 a.m., I had thought about every facet of my life—
twice.

I could try counting sheep, but that never worked for me.
I wondered who'd thought of imaginary sheep counting in the
first place, and did it work for anyone?

This house was full of creaks and mysterious noises. I
heard someone in the hall.

Oh, great, it was Dad. Big surprise! *Prepare yourself,
Christina, it's going to be another one of those nights. And why
wouldn't it be?*

He was standing at my doorway.

It was pretty sick that I was actually so used to this now.

Well, there he was, by my bed, sporting the official red
bathrobe of molestation . . . and there I was, lying on my
stomach, facing the hall, squinting and fake sleeping. Just
another typical night in the world of Christina. And ya know what
the funny part was? I was at the point where I actually felt
relieved when it was only him and not his asshole son too. How
sick was that? When would it stop? I'd be a teenager in less than
a month! Lately, he'd gotten braver and stayed longer, and I had
to tug my covers even tighter before he went away. I guessed
after all those years of Mom not saying a word about Dad missing

from the bed, he figured he was safe. It was like she didn't care at all.

I fidgeted a little, hoping he would leave.

Hey, why would he leave now? He just got here.

The next time I looked at the clock, about a half hour had passed, and he was gone.

What was happening to me? Why didn't I remember what happened after he came into my room? I felt okay. My covers were still on. My hands were cut from holding the covers so tight, so I guessed he hadn't gotten through my sheets, but what had he done? I didn't know. This had happened a few times in Arizona too. Why couldn't I remember anymore? I hadn't fallen asleep. I was sure of it! But I didn't know what he'd done. Had I blacked out?

I stayed awake the remainder of the night. The radio alarm went off at six in the morning with WPRO DJ, Salty Brine, announcing the fall TV schedule featuring a new show about people that fall in love on a cruise ship.

The temporary living arrangement went from weeks to months, but Mom and Dad still had high hopes for the perfect country home. Sunday afternoons were spent driving to an unpopulated town called Forestville. You could drive for miles and miles, some roads still unpaved, and not see a single house. Every now and then there'd be a driveway visible, leading to farm homes. Forestville felt like a beautiful painting, not real life.

"This house isn't ours yet. So, don't do anything or touch anything, just keep your traps shut, understand?" Dad instructed as we pulled up to a house for sale.

"Okay, Dad," everyone replied.

The realtor and the homeowners met us outside, gave us a tour of the picturesque red farmhouse property, and then led us inside. The house looked like something out of a country magazine. The walls were covered with wallpaper of young Huck Finn-type boys and old men fishing, and homemade crafts were everywhere. This wasn't an "us" house. I didn't think we'd fit in.

"This house needs a lotta repairs," Dad said.

They talked about that for a while, and then Dad said they'd like to make an offer on the house. I couldn't see us living in a *Little House on the Prairie*-type home, but hey, what did I know.

A few nights later, we were all sitting at the dinner table when Danny, as if responsible for making crucial family decisions, suggested, "We should start packing soon so we'll be ready to move when the realtor calls."

He'd probably pissed off some kid, something that happened at every school, and was now anxious to get out of here.

The next thing we knew, Mom was banging pots and pans around and making loud noises, throwing silverware into the sink. Everyone stopped talking and eating and sat frozen-tag still.

Danny knew he had set her off, but he didn't know why. Dad was the only one that seemed unaffected; he just kept on eating his ziti as if everything was fine.

"You don't need to pack anything! Because we didn't get the loan for the fucking house! I can't believe after all I've been through and given up for this goddamn family, we still didn't get that house. I think I deserve a nice house in the country, but I guess marrying a guy with three little babies isn't enough! Now I have to live in a house that belongs to a fucking relative! When is it going to end?"

We quietly cleared the dishes, then scattered toward anything that remotely resembled an exit. Zac and Andy went upstairs to watch TV, Danny and Mikey went outside, and I escaped to my room. Dad stayed at the table, eating his ziti.

Because my bedroom was directly across from the kitchen, even with the door closed I could still hear her. I started to cry.

Why couldn't she be a regular mom? Why couldn't she be someone I could confide in? Instead, she had more problems than me! My parents were so messed up.

1977 – thirteen years old

Chapter 9

Dear Diary,

They found a house so, surprise, we're moving again! I was just getting used to this jr. high and even had a chance to go to Washington, D.C., with the chorus, but that's not happening because we're moving AGAIN! Mom said it wouldn't have mattered if we were staying, because there wasn't any money to send me anyway. I guess it's okay, because I would've been really embarrassed to tell the teacher that I couldn't go because we don't have money. I am going to try my best to learn as much as possible, and when I grow up, I will always have a job where I can take care of myself. I don't want to have to rely on some loser guy like my dad to support me.

Christina

I'd be in my fifth junior high school once in this next house, so nine schools total since kindergarten. I had met so many different kinds of people but mixed in with all of the moving and different types of kids, one thing always stayed the same: him.

And even in that small awful-smelling house with their bedroom so close, Mom still never woke up to save me. Why? Had I been a horrible person in a previous life and this was my payback?

Last night, before the abuse, he'd looked through my dresser drawers, for what . . . money? Just creepy. He'd looked in my underwear drawer, then he'd gone through my other drawers. He'd even gone through the stuff on top of my dresser.

***

By the time Christmas had arrived, we were in the new house, but this year was different. There weren't many gifts due to lack of money, but we did chop down our own Christmas tree from the woods in our backyard. I had to admit, our new house was far-out! Our property covered five acres, and the house sat atop a small hill, making for a great natural winter snow slide, and the brook flowing through the yard down to Wilby's pond was excellent for ice skating in winter and swimming in summer.

We'd only lived there a week, so I hadn't met anyone yet, as most of our free time was spent cleaning and fixing up the house. The boys' rooms were on the second floor. My room was opposite Mom and Dad's . . . of course.

The hopes of my father leaving me alone at night had long since passed. I'd taught myself to deal with it, and as far as I was concerned, that was a different me. Not my real life. My hatred for him grew every waking day, making it almost impossible to keep inside.

When I was younger, I hadn't understood. Now at thirteen, I knew better, and I literally detested him. I believed Mom knew what was going on but wouldn't admit it because she liked her life with him and was more afraid of being on her own than saving her daughter.

Mom wasn't the kind of person who could take care of herself. She needed to depend on people, especially him. I never wanted to be like her. Between moving all over the country and not having a mom to lean on emotionally or for any real need, it'd made me independent. I liked it that way.

The school bus stop was on our road, at the bottom of the hill. The bus arrived at 6:45 a.m. Danny, Zac, and I arrived first. Andy, not far behind, was still looking for his shoes, which he seemed to lose every morning. Aside from Jed, a boy that Zac and Andy had met, I wondered if there'd be anyone else at the stop. Jed lived across the street. He had wavy dark-brown hair and always wore a flannel shirt, crisp blue jeans, and hiking boots. He looked like a short, stocky, meatball-shaped lumberjack but seemed okay. He fit right in with Zac and Andy— just another teenage boy looking for mischief!

Andy, hormones raging, came running down the hill, shouting, "Hey, Jed. Where're all the hot girls you said live nearby?"

"Yeah, Jed . . . ," Danny and Zac said in unison.

Oh, boy, just what I needed . . . three girl-crazy brothers and a human meatball, scaring away my chances of meeting new friends.

Before Jed could answer, a girl walked down the street toward us. Jed didn't say anything. He just pointed as if to say "See, I told you so." We watched as she neared the bus stop.

She either wasn't aware of us ogling her or didn't let on if she was. She walked downhill, facing the ground, kicking a rock toward the bus stop. If Jed hadn't spoken, I think she would have kept walking for hours and missed the bus.

"Hey, Maryann," Jed said, all proud of himself because he knew her name.

She was kind of short, with a happy sort of Girl Scout face and a super-cool blonde version of a Dorothy Hamill haircut. She must have gotten new clothes for Christmas, because she was wearing a brand-new pair of chocolate-colored Levi corduroys and scuff-free Earth Shoes.

Looking up and seeing new people at the bus stop changed her expression from not interested to . . . interested! Wow! She was so white, with little freckles on her face. Her eyes were big and blue, and she had wicked-cool blue mascara that my mom wouldn't even consider allowing me to use.

"Hey, Jed," she said, very monotone, then turned to me and smiled before speaking. "Hi, I'm Maryann."

"I'm Christina, and these are my brothers: Danny, Zac, and Andy."

They all replied hi back. Zac and Andy scampered off to the side, whispering things with Jed. Danny just stood there, acting as if he was far too important for Maryann to miss.

"Did you meet Molly yet?" Maryann asked me.

"No, I haven't met anyone except Jed," I replied.

"Don't worry. Not everyone from Forestville is like Jed. Some of us are normal." She laughed.

"Hey, I heard that!" Jed yelled.

"Sooooooo?" Maryann replied right back.

As the bus came down the hill, I told Maryann about where we lived and that we had moved in during Christmas vacation.

As we stepped up onto the bus, two more girls approached the bus stop, both yelling, "Wait!" in hopes the driver wouldn't leave without them. Maryann was laughing.

"Here come Molly and April," she said. "Molly's my best friend. We've been friends since kindergarten. And April lives up the street from you, near the apple orchard. She moved here about a year ago. Her dad used to be in the military, but he's retired now."

Wow! I'd thought Maryann was short, but April and Molly were even smaller. Must've been something in that country air.

Molly looked nothing like Maryann. She had brown hair like mine but longer and straighter, with a petite and curvy body and the tiniest waist I'd ever seen. Molly wore glasses that made her pretty, big brown eyes even prettier. She looked smart but not nerdy.

If I hadn't known better, Molly and April could have passed for sisters. Same build, same height, but April had naturally curly long blonde hair and big blue eyes.

Both girls were wearing new corduroys and shoes identical to Maryann's. They'd definitely shopped together.

I guessed that was what friends did. I wouldn't know, as I'd never lived anywhere long enough to have one.

Maryann told me to sit in the seat in front of her.

"This is Christina. She just moved into the house across from Jed's," she said to the two girls that sat in the adjacent seat to hers.

"Oh yeah, I know which one. Hi, Christina, nice to meet you," Molly said, then went on talking to Maryann about Christmas and other things.

"Hi, nice to meet you," April said.

I didn't say much during the ride, but I felt good because they stopped every now and then to ask me a question out of politeness in an effort not to leave me out. They were friendly, and I learned lots about their families from listening to them gab.

Our daily bus ride was forty-five minutes long. Some roads were unpaved, and some had deep dirt potholes with leftover snow and ice everywhere. Cars shouldn't have traveled on those roads, never mind school buses. We picked kids up on roads that appeared to have no houses at all. At one stop, there was a kid with his books on the ground, standing by a tiny shoveled path leading out to nowhere. Just trees and clouds! I wondered where he lived. He looked healthy, so he must've had a house.

One of the last stops was a driveway with a large house set way back. It had horses in the yard and a snow-covered tennis court by the road.

"The dad is the vice president of some bank, and they're wicked rich. That's Randy. He's in our grade, and he's a hunk!" Maryann said, pointing to the kid waiting for the bus to stop.

The bus arrived at Tomahawk Middle School, and we piled off in single file. Maryann was the same age as me; Molly and April were a year younger.

"Hey, I'm going to walk Christina to the office so she doesn't get lost. I'll catch up with you later, okay?" said Maryann, waving to Molly and April.

"Okay, I'll meet you at the lockers," Molly replied.

Maryann gave me a tour on the way to the office.

"This is the office, where you'll get your daily schedule. Maybe we'll see you at lunch."

"All right, thanks. Everyone has been so nice. My other schools weren't like this at all," I said.

Maryann replied, smiling proudly, "That's because this is Forestville. You live in the country now. That's where all the nice people live!"

I smiled approvingly and walked into the office.

"Hi, my name is Christina French. My mom registered us before Christmas vacation. Me and my brothers are new," I said to the gray-haired lady behind the counter as my brothers walked in behind me.

"Hi, Christina, and you meant to say 'my brothers and I,' right? Please have a seat, and we'll get all of you your schedules and get you going as soon as possible. Okay?"

"Yes, I did. And okay. Thanks," I said, and we all found seats in the office waiting area.

It was amazing that despite how different we all were, when it came to another first day in another new school, we all had the same initial reactions: be polite and quiet.

The secretary gave us schedules and maps, then off we went to our classes. This school was much smaller than our other school, and sixth graders were in junior high with us. Maryann said it was because there weren't many kids that lived here, and the school district consisted of two entire towns. Some of the kids I was going to school with lived twenty or more miles apart.

I wasn't as nervous as I usually was on the first day at a new school. I didn't know if I was becoming accustomed to moving or if something about the country was relaxing.

When I opened the door to my new class, the relaxed feeling faded into a scene that had become routine in my life. Class had already begun, and upon walking into the classroom, the entire class went mute, looking at me as if I was a botched science experiment. I stood by and waited for the teacher to break the ice.

"Well, class, it looks like we have someone new joining us. And your name is . . . ?" the teacher asked.

"My name is Christina French." I had said this so often that I thought I'd be a great contestant on To Tell the Truth.

"Christina, my name is Mr. Nimble. Welcome to Tomahawk Middle School and my history class. Please have a seat at an empty desk."

Mr. Nimble seemed a little . . . off. Maybe it was his appearance? His head was round, his hands were round, and even his feet looked round. How did one squeeze round feet into regular shoes? This man was perfectly round—not flabby, more like a solid helium balloon with shiny, greasy black hair oddly combed over to one side. I wasn't sure if I was holding back a giggle or a gasp.

I sat in the first desk that my legs took me to and exhaled as if I'd just stepped off a twisting roller coaster ride.

"Hey, I'm Parker." The boy at the desk in front of mine smiled.

His voice was so deep it nearly took my breath away.

"Hey," I responded.

Parker was big, like a football player, with shoulders so broad I couldn't see the blackboard without leaning to one side. He had dark eyes that twinkled when they looked at you. Parker was cute!

I didn't remember much of what Mr. Nimble said during class because I was too busy checking out the rest of the kids. One boy in particular stood out. His name was Wyatt. His primary goal seemed to be to torment Mr. Nimble, and he accomplished that goal in spades. After several smart-aleck answers, a few well-placed spit wads, and lots of classroom laughter, Wyatt was in trouble and sent to the principal's office.

By the end of the day, I had decided I liked these kids and this school. There was something safe about it, safe enough to take a risk and climb out of my shy shell. It was time to make the first move and speak up.

Getting on the bus, I heard Maryann yelling behind me, "Hey, Christina, wait up!"

I turned to make sure she was actually speaking to me . . . and she was!

"How was your first day? Are you on the A side of school or the B side?" she asked.

"I'm on the A side. What's the difference?" I answered and asked.

"Nothing, just a different group of teachers than us. The class is split in half. I have no idea why."

"Oh. So, you don't have Mr. Nimble?" I asked.

She laughed and corrected me. "Oh, you mean Mr. Numbskull. No, we're lucky. We don't."

"Boy, is he a weirdo! Some kid named Wyatt Roberts went off on him today."

"You're in a class with Wyatt Roberts?" she asked, surprised.

"Yeah, and some wicked-cute guy named Parker," I said, fishing for gossip.

April had gotten on the bus and was sitting with us too. April, listening as if she heard stuff like this every day. I got the feeling that Maryann was the self-appointed information central, and for now, that was okay with me.

"Well, let me tell you about Wyatt and Parker . . . ." And she was off.

By the time she was finished, I had more than enough info about a lot of kids in our class.

For the first time, riding home as the new kid in school didn't feel so lonely.

I think I am going to like it here.

1978 – thirteen years old

Chapter 10

Dear Diary,

I have a date! Bobby Winter asked me to the eighth-grade semiformal! He's so cute, AND Mom said I could go! Maybe I'll finally get to REALLY kiss a boy! I hope my stupid parents don't decide to move again, because this is my favorite school so far. The kids here are wicked friendly. April and I hang out after school almost every day. We're super close. I love having a real friend.

Christina

The school dance night was finally here! In another hour, Bobby would meet my parents. I couldn't wait to see him, and I was so nervous! I hoped my jerk-ass father wouldn't be mean to Bobby.

I loved my new dress. It was yellow and white with a lace top and spaghetti straps. I wanted something that would match my new pink satin jacket, but the only dress that matched it was way too expensive. It was okay, because Bobby thought disco sucked anyway, and he kept teasing me, calling my satin jacket my Saturday Night Fever jacket. Bobby didn't understand. It wasn't so much about disco as it was about John Travolta! Nobody in KISS or Led Zeppelin was John Travolta cute.

I heard knocking at the door.

Oh no, he's here! Okay, Christina, wait in your room until someone calls for you. Don't let him think you're too excited.

"Christina, are you ready? There's someone here to see you . . . ," Mom teased from the other room.

"Coming," I answered nervously.

I caught a glimpse of Bobby as I rounded the corner from my bedroom to the living room, and my face felt as if I was on fire.

Bobby looked—wow—hot!

His normal blue jeans and concert T-shirt had been replaced by a perfectly fitted powder-blue polyester suit, and his eyes sparkled against the fabric. His blonde hair was neatly combed, perhaps for the first time since we'd met, and he was smiling from ear to ear. My insides melted.

"Hey," Bobby said, happy and fidgety.

Oh good, he's nervous too. "Hi, Bobby. Have you met my parents yet?"

"I met your mom when I came in," he replied, pointing toward my mother.

Then Dad walked into the room, followed by Danny, also dressed in a suit. Danny had told Mom and Dad that his date was meeting him at the school. Total lie, Danny didn't have a date. Unfortunately, that left us riding to the dance in the same car.

"So, you're the guy that's taking my daughter to the dance, huh?" Dad said jokingly . . . sort of.

"Hi, Mr. French, I'm Bobby Winter. Nice to meet you," he said, sounding overly polite.

Danny smirked, as if he anticipated Dad would be mean to Bobby.

"Nice suit there, Bobby," Danny said sarcastically, attempting to belittle Bobby.

I wondered what Danny saw when he looked at himself in the mirror. I thought he saw himself as Ponch from CHiPs, but in reality, the only thing he had in common with CHiPs was eating them.

Bobby surprisingly replied politely, "Thanks, Danny."

"Come on, kids, let's go outside and take pictures. I'd like to have pictures of my daughter's first school dance," Mom said, leading us outside.

We spent several minutes feeling awkward and smiling nervously. I had my picture taken alone, with Bobby, with Mom, with Mom and Dad, and with just Dad, who grabbed me close, put his arm around me, and touched my ass. I ground my teeth to keep from punching him in the face. They even made us take pictures with Danny. Finally, we got in the car.

"Okay, kids, I'll meet you outside at eleven o'clock. And Bobby, I don't want to hear any stories about you trying to go too far with my daughter, ya hear?" he said, laughing.

Yeah, right. God forbid anyone else touches me, you scumbag!

We waved good-bye as the car door slammed, and Dad drove off. That left Bobby and me standing alone as Danny strutted his sorry self into the gym.

"You look pretty."

"Thanks. You look nice too. Let me guess, there's a Led Zeppelin T-shirt underneath that white dress shirt, right?"

"Nooo, there's not," he said, shaking his head. "It's a KISS T-shirt."

We both laughed.

"Hey, at least I'm not wearing a pink satin jacket," he teased back at me.

Walking toward the gym felt like being in an episode of the Twilight Zone. Our friends, all dressed up too, were standing side by side with their dates, leaning against gymnasium walls, as if required. The guys stared blankly at the floor, while the girls appeared a bit more in control of themselves. Maybe because we girls felt great in our formal outfits. The guys looked as if they were all wearing suits made of wood, still trying to be cool but not really pulling it off.

"Wanna go sit on the bleachers?"

"Okay," I replied, because I didn't have a better idea.

"I was really happy you said yes when I asked you," Bobby said. "All my friends said there was no way that you would ever say yes."

"Why did they think that?" I asked him.

"Well, rumor has it that you are the kind of girl that guys are supposed to stay away from."

"What does that mean?" I asked, wondering just that.

"It's just that most of the guys are afraid to talk to you," he said.

"Well, I'm glad you asked me," I said, smiling.

"How about thanking me during the next slow song?" he asked.

As the night went on, I danced with my friends, and Bobby and I experienced our first slow dance. We were both so nervous, I don't think either one of us remembered dancing. By ten o'clock, most couples were in the bleachers, making out.

I wanted to kiss Bobby, but not in front of everyone on those bleachers. I'd be uncomfortable making out in front of the entire class. We were fidgeting against the gym wall as the DJ announced the last slow dance of the night. We giggled, watching couples rise like zombies from the bleachers to the dance floor.

Bobby took my hand and led me to the double doors in between the exit hall and the classrooms. Instead of continuing toward the exit, he took a sharp right down the corridor. Once away from the crowd, Bobby stopped and propped himself against the glass between the wall and a door. He was facing the classroom hall, and I was facing the exit, watching my friends leave as if there had been a fire drill.

"What are we doing here?" I asked.

"Don't worry, we won't get in trouble. I wanted to find a quiet place to talk," Bobby explained, taking my hands, bringing my body close to his.

As our bodies touched, I could feel my face turning bright red. Jesus, I was nervous! I could barely hear what he was saying, and I was too shy to look him in the eyes. To avoid going completely limp, I focused on watching the rest of the kids exit the gym.

Why am I so nervous? Is it because I know, at any moment, I'm going to experience my first real kiss? I could feel my heart racing and hoped that Bobby didn't feel it too!

Bobby continued talking, but I still had no idea what he was saying. The butterflies in my stomach and the loud beating in my chest consumed every ounce of brainpower. I was so busy wondering when it was going to happen that I didn't even know how it actually happened; the next thing I knew, his lips and mine had become one, and we were kissing!

I began talking to my brain: Stop looking at the kids leaving and relax! Enjoy it. There's nothing wrong with this. He is NOT your father. This is okay.

I turned away from looking at the other kids, let my eyes close, and allowed myself to feel his kiss. I realized the butterflies in my stomach weren't butterflies at all but instead little raindrops of happiness, and that happiness was coming from Bobby. He was sharing that with me! It was beautiful. This was different. This wasn't wrong.

Moments later, I opened my eyes and found Bobby looking right into them.

"That wasn't so bad, was it?" he asked.

"No, actually, it was quite nice," I replied, and we kissed again.

The ride home was a bit of a blur. It felt as if I had little red hearts floating in my eyes like Pepé Le Pew, the cartoon skunk. On the ride home, I was vaguely aware of Danny bragging to Dad about how great everyone thought he was. I didn't care. All I wanted to do was get home and write in my diary. Once back, Mom had lots of questions. I didn't even know what she'd asked; I was still on cloud nine.

Dear Diary,

Tonight, April 7th, 1978, was awesome. My first official date, dance . . . and a REAL kiss! Everything was wicked cool. I really like Bobby. I can't wait until I'm old enough to move out of here. I want to feel like this all the time. I could tell Dad wasn't happy about my date, but I don't care. I hope he was furious, and that made me feel good! I can't wait to tell April! Good night!

Christina

1978 – thirteen years old

Chapter 11

Mixed with doses of good and bad, the next few months went by fast.

The good was Bobby. The bad, instigated by Danny, was Mom. I had a suspicion he'd been telling Mom and Dad things about Bobby and me that were not true just to hurt me. Mom was on my case constantly, asking about what exactly Bobby and I did together. We didn't *do* anything together. I couldn't figure out what she could possibly think we did while we were at school. It wasn't like I saw Bobby at night or we went anywhere together.

But she decided I was too young to be seeing one boy. Furthermore, Mom had also decided that I shouldn't be going out with *any* boys at my age because people would think her daughter was a pig, and that would reflect poorly on her.

"That boy is going to take advantage of you," she said.

"What do you mean, 'take advantage of me,' Mom?" I asked, almost in tears.

"Well, what kind of girl has a boyfriend in the eighth grade? Your father and I don't approve of it!" she insisted.

"But Mom, you should trust me. I know the difference between right and wrong!"

"How am I supposed to know that? Bobby's a boy, isn't he?" she asked, as if I had no brain or common sense of my own.

"Yes. And I'm a girl who knows better. Don't you trust me? You're not being fair! I have never, ever given you a reason not to trust me!" I answered, now crying.

"I don't have to be fair! I'm your mother! I know better than you! It's simple: you're a young girl, and he's a teenage boy. You don't have to tell me what happens. Believe me, I know! And he's not fooling your father either. Your father is worried, and we don't trust him!" she yelled.

"You don't have to trust him! You have to trust me! What have I ever done for you not to trust me?" I was yelling now.

She always sided with him! Why did I bother to argue with her? It was never going to get any better, and being with Bobby would make my life worse. Dad and Danny would make sure of that. In reality, she was his wife first and my mother last!

As she continued to yell about the awful daughter she was bringing up, I stormed off to my room and cried myself to sleep.

On the way to school the next morning, I told April what had happened. She couldn't understand why my mom acted that way, but I could never explain what my nights at home were like. The older I got, the more that monster won.

I really liked Bobby, but realistically, I was only in eighth grade. Was I going to move out and marry Bobby? Of course not! Could I move out on my own and support myself right now? Unfortunately, no. So, why did I put myself through all this agony? I wasn't kidding myself; I was completely aware that I was rationalizing a breakup with Bobby because it was the path of least resistance.

Bobby and I had initially planned to take the last bus home, as this allowed for time together after school.

I sat on the school's front lawn by the curb, waiting for him, silently rehearsing my breakup speech. I knew he had sensed something wasn't right, and he'd been asking me what was wrong all day. I'd repeatedly replied, "Nothing," but I could tell that he knew it was something.

And the look in his eyes when he approached me was proof.

"Your eyes are a little bloodshot. Rough afternoon?" I asked sarcastically.

The only deflection I had to work with was Bobby's habit of smoking pot. Like a lot of the kids in school, he smoked pot—a lot of pot. I smoked nothing. Our understanding was I would never bother him about it, and he would never smoke while I was around.

"I thought you weren't going to smoke that around me?" I asked. Maybe if I acted upset about it, he'd get angry too.

"Yeah, I know, but I had the feeling that something was really wrong today, and I just felt the need. I'm right, huh? Is it your mom? Is she driving you crazy again?"

"Well, yes, she is, but that's not what's wrong," I said, stalling.

"Then what? Did I do something wrong?"

"No. It's not you. It's me. I guess I'm just not ready for this," I said, trying to sound convincing for both of us.

"Ready for what?"

"For being a couple, I guess."

"But why all of a sudden? Yesterday, everything was okay. Except your mom, of course. She's never okay," he said, trying to laugh.

"Well, she spent most of yesterday screaming at me about what a pig I am and how I shouldn't be going steady at my age."

"Who cares what she said? Everyone knows you're not a pig!" he argued.

"Yeah, I know, but you don't live with my mother. She makes my life a living hell."

"So, what do you plan to do about her?"

"There's nothing I can do except give in . . . or move out, and unfortunately, I'm not exactly in the position to do that." I sighed.

"What exactly does 'give in' mean?" he asked nervously.

"I think we have to break up. I just can't deal with that woman anymore. And besides, she's right about one thing. We are only in the eighth grade," I said, trying to justify it.

"That's not right! She can't make you break up with someone! And so what if we're only in eighth grade? I'm still going to love you even when we graduate!" He was yelling and standing now.

Okay, this wasn't going as I'd planned. I'd thought Bobby would listen and feel bad but agree, then probably find another girl that didn't have such a screwed-up family. And what was this about love? Love? Yikes! Love scared me!

"I don't know what to think anymore, Bobby," I said with tears rolling down my face. "Can we just give it a rest for a while and let me think about everything?"

He wasn't happy, but it was better than nothing.

"Okay. School's out for the summer next week, and I'm going to visit my cousins in Maine for a couple of weeks. Can we talk when I get back?"

In Maine? What a break!

"Sure. It's a deal. We'll talk in a couple of weeks."

I kissed him on the cheek and told him how sorry I was that this was happening.

"Hopefully it will all blow over. I love you, ya know," Bobby said, looking directly into my eyes.

"Yeah. It's just too much at once, okay?" I said, hoping he would understand, but inside knowing that he never would.

"Yeah, it's fine for now. I'm going to catch a ride with one of the guys over at the high school. You okay to ride on the bus?"

"Yeah, I'm fine. I could use the long, bumpy ride." I smiled.

"I'll see you in a couple of weeks."

I watched him walk away, feeling responsibly sad inside.

***

I couldn't believe I had a job! The owners of the town market had been looking for someone to babysit their little girls and cashier at the same time, and I was more than happy to accept the offer.

I made three dollars an hour, way more than I'd made for babysitting in Arizona. It was about a mile walk to get to work, a small price to pay to get out of the house. The first thing I was going to buy was a ten-speed bike. I'd asked for one for the last two Christmases but was told we didn't have enough money to buy gifts like that.

Back in Hillsgrove, it'd seemed like our family always had enough money, but now it felt like the opposite. Mom and Dad were constantly arguing about money, and more than once during the winter, I'd taken a freezing-cold shower because we'd run out of furnace oil. I was so happy to have a job. I didn't want to be like my parents, never knowing where the next dollar was coming from.

Once I was working, Dad was quick to point out that I'd be buying my own school clothes. Fine by me. As far as I was concerned, the fewer things I had to ask of him, the better. I could buy my clothes *and* a new black ten-speed bike with curled handlebars.

Between school and work, the time went by fast. And before I knew it, I had enough money to buy my bike! I couldn't wait to get home from school because Dad was going to give me a ride to the bike store so I could pick it out!

I ran up the driveway and bolted into the house and yelled to Mom, "Hey, Mom, where's Dad? Is he going to be home soon?"

"He should be home shortly, and he has a surprise for you!"

"I can't wait to get my bike!"

I had been giving my parents money toward my bike savings so I wouldn't spend it.

So far, I'd saved $130.

"Next week, I'll have enough money to buy a bag for the front!" I said.

I was going to get a shiny new black ten-speed bike!

Minutes—though it seemed like hours—later, Dad pulled up the driveway.

"Hey, Dad, can we leave now?" I asked impatiently.

"We don't have to. I have a surprise," he said, walking outside toward the Suburban.

"What kind of surprise?" I hesitantly asked.

He opened the back of the Suburban and pulled out a green ten-speed bike.

"Look, I went and picked it out for you. I figured I'd save you the time. Isn't it great?" Dad said, looking at Mom, all proud of himself.

"But I wanted to go to the store and buy it myself. I wanted to pick out my own black ten-speed bike," I said, trying hard not to show the overwhelming disappointment.

"Well, it doesn't make any difference what color it is. It's still a ten-speed. You can ride it to work today."

I could see Mom looking at me out of the corner of her eye, prepared to yell if I even thought about complaining.

"Thank you," I answered, defeated, then got on my bike and rode . . . and rode . . . and rode, wondering why he'd decided to buy my bike without me. All things considered, for $130, I was riding a new ten-speed bike . . . and it felt great.

"Hi, Mr. Moppit. Anything special we need to get done today?"

"Yep, we got a big delivery that needs to be put away. Sammy has already started. He'll help you, okay?"

"Okay, Mr. Moppit. Hi, Sammy. Where can I start?"

"Hey, Bird. Just work with me. I'll show you as we go."

Sammy had given me the name "Bird" because he thought my feathered hair looked like the wings of a bird . . . but mostly because he knew it bugged me.

Sammy was cool and cute, taller than me, and sort of thin for a guy, and he had a great butt. He had feathered hair too, but I didn't call him "Bird."

We spent the next few hours unpacking and stacking groceries. The store only had three aisles, and we had enough peas to serve seconds to the entire town.

Mr. Moppit was an interesting-looking character. He reminded me of Charlie Brown's uncle, if Charlie Brown was real and had an uncle. His head was perfectly round, and he combed his black hair from the left side of his head all the way over to his right as if it'd grown that way. He wore thick round black-rimmed nerd glasses that made his eyes look like tiny dots. His unusual appearance never bothered him, though, and he considered himself the best-looking butcher in the town of Forestville.

My job at Sweet's had become more than just a job, and I enjoyed working with both Mr. Moppit and Sammy. They were more than co-workers; they were my friends, and Mr. Moppit taught me that all adults weren't like Mom and Dad.

I walked out of work excited to ride my bike home but found the bike lying on its side only to discover a bolt on the kickstand was loose. I was about to walk back into the store to see if Mr. Moppit would tighten it for me when I noticed something else. There was a bright red sticker on the underside of the seat. I looked closer to see what it was, and on that bright red sticker, it read, almost mockingly, "$79.99"! I had given my father $130 toward a bike I wanted to buy myself, and now I saw why he'd gone to buy it for me. That bastard pocketed $50! It had *nothing* to do with being a good dad and everything to do with stealing my hard-earned money! What a scumbag.

I took the long way home as I replayed in my head every possible scenario of how to confront this. By the time I got home, I had come to the realization that confronting him would only make it worse for myself. So, like everything else, I let it go, simply grateful for the freedom of a bicycle. Any bicycle.

***

Today was the last day of ninth grade! I was cleaning out my locker when Tim Lawford, one of the guys on the football team, tapped me on the shoulder. Tim was super tall, with wavy blonde hair—nice looking, and way out of my league. He only hung out with the cool kids.

"Hey, one of my friends wants to go out with you," he said.

I stood still for a few seconds just to make sure that he hadn't mistaken me for another girl.

"Me? With one of your friends? Which one?"

"Paul Moretti. He said you're in his algebra class. He thinks you're pretty," Tim said.

"Paul, with the red pickup truck?" I asked.

Just the thought of that scared the hell out of me. Sure, he was cute, but what a reputation! My mother would kill me! Rumor had it he was having some kind of contest to see how many girls' footprints he could get on the ceiling of his truck. I wasn't into entering that contest. He'd sat at the desk in front of me, so for an hour a day, I saw the back of his head. He appeared to dress nice, wore tons of Brut cologne, and was always looking for the answers to everything. That was all I knew about Paul Moretti, and I didn't feel right about going on a date with him.

"Why won't Paul ask me himself?" I asked Tim.

"He's shy."

I laughed. "Shy? I've heard a lot of things about Paul Moretti, but shy isn't one of them! And I can't go out with a guy I hardly even know."

"Well, you're going to the church festival this weekend, aren't you?" he asked.

"Yeah. Why?"

"So are we. That'll be a good time for the two of you to get to know each other better. Right?"

Sometime during the conversation, April popped up behind me, furiously spinning the dial on her locker as though she'd forgotten the combination. She continued until he left. She was a bit obvious.

"What was up with Mr. Football?" she asked.

I filled her in on what she'd missed.

"What are you going to do?"

"You mean what are *we* going to do?" I laughed. "I don't want to go out with Paul. My mother would have a fit as soon as she saw his pickup pull into our yard . . . although his brother Luke is pretty hot," I said.

"Well, this should be quite a weekend! Damien's supposed to be there too. Do you think he likes me?"

"Likes you? No, those sparkles bouncing around in his eyes when he looks at you are a total coincidence. Of course, he likes you, you doofus!" I said.

"Hey, wanna sleep over my house the night of the festival?"

"Cool, great idea and a great way to avoid my parents that night!" I said.

April and I spent the next few days lying in the yard, drenched in Hawaiian Tropic dark tanning oil and trying on outfits we thought would look sexy but not slutty for the Friday night festival.

The St. Paul's Festival was sponsored by our church, so everyone would be going, including our parents, but it was still a far cry from staying home. To avoid arriving with our parents, April and I walked to the festival.

"April, those yellow pants look great with that ruffled shirt!" I said.

"Ya think so? I like your bell-bottom jeans too. They make you look skinny. I don't look fat, do I?" she asked.

"Fat? You're a toothpick! You look great! Now come on, let's go!"

We arrived just as it was getting busy. The festival was really a church parking lot full of homemade food, one cotton candy machine, carnival games invented by parish families, and a dunking booth, but for Forestville, Rhode Island, it was the event of the year. Some guy was continuously announcing upcoming events on a very scratchy speaker.

"Coming up soon . . . log cutting . . . Watch Forestville's strongest take a ten-foot saw and race against time. After that, human plows! That's right, folks . . . men instead of horses . . . pulling plows . . . followed by our famous arm-wrestling event!"

Arm wrestling attracted all the girls. Forestville was like living in a world of *The Waltons*!

April and I did our best to blend in and even hung out with our moms so we'd look inconspicuous while checking out boys.

"Do you see him?"

"See him? I don't even know what Paul looks like. Do you see Damien?" she asked.

"Yep. Damien is coming right toward us."

"Oh, my God! Do I look okay? I'm nervous!" she said.

"Your tan is now a bright red. You look great!" I laughed.

Damien Krusty was his name. Tall, thin, jet-black hair, zits, kind of cute, though. I noticed he'd probably spent as much time getting ready as we had. His new beige corduroys and green-checked shirt still had that stiff, worn-for-the-first-time look. And his straight black hair was neatly combed and gelled to his head as if he'd used Dippity-do. Damien went to a private all-boys school, so I only knew him from the few times we'd met at the pond. Whenever he was around, I got a funny, not-so-good feeling inside. There was just something about him that didn't seem right. He was a Mr. Know-it-all, but so were most of the boys our age. I couldn't figure out what gave me that weird feeling.

"Hey, April. You guys just get here?" he asked.

I listened to them nervously suffer through a bunch of small talk and couldn't help but laugh. I didn't think either of them had any idea what the other was saying; they were just happy to be standing in the same place. They tried to include me in the conversation, but I could tell they wanted to be alone.

"I'll be back later, okay?" I whispered to April.

She nodded at me.

"Good luck!" I mouthed, drifting away into the crowd.

"Hey, where's your other half? She get kidnapped?" said a male voice from behind.

"Other half?" I asked, not knowing whom I was answering.

I turned around. I could feel myself blushing. It was Luke! Dark-haired, blue-eyed, broad-shouldered, tall, awesome-smelling, brother-of-Paul Luke.

He looked at me and laughed.

"Did I scare you?" he asked.

"Actually, yes. I thought you were Paul," I answered.

"Paul? My brother? That's understandable, he is scary!"

As brothers go, Luke and Paul were total opposites. Paul, though not a big guy, was on the football team. Everyone in school knew Paul Moretti. He was very outgoing and definitely not shy, and he had a twin sister, Penny. They were a year ahead of Luke and me.

Luke wasn't outgoing like Paul, but he wasn't quiet either. Luke didn't play sports and certainly didn't have the reputation with girls that Paul did, but everyone knew Luke too. Luke was very likable and a bit sarcastic, but in a fun way. Luke was intriguingly different. And the fact was, I was extremely attracted to him.

I shared the conversation I'd had with Tim Lawrence and made it clear to Luke that I wasn't interested in Paul. Luke listened and joked about Paul's reputation, occasionally teasing me about him. We spent the next hour or so dodging Paul and getting to know each other. We went for a walk on the path in the woods adjacent to the festival. I knew it would ruin my new Earth Shoes I'd been so careful not to scuff up, but now I didn't care.

Walking out of the woods, we noticed Paul had found himself another girl. Hand in hand, they headed toward his infamous red pickup. We both laughed.

"Well, I guess I wasn't all that special after all."

"Yes, you are. You could have been the one in that truck, but you *chose* not to be. That's special. Most girls would jump at the chance to have a football-player boyfriend with his own truck," Luke said.

"Thanks." My heart was beating too fast to say anything else. "It's getting late. I have to meet up with April soon. Hey, the CYO is going to Rocky Point Park this Wednesday. Wanna go?" I asked.

Wow! Where did that courage come from?

"Sure, but I gotta see if I can get Wednesday off from work. It's not that easy when your dad's your boss," he said.

Luke had educated me on his family while we walked. He worked with his dad, who owned an excavation company. It was like construction but with giant-sized Tonka trucks, and Luke and Paul got to drive those crazy things. Luke said he and his dad didn't get along at all. I felt bad.

"That's okay, I understand. Well, give me a call if you can come?" I asked, heart pounding, face on fire.

"How 'bout I call you either way?" he said quietly.

"Yeah, that'd be cool."

"I'll see ya later, okay?" Luke said, and slowly walked out of my sight.

"Okay," I answered back to the empty space.

Wow! I really liked him.

1979 – fifteen years old

Chapter 12

Luke and I had been going out for four months, but so far, he hadn't even tried to kiss me.

April and Damien had been dating the same amount of time, and they were thinking about going all the way.

I met April at the bus after school.

"Where's Luke?" she asked.

"Oh, I said good-bye to him in the parking lot. He's riding home with his sister, Penny," I said.

"You didn't have to ride the bus just because of me," she insisted.

"Yeah, I know, but my mom is starting to hassle me about spending too much time with Luke. The less she sees me with him, the better. And if I ride home with Penny and Luke, Danny will want to squeeze himself into the car. It's just not worth it," I said.

"Yeah, I understand."

"So, big plans with Damien this weekend?" I asked.

April blushed and smiled like she was hiding something when she answered.

"Chris, I'm so nervous, I don't know what to do!" she whispered.

"Why?"

"Well, the other day, when his mom went to the store, we went up to his room. We were making out on his bed, and he wanted me to touch it!" She made a funny gesture with her hands when she spoke.

I knew what she meant, although it wasn't because of her hand gesture, which I imitated, and we both laughed.

"It's a good thing our conversations don't depend on charades. So, what did you do?"

"Well, at first I said no, but we were lying on the bed really close to each other, and I could feel it right through our clothes! I wanted to touch it, but I was afraid that his mom would come home," she answered.

I kneeled up on the bus seat and looked down at her like a vulture ready to attack its prey and whispered, "What do you mean, 'at first' you said no? Come on. Let's hear the reeeeal story, because Lord knows I have less than no stories to share!" I tried to be serious, but I couldn't help giggling.

"As I was explaining my fear of his mom coming home, he started getting undressed right in front of me! And I couldn't help but look!" she said.

"You're kidding!" I was at the edge of my seat now.

"No, I'm not," she said.

"Well, what did you do?"

"Nothing, I just sat there in a daze. Then he asked me if I wanted to touch it! I said no way! I was too scared, and those things are pretty ugly!" she said, her face all scrunched up.

"No, April, I don't know!" I lied, thinking my abomination of a father didn't count.

"Oh, yeah." She laughed.

"Hey, at the rate Luke and I are going, I may never find out," I said.

"Total bummer."

"Well . . . what happened?" I asked impatiently.

"He didn't give me much choice. By this time, we were standing up, and he had me backed against the corner. And there I was, with *it* . . . stuck between us. I was so scared, I almost cried. I couldn't imagine actually touching that thing. It looked like a hard turtle's neck!" she whispered.

"Ewww" was all I said.

"Then he told me that he loved me and said it was natural for people to touch each other when they were in love. He said he wanted to show me how much he loved me. And he said his mom wouldn't get mad because she thinks guys should know about this kind of stuff," she said.

"Did his mom really say that?" I asked.

"Yeah, I think so. Damien's mom said if he was still a virgin when he was sixteen, she'd *get* a girl for him, if you know what I mean," she said, making this funny kind of face.

"You mean like a hooker or something?" I asked.

"Yep, can you believe that?"

"Wow, that's really weird," I said.

"Yep."

"Well, what happened next?" I asked, totally intrigued.

"I didn't want him to break up with me, so I touched it," she said, almost in tears.

"Oh, my God, April! Do you really think that Damien should have been that pushy?" I said, feeling really bad for her.

"Oh, it's not him, it's me. I think I'm too frigid. Damien said so and told me I should be much more mature at this age. He's right, and I really do love him," she answered as if she'd been schooled.

"What happened after you touched it?"

"Well, he told me to rub it back and forth. I didn't know how, I was so scared, but he showed me. Then after a while, he made a gross noise, and it was all over. And before we could do anything else, we heard his mom pull into the driveway."

"Are you sure you're okay with all this, April?"

"Yeah, I think so. I think we're gonna do the real thing this weekend. My mom and dad are going away," she said.

"Please be careful, okay? And don't do it if you're not absolutely sure how you feel," I said, well aware of how hypocritical I sounded.

Yeah, sure . . . Give your friend great advice, but treat yourself like a complete doormat. Maybe she can't say no? Perhaps she doesn't know how to say no? Just let her be, not every guy in the world is like your dad. Still, something about Damien doesn't sit right.

"Don't worry about me, okay? I can't deny I'm scared, but I really do love Damien," she said.

"Okay, but call me if you need me, okay?" I said, trying to smile.

"Okay. So, how's Luke, anyway?" she asked.

I snickered.

"Still good and at least three feet apart. Nothing like your exciting life. I honestly don't know why he hasn't touched me. We talk on the phone every night, and he's always talking about how we're going to be together forever . . . . Maybe he means as best friends or something?" I laughed.

April laughed too.

"I see the way he looks at you. You're definitely more than friends," she said.

"Well, we're supposed to be going to the drive-in tomorrow with his oldest sister, Tricia, and her boyfriend. Maybe he'll actually hold my hand or go for the big one . . . a kiss right on the lips." I smiled as I made the sign of the cross and looked up as if I was speaking to God.

The bus came to my stop.

"Good luck. Whoever gets up first on Sunday has to give the other one a call and plan a place to meet, okay?" she said as she waved bye.

"Okay. Good luck," I answered, and headed home.

Walking into the house, I heard Mom's voice.

"Well, what do you know? It's about time you decided to come right home from school for a change," she said sarcastically, leading me to believe there was more to come.

I had gotten myself into every after-school activity I could sink my teeth into. Between work, cheerleading, dance show recital, and the occasional volleyball or basketball game, I really wasn't home much, and that was the goal.

Aware of what was coming, my stomach twisted into knots.

"I have a paper due on Monday, the football game on Saturday, and work on Sunday, so I came home early today to get my homework done," I said, trying to swallow the lump in my throat and hoping she would lighten up because she was holding a cast-iron frying pan.

"It's nice to know all you think about is yourself! What about me, your mother? Don't you think I need help around this house anymore? Or are you too preoccupied with that boyfriend of yours? God knows what he's got you doing! I've just about had it with that situation! Do you hear me?" she yelled.

My heart felt as if it was beating outside of my body, because I knew this was about to get worse. I was afraid she'd lash out and bash me in the head with the frying pan. I needed to say just the right thing. Something that wouldn't set her off any more than she already was, but I was at a loss because I had no idea where all the anger was coming from.

I played it safe and responded meekly with, "I'll help you, Mom. You just have to ask. What do you need me to do?"

As those words left my mouth, her expression changed to one I'd come to know all too well. If I died and went to hell, that was the face I would see for the eternal afterlife.

That was the point of no return. I had no idea what went on in that broken brain of hers.

I definitely had not responded with the right words.

"Ask? Just ask? Huh! How many fuckin' mothers out there have to ask their daughters to help? How many? Just one! Because after everything I've done for my daughter, she still doesn't appreciate her mother. I've been through so much; I should be sainted! My daughter doesn't think enough of me to pick up a fuckin' rag without me asking? You know what your problem is? You're too busy with that fuckin' boyfriend of yours. I can only imagine what you've been doing with him! And his sister's boyfriend drives a van! What kind of mother allows her daughter to date a guy with a van? Now my daughter is hanging around with some pig! I don't deserve to have a pig for a daughter, do you hear me?" She was yelling like a possessed woman.

I needed to stand up for myself! Maybe if I explained it, that would make her feel better? But before I could utter a word, she slammed the frying pan down on the counter.

"Mom, I'm sorry. I didn't mean for you to have to ask me. I'll do the dishes. And Luke's not the kind of boy you think he is. He hasn't even touched me! And Tricia and her boyfriend are nice. He drives a van because that's what he uses for work. Don't you trust me? It shouldn't matter what you think they're doing. You should trust *me*. I've never done anything for you not to trust me. I never get into trouble!" I was pleading now.

She looked at me as if I was speaking in a foreign language. I just stood there, afraid to make a move. I wanted to walk away so badly, but I was scared she would turn into that chick from the *Exorcist.*

She stopped just long enough to glare at me, speaking in a nasty, bitter, hateful tone.

"You must really think I'm some kind of fool. Do you think I'm fuckin' stupid? You've been with this boy for months now, and you expect me to believe he hasn't even touched you?"

"But he hasn't, it's the truth. I have never lied before. It's not fair!" I was crying now, out of both fright and hurt.

It hurt so bad inside. All I'd ever tried to do was make *her* life less stressful. I hadn't seen anyone after Bobby for fear it would turn out exactly like this. I went out of my way to make sure that I was kind to Dad and tried to do everything they asked. I even ignored all the terrible things that Danny did.

"Why don't I believe you? You're a fifteen-year-old girl, and I know what fifteen-year-old girls do! Your father is worried sick. He doesn't trust this boy, and I don't like him either! I think you need to slow this down. You hear me?" she lectured, having ignored every word I'd said.

I looked up with tears running down my face and just said, "Yes." Then I slowly walked out of the kitchen and into my room.

Oddly enough, my room was the safest place for me to be before the lights were out and the worst place in the world when I went to bed. My brain had divided my bedroom into two completely different worlds. I closed my door whenever I was awake, and my room became my private little hideaway. But the minute it was time to go to sleep, I left the door wide open. Since I'd started working for Mr. Moppit, I had used my own money to buy a small TV and install a telephone line, because as my father had put it, if I wanted to talk on the phone and watch what I wanted, then I had to provide those things for myself. In this case, his self-serving ways worked out better for me. Every night before and after talking with Luke, I chose to live in TV land with Mork and Mindy, the Fonz, and the *Eight is Enough* crew. It helped me forget where I really lived.

The pages in my diary were almost full. And every now and then, I looked back and read what I'd written over the years. Other than my change of feelings toward boys, there were a lot of consistencies. I mentioned the visits from Dad less and less because I'd conditioned myself to put it out of my head. It'd become such a regular thing that it almost didn't matter to me anymore. I was numb to it. Besides, that was a different Christina, not me. And my relationship with Mom continued to grow worse and worse.

On the upside, I thought I'd become a stronger person than the two of them combined. I was older now and had a good grip on handling my crazy homelife situation. Most kids' parents were the backbone of their lives, but not mine. As far as reliability went, they were actually regressing! Making me buy my own school clothes was one thing but needing to borrow thirty dollars for food or asking for heating-oil money so we'd have hot water while buying things to make you look rich and acting like you were the perfect family on the outside was a whole new level of sickening. Food, shelter, and clothing are necessities of human survival. I didn't think we'd end up homeless, but we sure as hell were not living the life that people thought we were. They had a lot of nerve making fun of other poor families in our town.

My friends were my life, and I liked it that way. They were the ones that made me feel secure. My friends didn't want me around to pay their bills or abuse my body. My friends cared about my thoughts and feelings. I was grateful for my friends and so thankful my insane parents hadn't had the urge to move in a while. As wacky as my life was, this was the best it'd ever been. Growing stronger was part of what I did naturally now, and growing older was the best thing in the world because it brought me closer to moving out.

1979 – fifteen years old

Chapter 13

It was New Year's Eve, and Mom and Dad had plans with some of our aunts and uncles to go to El Morocco, a swanky Italian restaurant with live entertainment in Atwood. Mom bragged about El Morocco being owned by one of her third cousins and that a Mafia family wedding took place there. She thought she was hip because she was going to the same place that mobsters went.

They were both in unusually good moods. Mom had been prancing around the house all day, singing some Guy Lombardo song, Danny was going to sleep over at a cousin's house, and the rest of us were allowed to stay up as late as we wanted. We were going to watch the ball drop as Dick Clark counted down to midnight in Times Square. I couldn't wait for them to leave.

I wanted to spend the night talking to Luke and watching TV in my room. Mom and Dad were really on my case to the point where it was unbearable. They controlled the time on the phone with Luke, and I was always walking on eggshells to make sure I didn't upset them for fear I might get grounded. Danny had to make sure he used every opportunity to instigate and get me in trouble. Sometimes I caught Danny and my father sitting together, whispering to each other and looking at me. They totally creeped me out. I'd called them out a few times and asked what they were whispering about. Dad's response was always the same, but he'd been getting angrier. He'd say, loud enough for Mom to hear, "Children should be seen and not heard." Then Mom would yell at me without even asking why and tell me to mind my own business. I hated both my dad and Danny.

Tonight would be like a breath of fresh air. No parents and no Danny. My younger brothers weren't any problem. As long as the TV worked and there was enough to eat, life was just fine with them.

By six o'clock, Mom, Dad, and Danny were gone. Luke had to work during the day, so we planned to speak later on. I admired the way he worked. Luke's dad had divorced his mom and left her with five kids so he could be with some other woman who lived nearby. Now his dad had kids with that woman too. But even with his parents being divorced, his family had something I'd never experienced before. It was hard to explain, but I'd thought a closeness like that only existed on TV. Luke's mom and family made me feel welcome when I visited his house, and I knew he didn't feel the same at my house.

I thought about how the year had changed for both me and April in so many ways. And how, secretly, it was still the unspeakable equivalent. I didn't think April would ever be the same after that dreadful afternoon with Damien.

I wish I could have helped prevent that horrible day for her. No one should ever have to feel that way. Ever. If there is a God up there, why doesn't He know that some people can't handle tragic events in their lives? Every time I think about that phone call, the entire day runs through my brain wondering why this had to happen to my friend.

I remember the phone ringing, and I expected a happy call from April.

"Hello," I'd answered.

"Chris?" It was April, and she was crying.

"April, what's wrong?" I asked.

"Can you come over now?" she asked, panicky.

"Of course." I'd hung up and flown out of the house, down our driveway, and up toward the apple orchard. I didn't stop running till I was at her front door.

We'd walked down to the pond and sat on the rocks by the water's edge, neither one of us speaking. I waited for her to speak first. She was a mess: her eyes beet red and swollen; blonde curls, normally sitting just right, were now aiming in every direction; and blue mascara, usually vivid and thick on her lashes, was running down her face like bad finger paint. April got hives whenever she was nervous. Her neck looked as if she'd been attacked by a thousand cats. I'd never seen it so bad.

"I don't know what happened!" Her voice was speaking, not her. "There was blood everywhere . . . . Then he just got up."

"April, what in the world are you talking about?" I asked. Now I was panicking too.

"We did it, and it was awful!"

It? Awful? Was she talking about sex, or had they killed someone?

"What do you mean, 'awful'?" I asked, baffled.

"We did it. We went all the way. But it wasn't like he said it would be."

I didn't say a word. I just waited for her to continue. The only thing I could think of was how awful I felt when my father did those things to me, but April was more fragile than I was. I just wanted to hold her . . . and kill him.

I held my breath and listened.

"We did it in my bed. In my room! My mom and dad were away, just like I told you. Damien and I planned it, but I was *wicked* nervous. I was afraid my parents might come home early and walk in or something. But he calmed me down, and the next thing I knew, he was on top of me and pushing it inside me. I was crying, but he didn't stop. It hurt so much. And then . . . then . . ." She stopped and cried for a while.

I was listening, but it was agonizing. I kept seeing Damien with April and flashes of my dad, and it was so hard to concentrate. I felt so bad for her. I was speechless. I just wanted to be there, back there with her so I could have helped stop it.

"It was so quick. The next thing I knew, there was blood everywhere. At first, I didn't know where it came from. Then I realized that it was from me, and I panicked. I couldn't have bloodstains on my sheets! What would my mother say?" She looked at me as if I had the answer.

"What did he do, April?" I whispered.

"He didn't do anything. He didn't hold me or say anything. He just got up and went to the bathroom. He was still all hard—it was sticking straight out. After a few minutes, he came back out. I was crying uncontrollably, but he just left. Just like that. Said nothing. Just left." She looked at me for more answers.

I didn't have any. The whole thing was spinning in my head. What kind of guy was he? What an awful person!

"April, he's not a normal guy. That's not the way it should be," I said, knowing far too well how something that awful felt.

I wanted her to know that she hadn't done anything wrong. But how? How could I make her understand that?

"I don't care how it should be. All I know is that I'm never doing that again!" April said.

"Oh, geez, April. I know there's no way to make you believe this now, but that isn't how it's supposed to happen. All guys aren't like Damien." I tried to sound as convincing as I could. I felt so sorry for her.

Things like that shouldn't happen to people like April. April wasn't emotionally equipped for that stuff. No one should be emotionally suited to handle that, but I was. I would have gladly taken her place if it meant she could just erase it all of it.

She heard me, but she didn't acknowledge it.

"I took the sheets and blankets off my bed and washed and scrubbed them three times till they were clean. I didn't want any sign that it ever happened," she said, as if there was no one there.

All of a sudden, fear swept through me. What about protection? Had he used it? What if April got pregnant?

April looked at me as if she could read my mind.

She answered my thoughts. "I got my period this morning, so at least I'm not pregnant."

"Ohhhh . . . that's good." I sighed.

"You know, he hasn't even called me! I mean, not that I want to talk to him or anything, but he hasn't even bothered to call," she said in disbelief.

We'd walked back to her house in silence. Both of us in our own worlds but comforted by the fact the other was there. There wasn't anything to say, just the brisk breeze quietly sweeping through our minds as we took each step away from words spoken, never to be brought up again.

Entering her house had been like walking onto a theater stage. Act II was visible, new, and fresh. Act I was behind us, forever gone.

"So . . ." She'd smiled. "What happened at the drive-in last night?" she'd asked with a smirk.

I'd smiled back and giggled. "The shy guy kissed me!"

We'd sat at April's kitchen table and eaten microwaved apple crisp, our favorite dessert. We'd chatted about Luke making the official jump from friend to real boyfriend and never mentioned what had happened in April's room ever again. That day, April left a permanent and indelible impression on my life and heart.

I looked up to the imaginary being we called God and prayed that April would have a happier new year ahead.

I spent the next few hours daydreaming, watching time run in the corner of the screen, counting down the minutes till midnight. It was almost here! Luke was going to call any second to wish me happy New Year. The boys were in the living room, watching the other TV and waiting for the ball to drop in Times Square. I watched it on my TV, simultaneously listening to everyone counting out louder as each second drew closer to midnight. "Five, four, three, two, one—happy New Year!" Wow, there were so many people in that city. Thousands of couples, all kissing and hugging at the same time while tons of streamers and balloons floated down onto their heads, filling the city with a festive mood so powerful I could feel it all the way in my room. I sure wished I would be that happy someday.

I heard a knocking at my door.

"Christina, can we come in?" they asked.

"Yeah. Sure," I said.

Zac, Andy, and Mikey were at the door, all smiles and hugs, to wish me happy New Year. We hugged and kissed and watched Dick Clark talk about the people in Times Square while we viewed from home. Seconds later, Luke called to wish me happy New Year.

"Hey, kid. Happy New Year!" he said.

"Happy New Year to you too!" I replied.

"I waited until just the right second to call. I can't talk long, Ma needs to use the phone. I just wanted to wish you a happy New Year and tell you that I love you," he said.

"Me too. Good night," I replied.

For some reason, I still couldn't bring myself to actually say the words "I love you." I didn't know why. Was it because I didn't really know what that feeling was like? Or was I too scared to be so attached to someone in that way?

Somewhere around three o'clock, Mom and Dad staggered in. They were really loud, especially Mom. She was singing, yelling "Happy New Year," and laughing like a wild hyena. I thought she was drunk. My parents rarely drank; maybe that was what adults did on New Year's Eve? By the time Mom and Dad got to the hallway area, Mom was quiet and went into the bathroom. I couldn't exactly tell what happened next, but I was pretty sure Mom got sick, then Dad helped her to their room.

I lay still, listening intently to each move. I heard Dad put Mom to bed, then the rustling of bureau drawers and the door creaking open again, then Dad's feet heading toward the dining room. He woke the boys, who had fallen asleep on the living room floor, and sent them to their rooms.

Within minutes, I heard the second-floor stairs creaking and knew the boys were gone. Now it was just me . . . and him. I could feel my heart starting to beat rapidly as if on cue, knowing what would probably happen next. Mom was passed out in their bedroom, and it was just too much of an opportunity for him to let pass.

I brought the covers up to my neck as far as possible and squeezed my hands together tightly. I could feel my fingernails digging into the palms of my hands.

Why was I shaking so much tonight?

Tonight, I was wide awake, anticipating his arrival. I could feel my heartbeat rise as he grew closer and closer. Most of the time, my subconscious woke me to let me know he had arrived, so the entire adrenaline thing didn't feel quite as intense as it felt tonight. This was awful. I literally wanted to kill him. Why, of all nights, had Mom passed out, becoming even more oblivious to what was happening to her daughter? Maybe that was why I felt worse than usual. Tonight, I knew there was no way in hell she was waking up. Even years into this, every time it happened, there was always some shadow of hope inside thinking she would burst into my room and save me from this repulsive beast she made me call Dad.

Life began to happen in slow motion. I heard every move those fat, Fred Flintstone feet made.

Step . . . step . . . click . . . close.

There went the kitchen lights and the door leading to the upstairs. Now my brothers were cut off.

Step . . . step . . . click.

The dining room light was off.

My heartbeat grew louder, and I lay with eyes wide open as if I was actually seeing each move he made.

Step, step, step . . . click, click.

Now the last of the lights were off in the living room, and he was headed toward the hall.

Maybe he won't come into my bedroom? Maybe he's too tired, and maybe he'll go straight to bed. Please, God. Please! Make him go to bed! I'll do anything you want. I'll make sure I do whatever Mom says, and I'll never argue with her again, no matter how mean she is to me. Please make him go to bed!

The hall light was the only light on in the house. Usually, that light stayed on all night, just in case someone got up to go to the bathroom. I liked having that light on. It lit up my room and the hall area.

I heard him approaching the hall now.

Step, step . . . click. And off went the hall light.

Oh . . . God, please be with me tonight . . . .

As the light went out, I thought I stopped breathing. I was too scared. I turned over from my back to my stomach, the safest position I could be in, and held my covers tight. My head faced the doorway to my room. My eyes were closed but slightly open so I could see him enter my room. And the living nightmare began . . . .

There he was, like a tiger about to feast on his prey. There was no remorse in his eyes, just business as usual. But he didn't head directly for me. He entered my room, stood at the foot of my bed, and turned toward my dresser.

What's he doing there? What's he looking for?

When he got to my dresser, he stopped and waited. Maybe he was just double-checking to see if I would wake up? I didn't move an inch, but I was curious, and for a brief second, my heartbeat slowed as if I was watching a movie and not real life. He opened my jewelry box, rifled through it, and slowly closed it up. Nothing there of interest, I guess. Then he began to open my dresser drawers.

What on earth is he looking for? Notes from Luke? Good luck, asshole! You think I'm dumb enough to leave them in an obvious place like that?

I almost laughed. He went through each drawer, sifting through the contents as though he was looking for evidence left by a murder suspect and carefully caressing each pair of panties. But so far, he had found nothing that seemed to be of any use.

Maybe he's just more perverted than I thought. Is that even possible?

The last drawer he searched was what I called my junk drawer. It had lots of goofy little sentimental things from dates, like movie tickets and whatnot, and a rare, oversized 1912 penny I had found in the backyard one day. I also kept my diary in that drawer.

Is that what he's looking for? My diary? Oh, no! Please don't!

My heart rate flew right back up to where it had been and continued to rise. His fat, stubby hands randomly rustled about in my drawer as I waited for his fingers to reach my diary.

Oh, no. He has something in his hand! What is it? I can hardly see it!

But neither could he, so he turned and leaned toward the door, as if looking for a light that was not there, and then I saw it! He had my penny! My big penny, the one with the Indian on it. But why? I had shown it to him when I found it, and he hadn't thought it was a big deal. I thought it was cool because it was bigger than a quarter. What did he want with that? Moments later, he turned and put it back, rustled through the drawer some more, and stumbled upon my money. He took it out of the drawer, counted what I had, and put that back too.

Boy! What a nosey son of a bitch!

He then turned and headed for my bed.

There he was, plain as day. Red bathrobe now open, fat knees and all. I could see he wasn't going to give up as quickly as he sometimes did. Sometimes if I held my blankets real tightly, he eventually went away, but not this night. He was ready for a tug-of-war! And the hate I had for him grew to heights I didn't think were possible.

I wondered if he knew I was awake. Did he know I knew? Was that some sick satisfaction he got on top of everything else? Or did he think he was so slick he was actually putting one over on me? It was so hard to tell.

My insides were screaming, *GET AWAY! GET AWAY!* But he wouldn't leave.

I gripped the blanket tighter and tighter. I could feel my nails cut my palms. Then he stopped tugging at me. Was he going to leave?! *Please leave, please leave!* But he didn't go. He just stood there, contemplating his next move. I lay there as quiet as a mouse, slowly turning entirely onto my stomach, pulling my hands into my chest with the rolled-up blanket that had become a part of my palms.

There was no way in hell he was going to turn my body over! He had to leave . . . or stand there and do disgusting things to himself. Either way, I was safe.

Or at least I thought . . . .

What was happening now? Why was he climbing onto my back? My covers were on! What could he do? Why . . . why did this have to keep happening?

Now he was moving up and down on me, but there were covers between us.

What a fucking idiot! What a sad fucking idiot!

I was trapped under him. I waited for what seemed to be an eternity until finally, he was done. He was so heavy, and I thought I was going to suffocate—what a way to die.

It hurt so bad. It felt like he had crushed my ribs.

After he left, I opened my eyes, saw the darkness around me, and began to shake. I felt my entire body shaking so much it rocked my bed. I wanted to cry, but I couldn't. I tried to breathe deeply and slowly, but I couldn't. I wanted to scream at the top of my lungs and tell the world what an asshole he was, but I didn't.

I lay there wondering what I must have done in some earlier life to make this one so bad. I'd tried so hard to do everything right for those people I called parents. Mom knew that as soon as she raised her voice, I would back down and do whatever she wanted, even when I knew it was wrong.

Why am I like this? Do all daughters have to go through life like this? When will it end?

Finally, the shaking stopped.

Dear God . . . please help me make it through all of this. I promise I will be the best person that I know how to be. I promise I will always go above and beyond what anyone could ever expect. I just want to be a decent, normal person. I want to be responsible for myself. I want to be in control of my own life. As strange as it is, I know you're always there, because if you weren't, I'd be some messed-up kid with lots of drug problems and stuff, but I'm not. If he would just stop, everything would be okay. Maybe things will change soon . . . .

Happy F-ing New Year,
Christina

1980 – fifteen years old

Chapter 14

We'd been back to school for a few days, and the homework was piling up. Cheerleading season and dance recitals were over, so there weren't many reasons to stay after school. Going home every day sure was a bummer.

"Hey, kid, you gonna ride home with Penny and me today?" Luke asked.

For some reason, Luke always called me "kid."

"Yeah, even though my mom will have something to say about it, with you being such a bad influence and all."

"Geez, I really don't know where in the world she's coming from. I'm as harmless as they come. You know that, right?"

"Yeah, of course I do, and I've told her that a million times, but she doesn't believe me. In her eyes, life isn't normal unless there's some kind of tragedy. And of course, I'm usually the cause of all of it." I shook my head and laughed in disbelief.

"Hurry up, you two! I've got to get to work. Wow! Chrissy's riding with us today! And what does Mom think of this?" Penny teased.

"Oh, I don't know, but I'm sure I'll get her opinion as soon as I get in the house," I mumbled.

"God, does she think we're a bunch of sex-crazed maniacs?" Penny said, with more than a bit of sarcasm.

She was definitely the outspoken one in the family. She was the smallest in size but the biggest in attitude, and she wasn't afraid to show it. Especially when it came to her family.

"I don't know, I think she just needs to find something wrong with everything I do. And my asshole brother Danny told them that we've been making out in the halls and that Luke had his hand up my shirt. As if," I answered, with just as much question in my voice as she'd had in hers.

"There's something wrong with that freakin' brother of yours. Why don't your parents see it? He's a total creep!" Penny said.

Luke sat quietly, but by the look on his face, it was clear that he wanted to bash Danny's face in.

As Penny's worn-out gray 1972 Mustang pulled into our driveway, I could see my mother through the kitchen window, washing dishes. Luke got out, then helped me out of the back seat.

I turned so my back was facing the house.

"She's watching us," I said to Luke.

"Yeah, I know, I can see her. Don't worry. I'll be good," Luke said, and quickly kissed me on the lips.

"Bye. I'll talk to you tonight. Thanks, Penny."

"You're welcome. Good luck in hell!" She laughed.

Luke got into the car, looking at me as if to say "I wish I could make it better, but I can't."

I looked back and nodded "I know" and headed for the house.

I opened the breezeway door and felt the tension; my heart was already racing. I closed my eyes and deeply inhaled as I entered the kitchen.

"Hi."

"I really don't think I like my daughter getting a ride home from him. Don't you have any respect for me at all?" And just like that, she was off.

This was the part I hated most of all. How could I answer a question that had no logical answer?

"Mom, I wasn't getting a ride home from Luke. Penny was driving, so we weren't alone. When she gives me a ride, I get home sooner than taking the bus. We drive right home!"

Why did I even open my mouth? I knew it was just going to get worse.

"I don't give a shit who was driving! You're still a fifteen-year-old girl! Do you hear me? I saw the way he kissed you! There is no need for that at your age. That boy is turning you into a pig! It's about time this ends! Do you understand that, missy? It's a good thing that your father wasn't here to see that! And from what your brother has told us, there's a *lot* more going on than that! This has got to stop!" she screeched.

Tears were rolling down my face. I didn't want to argue, and I couldn't compete with her reasoning. I stared blankly at the floor and spoke quietly.

"I'm not a pig. And you have no idea what kind of boy he is because you won't listen to me."

I walked to my room, closed the door, and prayed that she wouldn't come barging in. I just wanted to fall asleep and wake up far, far away, like in the Land of Oz, and never have to come back.

I didn't come out of my room until I was called to help set the table for dinner, which I did in complete silence. I made it through dinner without speaking or being spoken to. Instead, I listened to Danny brag to Mom and Dad about how he was going to be the captain of the football team next year because all of the kids in school thought he was the best. I couldn't figure out why he would even say that, because he had to know it wasn't true. His lies came as naturally as breathing.

I went back to my room as soon as dinner was over. Thank God for my TV. It had been a savior lately, and tonight was my favorite night of the week: *Mork & Mindy, Bosom Buddies,* and *Magnum P.I.* Luke would probably call during *Bosom Buddies*, because he knew *Magnum* was my favorite. Luke was cute, but he was no Tom Selleck. The night was going a lot better than I had thought. I had expected a yelling match when Dad got home, but nothing had been said.

Luke called at eight thirty, as usual.

"Hey, kid. How's life on the inside?" he asked.

"Could be better," I said, and filled him in on what had happened.

But tonight, I couldn't keep my head focused on the conversation. Mom's voice from that afternoon was still replaying my head. Luke was talking, and I was thinking.

I can't put up with too much more of this. Maybe I should just call the whole thing off.

"Boy, I can't wait till I'm eighteen and I can get out of here!"

"Awww, come on, hon. By the time we're eighteen, this whole thing will have blown over. Your mom will get used to me. She has to—she has no choice!" he said, assuming it was no big deal.

Oh, my God. He said when we're eighteen. That was almost three years from now! I hadn't thought about us that far ahead. *How do I deal with my parents for the next three years? I'll be in a mental hospital! This house is unbearable now.* Between Danny's lies, my father's disgusting jealousy, and my own mother's inability to see the truth, this was really starting to feel hopeless.

Everything was running through my head as he talked about problems he was having with his dad, and just as I realized I hadn't been paying attention, my father burst into my room.

Before I could even say anything to Luke or to him, he grabbed the phone out of my hand.

"You will stop seeing my daughter immediately, and don't you EVER call this house again!" Then he slammed the phone down.

He looked at me and said, "It's over. I don't want to deal with any more of this shit, do you hear me?" He turned, stormed out, and slammed the door.

What the hell just happened? Did he really just say that to Luke?

I sat frozen for a few minutes as it sank in. Then the steam began to build inside, and I decided I had nothing to lose. I got up and headed for the living room.

"Why did you just do that?" I yelled at him.

"Because it's about time this nonsense stops," he angrily answered.

"But why like that? Why didn't you come to me first?"

The phone in my room began ringing.

"Come to you? Why, so you could lie to us? You think we're stupid? I've heard all about this boy and the things the two of you do, and I'm not going to have my daughter doing anything like that. That's the end. I don't want to hear another word about it, do you hear me?" he said like a proud peacock.

The phone was still ringing.

"No. This is not the end! I don't care if you're my parents or not. That was wrong, and the way you did that was so disrespectful! If you have a problem, you should have come to me first. You're talking about a boy that didn't even hold my hand for the first six months. He's probably the safest boy in school! I can't believe what you just did—that was just ROTTEN!" I couldn't stop yelling.

Saltwater from my tears was dripping into my mouth, stinging my throat. But I didn't care. I wanted them to know what they had done was wrong.

"Don't give me any of this crap about him being so shy! Your brother has told us all about the drinking you do on your double dates. I've seen the way he kisses you, and your brother says he does a lot more than that in the halls between classes! Don't you lie to me! And I don't have to come to you first. I'm the fuckin' parent here. Whatever I do is right, do you hear me?"

"Everything Danny told you is lies, and you believe him! He's the biggest liar in the family, and you still believe him instead of me! It's not fair, I have never given you any reason not to trust me! And I don't care if you're a parent or not, you can't stop me from seeing him!"

I yelled, without thinking, and the last statement flew out of my mouth.

Oh, boy. Now I've done it. I froze as I watched him rise from the couch and then flinched as he passed me, relieved that I didn't end up on the losing end of a parent-child K.O.

What now? Why is he leaving the room?

Mom just sat there through all of this as if she'd written the script.

Why is he going in my bedroom?

"What are you doing in my room?" Now screaming loud enough for the whole town to hear.

He made no effort to answer. All I heard was rustling and banging, still too scared to move from my spot in the living room. Mostly because I feared the sudden movement might set Mom off, and *that* I knew I couldn't handle! Moments later, out came Dad, looking as if he'd lost a battle with Godzilla: hair sticking up in all the wrong places, face red as a tomato, and the bottom of his T-shirt tucked under one of his old-man breasts. He was carrying my phone he'd ripped out of the wall and my small TV. I wanted to kill him. Instead, I just stood there, dumbfounded.

I spoke in a voice just above a whimper, "Why did you do that?"

"Because you spend too much fuckin' time in that room of yours. It's not healthy! And I don't want you sneaking off and calling him! Without a phone or TV, you'll have no choice but to be a part of this family. And don't even think of trying to see him behind our backs!" He was in his glory.

The phone in the living room started ringing.

Mom picked it up as if everything was just peachy here at the French household.

"Hello?"

After what seemed like an eternity, she began speaking again.

"Listen, Chuck, I don't know what you've been told, but Al and I think our daughter is too young to be seeing your son. That's all there is to it," she told Luke's dad.

Wow! Luke's dad is calling! He must be raging mad to have his dad call.

"No, he can't talk to my daughter. She's grounded until further notice."

More silence.

"I don't care what you think. From what I've heard, you're not the greatest father either." And she slammed the phone down.

Great. And now it was worse.

Mom recited word for word what Luke's dad had said to her. Dad agreed with her, of course. Then the room went silent, the kind of awkward silence when it feels strange just to move an arm or even blink. I wanted to go to my room, but I knew better.

She spoke.

"Sit down and become a part of this family for a change."

I sat on the couch as far away from either of them as humanly possible.

Other than the sound coming from the TV, it was entirely silent. Zac, Andy, and Mikey had vanished to their rooms as soon as the yelling started. They weren't stupid. Danny was conveniently out somewhere. I couldn't wait to get my hands on him. I hated him.

How could they believe him over me? He was the biggest friggin' liar ever! They'd grounded me for a month last year—a month—because he'd said I was making out with someone at the movies. I hadn't even been with a guy; I'd been with my friends, and they'd still believed *him*! Everyone knew he had a lying problem. But God forbid that Dad ever admitted his precious son had any problems!

I sat on that couch, staring at the cushion until I became one with the tacky orange, tan, and red tweed. I wanted to leave, but where would I go? I didn't make enough money to live on my own.

What if I tell on Dad! No, Mom would never believe me. And even if she did, I'd end up in some home away from my friends and school. Those're the only things that I like about my life: school and my friends. How am I ever going to face Luke again? My life is absolutely over!

I heard the door open. Danny the liar was home.

He walked in that living room, acting as innocent as Richard Nixon during Watergate.

Danny waved his arm and happily said, "How's it going?"

He knew damn well how it was going, and he was enjoying every minute of this!

"You know exactly how it's going, you big, fat liar! You told Mom and Dad all kinds of lies about Luke and me! We've never even had one drink, but thanks to you, they think I'm a lush! I'm not even going to get into all of the other lies. How do you keep track of what you say? Everyone knows you're a big, fat loser, always asking Luke all kinds of sex questions about us! You were hoping you'd hear all sorts of stories. And then you got pissed because he told you to screw off! So, you're getting back at us by making up lies? Ya know something? You're a pervert and an asshole, just like HIM!"

And as the last word left my lips, I saw it coming out of the corner of my eye.

I felt that big baseball mitt of a hand connect like a Hulk slap right into my face.

It hurt like hell, but I didn't even look at him, say a word, or cry. Instead, I continued staring into Danny's lying eyes, waiting for a response.

"That mouth of yours is going to get you in a lot of trouble someday! I'd watch it if I were you!" Dad said.

I turned and looked back toward my father and saw both fright and anger. He was expecting me to blow it for him, but he was warning me to keep my mouth shut.

Does he know that I know? God, I hate him!

"I never lie. I heard all about the stuff you two do from Luke. Luke told me!" Danny said.

To this day, I can't believe how Danny could look someone right in the eyes and lie. He either believed his own lies or had no conscience whatsoever—or both!

"How can you believe him?" I screamed.

"That's it! I don't want to hear any more! End it!" Mom shouted.

"I don't want to end it! You trust him over me, and that's not fair! I would have broken up with him myself just so he"—I pointed to Dad—"wouldn't have done what he did!"

I didn't wait for her response.

"Can I please go to bed now?" I asked.

"Go! And I don't want to hear another word about this!" she said.

Dear Diary,

This has been the worst day of my life. My parents are awful. My brother is evil, and I don't want to be here anymore. But I don't have anywhere else to go. I have to see Luke tomorrow, and I don't know what to say. I feel so terrible. Why won't this end? I have a real dad out there somewhere. Why doesn't he ever try to find me?

Christina

The school bus ride was excruciating. I tried explaining everything to April, but I just didn't have the energy to go through it all again. And Danny conveniently sat right behind us, listening to every word. This was not going to be a good day at all.

Somehow the news about what had happened spread throughout the school like wildfire. I didn't know if it was Danny or Penny or even Luke, but everyone was asking me questions. I didn't want to talk about it with anyone. No one could help.

In between each class, Danny, who I usually didn't see all day because he was in all the stupid classes, was always right behind me. Luke, so far, was nowhere in sight. I wondered if he'd even come to school.

The rest of the day followed just the same: blurry teachers, the consistent shadow of Danny, and no Luke. Finally, it was over. April met me at our lockers.

"How did it go?" she asked.

"Okay, except for nosy people asking questions. I haven't seen Luke all day. I don't think he came in today," I answered with mixed feelings, looking at April, watching her eyes open really wide. She was staring above me . . . and I knew it was time.

I turned—

And there was Luke. If I hadn't known better, I wouldn't have recognized him.

He looked devastated. I felt my heart break into a million pieces, and I felt as if I'd just swallowed poison. His eyes were so puffy I couldn't imagine how he could see.

"We need to talk," he said.

"I know."

We walked to our favorite spot, under the stairway near the parking lot entrance. We had met there every morning for the past five months. It had always felt comfortable until today.

"What is wrong with your father?" he asked.

Uh, that was a loaded question!

"I don't know—a million things. But the whole thing was started by my brother," I said, and briefly explained what had happened.

"I don't have a lot of time. From now on, I have to be on the first bus home. I can't even go to after-school activities until this blows over."

"I'm gonna beat the shit out of your brother! *Nobody* can break us up! You're my girlfriend, and it's going to stay that way!" he said defiantly.

This was what I was afraid of. This was why my parents shouldn't have done what they did. They'd just made it all harder for me.

"Luke, if I'm seen anywhere near you, even in the hallways, my brothers will tell on me. And as much as I'd love to see it, you can't beat up Danny, because *I'd* end up getting in trouble, do you understand?" I pleaded.

"No. I don't understand any of this. I won't beat up that dumb-ass, but I need to see you! I don't have any intention of stopping. Do you?" he asked, expecting the same answer.

"Luke, how is that going to happen? You don't understand how bad it is at home. They're making it impossible to do anything. We have to be apart, at least for a while."

I was crying. I didn't know if it was from feeling the hurt that Luke felt or the fear that someone would come around the corner and see us.

"We are not breaking up!" he said.

"Please, let me go now. I don't want to get into any more trouble, please." The tears were uncontrollable now.

"I'll meet you here tomorrow morning before school. Okay? We'll talk then," he said.

At that point, I would have agreed to anything just so I could catch the bus on time.

"Okay," I mumbled.

Then he grabbed me, pulled me close, and kissed me.

Nothing felt right anymore.

After weeks of arguing, crying, and literally tearing myself away from Luke, he became someone I seldom saw. He'd finally given up. I never saw him the halls at school. He avoided me at all costs. If it wasn't for the lingering emotional pain, I would've thought he'd never existed.

1981 – 16 years old

Chapter 15

Fall was in the air, and I was listening to "Another Brick in The Wall" by Pink Floyd as I got ready for my first day as a high school junior. The entire Tomahawk High class of 1982 consisted of 132 kids; everyone knew everyone. Tomahawk High felt more like a big family than a school full of kids. I loved this school.

Being a junior in high school also meant being sixteen and having a driving license! Nana had given Mom her old 1969 Catalina, but she didn't really use it much, so they'd offered it to me for $300.

I didn't see much of April anymore. We weren't mad at each other or anything. Being in different grades, we had both made new friends. April was a year behind me, so she hung out with people I didn't and vice versa.

Stephanie Williamson and I were in a lot of the same classes, got along great, and had become good friends. Steph was super logical and wicked organized. For her, everything needed to make sense. I was easygoing, not so black-and-white, and went with the flow. Combined, we made a pretty good team.

After school, Steph and I walked to the buses together. She lived on the other side of Forestville, so she took a different bus.

"What time do you want to head out to the roller rink tonight?" I asked her.

We'd gone to the roller rink every weekend for the past month. Sometimes, when I didn't have to work, we went on Sunday afternoons too.

"Meet around seven?" Stephanie said.

Mom was in one of her bad moods when I got home. I was so afraid I'd set her off and wouldn't be able to go skating, but I made it out by the skin of my teeth.

Steph and I got to the rink just before it started getting busy. Steph was wearing her usual skating outfit, Levi's jeans and a chamois shirt. She was very earthy yet somehow also preppy. We were about the same height, five-foot-sevenish, but Stephanie was much thinner than I was. She couldn't have weighed more than a hundred pounds. My body was more athletic, where Steph's was perfectly straight. She had long, wavy brown hair, with big brownish-hazel eyes and a perfect set of teeth that made her smile look even more wholesome. If Ivory soap ever needed a poster girl, Stephanie would fit the bill. Her whole family was wholesome, like *The Waltons*.

On this night, for whatever reason, we had a serious case of the giggles. I was laughing so hard I had tears coming down my face.

"You know, we really need to stop making fun of everyone else. There's probably someone goofing on us right now, and we don't even know it," I said, looking around at all the other kids skating.

As we finished lacing our skates, the lights dimmed, the mirror ball in the middle of the rink began to spin, and millions of tiny colors decorated the walls.

"All skaters clear the floor. The next song is ladies' choice!" the DJ announced over a scratchy-sounding speaker.

As the rink emptied, Steph and I checked out the guys coming toward our section. We sat right next to the break in the wall where skaters entered and exited.

The DJ began playing "Just the Two of Us" by Grover Washington.

"Hey, did you see that guy with the greasy hair that looks like a duck when he skates? If he sticks out his butt any more, he's going to crash headfirst into the floor!" I said, and we both laughed.

"Hey, did you see those two guys that kept looking at us while we were putting on our skates?" Steph asked.

"What two guys?"

"Those two, over there. But don't look now, because they're looking right at us!" she exclaimed.

I whacked her in the arm.

"How the heck am I supposed to know who you're talking about if you won't let me look?" I said, scrunching my eyebrows.

"Well, I don't know. Hey, the special's over. Let's skate. We can check 'em out from the floor," she said.

And off we went.

"Do I look okay?" I asked.

"You look fine."

I was feeling pretty cool in my white painter's pants, an expensive-looking green sweater, and mock white turtleneck borrowed from a friend, accented with my favorite gold metal rhinestone belt around my waist.

"Sooo, Stephanie, where are these so-called cute guys you were talking about?" I laughed and asked.

"Right behind us," she answered with a little smirk.

"Oh," I uttered.

The lights dimmed again. And the mirror ball began to spin.

The DJ spoke: "Next skate, couples only. All others, please clear the floor."

We heard the song "Reunited" fade in as Steph and I skated toward the benches.

"Hey!" I heard someone shout, and then I felt a tap on my shoulder.

We both turned around and stared like deer in the headlights at the two cute guys Steph had been rambling about.

We didn't get a chance to say a word before they spoke again in unison.

"Wanna skate?" they said as they split up and skated closer to us.

The tall blond one skated toward me, and the dark-haired guy glided toward Steph.

There wasn't much time to respond, so we began to skate.

God, this is strange with no Steph to talk to! She was already on the other side of the rink by the time I looked up.

"What's your name?" he asked.

Oh, cool. He was nervous too. He was blushing!

He was so cute! And tall too, at least six feet, and his blue eyes sparkled in the lights.

"Chris, what's yours?" I asked.

"Ben," he answered, and smiled at me.

What a cute dimple. Damn, he's fine!

"You know, me and my friend Riley have noticed you and your friend the last couple of weeks. I finally got up enough nerve to ask you to skate," he said.

"Thanks. I'm glad you did," I said, feeling my face turn a deep red.

"You're not from around here, are you?" Ben asked.

"No. I live in Forestville. How 'bout you?"

"No-school Forestville!" He laughed.

That was what everyone who didn't go to our school said because we had so many snow days. Every snowy morning, WPRO's Salty Brine would list all canceled schools, and Forestville would be first. Kids were jealous of our snow days, but they never thought about us when we were still in school in July.

"I live in Eureka, but I go to Henderson Private High. I'm a sweet and innocent boy," he said as he smirked with a twinkle in his eye.

I laughed. "Somehow, I'm not buying that."

"Awww, come on. You're supposed to think that so you'll like me." He smiled.

"Well, you seem cool so far."

"But . . . ," Ben said, as if he knew.

"But what?" I asked.

"But you're gonna say no if I ask you out," he said.

"Well, it's not that. It's just that my last relationship ended in a parental catastrophe, and that is not something I'd like to repeat." I laughed.

Ben didn't say anything. He skated us right off the floor, stopped, and looked me directly in the eye.

"So, because you had a bad experience with another guy and your parents, you won't go out with me or anyone ever again? That's the lamest excuse I've ever heard," he stated, still smiling and revealing that adorable dimple.

"I have parents from hell. They hate everyone I date. They make my life miserable when I'm seeing someone. Plus, I've only known you for ten minutes. For all I know, you could be an axe murderer." I smiled.

"Look at these eyes. Do I look like an axe murderer? And how do you know your mom and dad will hate me? I have an irresistible boyish charm!" he said.

He is tough! And soooo cute!

"I don't know, I'll have to think about it," I said.

"Can I at least call you? Maybe I'll convince you that I'm not an axe murderer?"

"Who's an axe murderer?" the friend asked, skating up to us.

"Apparently Chris here thinks that *I* might be. Chris, this is Riley," Ben said.

"Hey." Riley was cute too, but different looking from Ben.

Riley was shorter and stocky, with dark hair and dark eyes, and looked a bit serious, where Ben looked more like a raccoon ready to venture into the unknown.

"Steph, this is Ben," I said.

"Hi, Ben." She smiled and looked at him as if to say "Well . . . good luck."

"Yeah, yeah, yeah. I know, she's not into dating because her parents are from hell!" he said.

Steph laughed out loud. Riley looked confused.

"So, when are we going out?" Riley asked.

I glanced at Steph. She nodded. I guessed Riley was okay with her. But I was still nervous.

"After you call me," I said to Ben.

"Well, how about giving me your number? I'll get a pen and be right back," he said, and they skated toward the front desk.

"Oh, my God, Steph. I was sooo nervous! What do you think about Riley? Do you like him?" I asked.

"He seems nice, and he's cute, but I don't know him. What about Ben?" she said.

"He said he'd call so I'd feel more relaxed about going out. What do you think?" I asked.

"Riley's gonna call too. I guess we'll see what happens," she said.

"Yeah, I guess. I'm petrified about dating another guy and having my parents freak out again. Maybe I should just forget the whole thing."

"Oh, geez, Chris. It's about time your mom stops controlling you. You need to have a life too!" Steph said, not really understanding completely.

"Yeah. I guess you're right. Let's see if they call first," I said.

Ben and Riley skated back to us as we started for the rink.

Riley went off with Steph. Ben stopped me at the entrance.

"So, are ya gonna give this murderer your phone number or not?" he said.

"Okay, smart-ass." And I gave him my number.

"Riley and I have to take off as soon as he gets done skating with Steph, but I'll call you as soon as I get a chance, okay?" he said.

"Yeah, sure, that'd be cool." I smiled.

I watched him skate away. He sure was cute.

A Henderson guy. Wow! Henderson was a very cool all-boys school, mostly rich kids. But should I take another chance with my parents? And if I didn't take it now, then when? When I moved out? What the hell was wrong with me?

Oh well, maybe he wouldn't even call.

The rest of the weekend passed with no call from Ben. I got home from school on Monday, ran into the house, and rushed to my room with only ten minutes to get ready for work.

"Christina!" Mom yelled.

"Hang on. I'm getting ready for work!" I yelled back.

Oh, no. What did my mother want? I knew I hadn't done anything wrong, but maybe Danny had schemed up something awful again.

"Did you call me, Mom?"

"Yes, I need to tell you something," she said very seriously.

Oh, boy! What now? My stomach began to knot.

"What?" I asked in a voice barely above a whisper.

I walked into the living room and thought, *Mom really needs to do something with that frosted hairdo.*

Why in the world did women frost their hair? It certainly didn't look natural! Was I going to grow up to look just like her? Everyone said that all girls turned into their mothers! God, that couldn't be true for everyone! So far, we didn't look alike. Plus, I was five foot seven, and she was only five foot two, so that boded well for me. I'd always hoped I looked like my real dad. I had no idea what that was, but I didn't want to become my mom.

"Well, you know your dad and I have been having money problems. Right?" she asked.

Oh, boy. Here it comes. They need more money but would never think about asking Danny!

I winced. "Yeah."

"Well, if we don't do something soon, we're going to lose this house, and I couldn't bear to think about that. So, your dad and I have decided to put it up for sale. Dad is working with a guy in Hillsgrove, and he's got a special deal with the State Side Credit Union, so we think we can get a loan with that bank," she explained, like all this was no big deal.

"Move?! But this is the only place we've been for more than a year since grade school! We can't move, I like this school." I was devastated.

"I know you don't want to, but we have no choice. It's either sell the house or lose it. Either way, we can't stay here," she said.

I felt my entire life slipping away before my eyes.

Not again. I can't go through this again. And in my junior year of high school! What about work? What about my friends?

I felt tears welling up and spilling out of my eyes.

"This isn't the time to get upset or cop an attitude. Your father and I don't need this right now, do you hear me?"

I whispered, "Yes."

"Oh, by the way. A boy called for you. Actually, he called yesterday too. He said his name was Ben, and he was nice and polite. He told me all about his school and where he lives. He said he'll try calling back tonight. See? If he's as nice as he seems, we'll live closer to him when we move!" she said, as if she'd just solved all my problems.

Why was she being so sweet about a boy calling the house?

Did Ben really have that unique parental charm he'd bragged about? Right now, I really didn't care if Tom Selleck called. I just wanted to run away and die.

1981 – sixteen years old

Chapter 16

Ben and I had been dating for almost six months, and so far, everything seemed surprisingly fine at home, probably because I only saw him on weekends, and even then, it was usually just a single Friday or Saturday night. Ben had a long drive coming from Eureka to Forestville, and with our schedules, it was tough, but it worked.

Dear Diary,

Winter is finally over. Winter sucked because when roads were unsafe, Ben couldn't visit. Our house is still for sale. Lots of people have looked at it, but no bites. I have mixed emotions about moving because I love my school, but I love Ben too. It's a different relationship than with Luke. I guess whatever happens will be for the best. At least, that's what everyone says. My friends have been wicked cool. Steph says if we move, we'll never lose touch. Tomorrow night, Ben and I are going to see the premier of Raiders of the Lost Ark. I can't wait.

PS: Dad & Danny still suck!!!

Christina

"Christina. It's for you!" I heard Mom yell.

As I woke, I glanced at my alarm clock and saw that it was only 9:30 a.m.

Who in the world was calling me this early? It was Good Friday, so no school and a three-day weekend!

Mom came into the room.

"It's Ben," she said.

Ben? He was going skiing with Riley today. Maybe it got canceled and he'd decided to visit me!

"Hello?" I said, still a bit foggy.

"Hey . . . I got bad news . . . ," Ben said.

"What's wrong? Are you okay?" I was scared.

"Yeah. I'm okay, but my car isn't. I got into an accident last night. The car is wrecked," he said.

"Awww. Are you sure you're okay? Did anyone else get hurt?" I asked.

"No, no one else got hurt. It was just me, some black ice, and a big tree. I'm okay, but I can't come up tonight."

"Oh," I said, disappointed. "Bummer, I was looking forward to seeing you."

"Yeah, me too. When the hell are you gonna move? How long does it take to sell a house?" He sounded frustrated.

"Hopefully very soon," I said, aware of the partial lie. "I'm sorry about your car."

"Yeah. I am too. I'll call ya tonight, okay?" Ben said, sounding as if he really wasn't.

"Okay," I said, feeling awful inside.

"I think me and Riley are going to demolish a case of Heffenrefer tonight. At least we won't get pulled over for DUI." He laughed.

"Please don't," I said.

Ben was a typical teenage guy—loved to drink, loved to smoke pot, and loved to party. He wasn't out of control, but I didn't drink or smoke at all. Ben's standard line in introducing me to his friends was "Meet my level-headed girlfriend." But he never teased me about not drinking or smoking and never pushed me to try it, and I respected him for that.

"Please try and call tonight, okay?" I said, worried.

"Okay. I'll try." He said good-bye and hung up.

What an awful beginning to a day called Good Friday!

I spent the rest of the day bumming around the house, watching TV, and getting more depressed by the hour.

"Christina, are you ready yet?" Mom asked.

"Ready for what?" I said.

"It's Good Friday; we're going out to dinner. You're coming, aren't you?" she said, surprised that I might say no.

"I really don't feel like it, Mom. I'm not even hungry," I said.

I was lying on the couch in the living room, and Dad was standing in the entrance area. For a short, fat, perverted, scamming loser, he seemed extra sure of himself. Maybe it was because he was all dressed in that powder-blue shirt, navy polyester pants, and clip-on tie. He grossed me right out.

"It's Good Friday! The family is going out for dinner, and you are part of this family, correct? So, you are going," he said sternly.

The dinner smelled and looked great, but something in my stomach wasn't right. I just couldn't eat.

"Christina, what's wrong?" Mom asked.

"I don't know. Something feels really weird in my stomach. I'm just not hungry," I said.

I didn't finish, though I made a decent attempt at moving my food around the plate, leaving the appearance that I'd eaten some.

Zac, Andy, and Mikey fell asleep on the way home. Danny was babbling about how great he was at something, but I blocked him out, staring out the window. I felt unsettled.

As we approached our street, I couldn't wait to get out of the car. I just wanted to talk to Ben. Dad turned up our road, and Mom started yelling.

"Look at all those lights! What's going on?" she said loudly, and then—

"Oh, my God, Al, it's our house! Our house is on fire!"

Everyone immediately woke up. Mom was right. Our house was on fire, and there were trucks and people everywhere.

The next few minutes were a blur. Dad pulled into our driveway, and we all started running for the door, but people stopped us. Some were in firefighting suits, others were in emergency gear, and some were just neighbors. Everyone was shouting.

Someone I didn't know was holding me back.

"I want to go in! My father went in, I want to go in!" I screamed.

There were flames shooting from the rooftop. I stopped and stared for what seemed like an eternity. Everything was in slow motion. I saw Danny and my hysterical mom with a policeman dressed in blue. I saw Mikey, Zac, and Andy standing off to the side with some woman who shopped at the market—I think her name was Brandy. She was on the volunteer rescue team. The entire Forestville Fire Department was made up of volunteers, including guys our age, like my eighth-grade boyfriend, Bobby. This was insanity. Brandy stood by, holding on to the three crying boys. It was heartbreaking.

People were running everywhere with buckets of water while the town's only firetruck was busy trying to extinguish the fire before running out of water. Our house had become a full-on live-action horror movie. People were screaming and running with no apparent direction. The house itself had taken on a life of its own. We stood by watching it lose an agonizing battle to an angry ball of scorching red flames. Fire soared through our home as if on a mission to destroy everything in its path, leaving behind the resemblance of an enormous, disproportionately charred, sunken souffle instead of a family home.

Even with everything I was seeing, I still wanted to get inside. I desperately wanted my diary. I tried to move, but someone held me back.

I saw Dad near the house with a policeman.

"Let me go!" I said, still trying to get inside, but the person held on.

"Take your fucking hands off me! I need to get to my bedroom!" I yelled.

"Christina! That language!" Mom exclaimed.

I looked at the person holding on to my arms.

It was Father Porter, our parish priest.

"Sorry, Father," I said, regaining a bit of self-control.

"It's okay," he said.

Bobby approached.

"Christina, I've been in your room. Your room has more smoke and water damage than fire damage. I know this sounds crazy, but this looks worse from out here than it is inside."

"Thanks, Bobby," I said.

"You're welcome," he replied, and went back to work.

We had to sit and wait while other people tried to stifle the flames destroying our home. The smell was awful. It smelled like death. Wet, moldy death. By the time the last person left, our house, no longer a home, was a blistered skeleton of disintegrated memories.

At some point during the catastrophe, Uncle Jay, Mom's brother who also lived in Forestville, arrived. I was sitting on a rock near the end of the driveway, watching the last of the volunteers leave, when he spoke.

"Okay, kids. Let's pile up in my car, and you can spend the night at my place," he said.

"But I want to go inside. Dad went in. Why can't I?"

"Yeah!" one of my brothers said.

"It's still too dangerous in there. We'll come back in the morning," Uncle Jay said.

"But Uncle Jay, I need to see it. I need to see my room. I don't care how dangerous it is," I said.

He looked at Mom and the policeman for the okay.

They nodded, and someone spoke, "I can escort her."

"Okay," I said.

The policeman led the way; I followed.

"Please, be very careful. We can only step in certain places, and we can't go upstairs," the policeman said.

As we neared, the heat radiating from the smoldering sides of our melted pile of house instantly dried my eyeballs. At the same time, itsy bits of lingering ash carelessly landed on my tongue, as if they wanted to teach me that fire tasted like death.

I quickly learned that heat was nothing compared to the smell of the leftover house. I felt as if someone had shoved a dirty, wet ashtray up my nasal cavity, and it seeped down into my throat, one slow drip at a time, forcing me to digest that putrid odor.

We didn't need to open the door to walk inside, because there wasn't a door to open. We walked through a gaping hole onto a soot-filled floor of black ashes. Inside was dark, eerie, and evil, and it felt alive, with the heart throbbing from within the walls. If it'd been Halloween, I would've run back down the driveway, screaming for my life.

Concentrate, Christina, just gotta make it to your room!

We took each step apprehensively, like the next step in a funhouse. Were we going to fall right through to the basement? Was a hand going to come up from the floor and grab my ankles? The entire house was wet, dank, and gloomy, but there was the faint noise of fire crackling in the background, as if taunting to remind us that the something was still alive. The kitchen walls, smoke stained from the water, looked like a black-and-white version of the blood-smeared walls from *Carrie.* And as if that wasn't debilitating enough, the stench of wet ashtray had been mixed with the reek of melted plastic chemicals, and the whole kitchen felt like we'd walked into something seeming all the more chemically toxic, like a failed experiment in a morbid recipe class.

The wall by the kitchen table wasn't a wall at all, just a huge hole leading straight to the basement. What was left of the linoleum floor was curled up and singed on all ends. We continued to the living room, now a combination of itself and remnants of the rooms above, haphazardly decorated with water-logged, torn-apart Hardy Boys and Nancy Drew mystery books.

We walked through the hall to my room, ceiling dripping like a depressing, rainy night. Drops of water fell on my face and trickled down my cheeks like dirty black tears. This was a living nightmare. Bobby had been right. My furniture was still in place, but it wasn't the room I'd left.

Strategically placed *Tiger Beat* posters now stuck to the walls like sad, soggy abstract art. My room smelled like the rest of the house—dead—yet everything, although completely devoid of life, was still in place. I felt dizzy. I just needed to get my diary and get out.

The air in my room was moist and humid. Sooty water seeped into my sneakers, like being in a burnt swamp. I opened my top dresser drawer, but it was too dark to see inside. I reached in, using my hand as a fishing pole, hoping to snag my super personal book of thoughts. I reached all the way in, but I couldn't feel it! *Maybe it got shook around?* I grabbed frantically—no diary anywhere.

Oh, my God! It couldn't be gone! Bobby said he'd checked my room. Had he taken my diary? He knew I kept one. He'd teased me about things he thought I wrote, but I never thought he'd steal it! He had no idea what he was about to read!

It had to be there. I stood still in the middle of my room, wild-eyed, my mind frantically racing. I mentally sifted and sorted through the remains of my room, wishfully thinking my diary would appear from the drawer, like a baby reaching for its mother in safety. But no such luck. I exited my room, feeling faint and zombie-like.

Once outside and when the policemen were done talking, Uncle Jay piled us all into his car to spend the night at his house. It was a somber, quiet ride. I could barely keep myself breathing, never mind cry.

Our home was ruined, and when Bobby read my diary, all of my secrets would be out. Everyone would know who, what, and why Christina was.

Mom broke the silence of the ride and started sobbing hysterically, saying, "Why me, why me?"

This hadn't happened to everyone in the family . . . just her.

Uncle Jay, now divorced, lived in a mansion-like house on the other side of Forestville.

It was a huge, white brick home with incredible woodwork accents, and he had a built-in pool too, but I still would rather be at our house. After his divorce, Uncle Jay had divided the massive home into three apartments, and one was currently vacant. We'd be staying there until we could figure things out. Mom and Dad put me in a bedroom upstairs—next to what would be their room, of course. The boys would be staying downstairs.

I woke up early in the morning with the overwhelming need to brush my teeth. Still groggy, I headed for the bathroom.

My feet touched the cold tile floor, and the previous night slowly oozed back into my bones and consciousness.

Ugh. I remember everyone yelling, and the smell of nothing left. Our house has burned down. This isn't our bathroom, and I no longer own a toothbrush.

Was this what it was like to be helpless? To have nothing? I wasn't sure what it was, but I knew I'd never felt like this before. Someone or something had taken away everything we owned. My clothes, my stuff, even my toothbrush! And my private thoughts had been stolen by an ex-boyfriend! Uh-oh.

The bathroom walls started spinning, and the air went blurry. I held on to the sink as tightly as I could and didn't let go until I regained control of myself. As the world slowly came back into focus again, I walked back to the bedroom, realizing I still wore the smoky clothes from the night before. *How disgusting!* I looked at the chair next to the bed and saw a large T-shirt that was probably intended for me to wear last night, but I hadn't noticed. I sat on the bed, wide awake, and waited for someone to come in, because I had no idea what to do next.

"Christina?" Mom called from downstairs.

"Yes?" I answered.

"Are you coming down? Nana's here. She made us breakfast," she said.

"Yep. I'll be right down," I said, thankful I now had somewhere to go.

I sat down with everyone else, who were already at the table, eating French toast and eggs.

"Did you sleep okay?" Nana asked.

"Yeah," I said, although I didn't remember much. "What time is it?"

Mom replied, "It's about nine o'clock."

"Can I call Ben? He probably tried to call last night and doesn't know why I never called back," I said.

"Okay."

I couldn't eat yet. I was worried that Ben might think that I was mad or something.

I dialed and waited for the ring. His mom answered.

"Hello, Mrs. Honer, may I speak to Ben, please?"

"He's still sleeping, Chris. Is everything okay? You sound upset."

"Not really. Our house burned down last night. I think he might have tried to call, so I just wanted to let him know why nobody answered and that we're all okay," I said, as if things like this happened every day.

"Oh, my God! Was anyone home when it happened?" she exclaimed.

"No, no one was home. We were all out to dinner," I said, hoping Ben's mom wouldn't ask any more questions.

"I'll go wake him right now, honey," she said.

"Okay. Thanks," I replied.

"Hey," Ben said, still groggy.

"Hey, did you try and call last night?" I asked.

"Yeah, I tried like a hundred times till around midnight, but nobody answered. I was worried. Where were you?" he asked.

"Well, we ate dinner out and then went home, but unfortunately home wasn't there anymore," I said, sounding monotone.

"What?" He was awake but obviously confused.

I went on to explain everything I could remember except for the missing diary. I couldn't bear to mention that. We talked for a few more minutes, but I didn't want to stay on too long, as it was a long-distance call. We agreed to touch base later.

I went back to the kitchen. Everyone except Dad was still at the table.

"Mom, are we going to go to the house today too?" Andy asked.

Too?

"Mom, did Dad already go to the house?" I asked.

"Yes. Dad went to meet the insurance investigator and the detective to help determine the cause of the fire. We need to figure out how we're gonna survive," she answered as tears rolled down her face. "Mother, why did this happen to me? Now what am I going to do?" she said to Nana as she sat in the chair and sobbed uncontrollably.

I whispered to the boys, "Are we going to the house?"

"I don't know, she didn't answer," Andy said.

"I wanna go get my stuff," I whispered.

"Us too," Zac replied.

Zac poked me in the leg and made a face toward Mom.

"Ask her," he said.

I made a face back at him.

Why me? I didn't want to be the one to make her start yelling at us.

But then Mom spoke, "Why don't you kids go and get ready. I have to meet Dad soon. Nana's going to drive us."

Cool, we were going soon. Get ready? We didn't have any clothes other than what we'd worn yesterday, but we all got up and moved about, doing our best to act like everything was okay.

I headed upstairs, joking to Zac and Andy, "Gee, I wonder what I'm going to wear today?"

Making jokes at that point seemed like the only sensible thing to do.

If this God person is in total control, He's sending me down a bizarre path.

First, gives me a father, then takes him away before I'm old enough to know him. Then He allows my mother to marry another bad man, who legally adopts me and uses me as his private sex toy.

How does that same God condone burning our home to the ground and the disappearance of my diary?

Oh, and sometime during my life, my mother's gone batshit crazy!

It has to get better once I leave, right?

Every 9 Minutes

1981 – sixteen years old

Chapter 17

Living with Uncle Jay put us on a different school bus route, another reminder that life had changed so drastically. Everything, even the sound of the bus door opening, seemed foreign. With each step I sank deeper into another world—a world in slow motion. Once on the bus, I walked past the driver and down the aisle, feeling the stares from kids looking at me as if I was a circus freak.

My house burned down! I didn't!

I passed each seat, looking for an empty one, listening to the same questions over and over. By the time I sat down, I wanted to scream at the top of my lungs.

Yes! I'm all right! No, I have no idea what caused it! Stop asking!

I counted to ten—silently. Zac and Andy were loud and energetic, talking about the fire to kids on the bus. Danny had stayed home to help Dad.

I opted to sit alone and focus on the morning dew glistening on the trees outside, listening to wet leaves slap against bus windows as we bumbled over roads with divots so deep they bounced me inches off my seat. But I didn't flinch. I was lost in visions of smoke, flames, uncertainty, and fear.

What if Dad hadn't made me go out to dinner? Would I have prevented the fire? Would I be hurt or dead? Dad had said it was the washing machine. How did he know that? How did people determine the source of a fire?

Why did we live in a town where the people responsible for disaster control were our fellow civilians? Why on earth had Bobby taken my diary? How did he know where to look? My big penny had been inside the diary. Now he had that too. Was it worth anything? What was going to happen to me if everyone found out?

The entire day was a blur, and the next thing I knew, I was back on the bus again, heading for Uncle Jay's.

Where had the kids gotten all the exaggerated rumors about our house? Our house had burned down, it hadn't been swallowed up into the ground or vanished from existence. Why hadn't Bobby said anything about the diary? He'd stopped me in the hall, asked if I was okay, and said he'd done the best he could to make sure my room wasn't totally wrecked. I didn't get the slightest sense he had my diary. Was it possible he hadn't read it yet? I almost wished he had said something just so it would be over with and my stomach would stop turning.

When I got into the house, Mom and Dad weren't there, just Nana.

"How was school?" she asked, immediately followed by a question she asked at the end of every conversation: "Are you hungry?"

"Sit down, eat some eggplant," she insisted, as if no one in their right mind would pass up eggplant.

Zac and Andy were already home and at the table, asking for seconds.

"No thanks, Nana, I'm not hungry. I've got homework to do," I replied, knowing she wouldn't argue with schoolwork.

"Okay. But let me know when you want to eat. You need food to keep your brain working," she said, as though eating was one of the Ten Commandments.

"Okay," I said, shaking my head, wondering how she didn't weigh five hundred pounds.

I just wanted to go through the things I'd salvaged from my room. We had spent Saturday gathering savable items. I ended up with a few clothing items from my dresser drawers and a handful of irreplaceable items.

I sat on the bed, my box of rescued keepsakes beside me, thinking it was odd that Uncle Jay had never remodeled the Holly Hobbie-wallpapered, pink-trimmed room after his wife and kids left.

I opened the box and looked down at what was left of my possessions. It wasn't much; most were ruined and should have been thrown away, but those things meant a lot to me, like the scrapbook I'd started back in Hillsgrove when I was in grade school. Now it was edge-burnt from fire, stank of smoke, and warped from the water damage, but the inside contents toward the center were still somewhat recognizable. I reflectively thumbed through the pages of my life. I smiled, looking at the photos of friends long forgotten, and relived a few stops along our cross-country trip. All in all, the journey back to memory lane made me feel both happy and sad.

Mixed in between the old friends and vacation stops were photos of homes we had lived in along the way. At the time, I'd thought they would bring happy memories of each place we'd lived, but now I found that was not the case at all. I took the photos out, placed them in a pile on the floor, and stared at them. Then slowly, one by one, I picked them up.

Our first house in Hillsgrove was on top. The photo brought back haunting memories.

I heard the creaking of the stairs as the weight of those fat feet neared my bedroom door. Vivid, horrifying, repetitive dark memories played over and over again, fading into visions of our family packed together in our orange Suburban, leaving for what I'd believed would be a happier place.

I put that photo down and picked up the next of our home in Phoenix, Arizona. It took my breath way as I relived, in graphic detail, the disgusting scene of my father and brother, naked, leaning over my bed. I released the photo as if on fire and watched it fall to the floor, sitting still until I no longer felt faint.

I even had a photo of me and my younger brothers in Halloween costumes on the front step of our rented mothball-smelling house. The memory of that home was as brief and consistent as the holiday itself.

The last photo was of our home in Forestville, now gone. In that photo, I saw my older self being crushed by a heavy body, but I was tired, worn, and unable to get up. I saw myself trying to scream, yet nothing came out. I saw both parents yelling and screaming in my face. Then I saw my father holding on to my ten-speed bike, laughing like a horror movie clown. Next were visions of his naked body standing above me on my bed as my life slowly faded to black, only to rush back as vigorous flames of fire red as I watched our home burn to the ground.

Stuck between a trance and a mental breakdown, crying so hard tears ran down my face and arms, I picked up the pile of memories and gripped that hunk of hate at tightly as possible. I sat still and watched as my tears descended and destroyed those photos, turning colors and details into blurred memories I hoped would eventually disappear but knew never would.

I wiped the tears from my eyes, grabbed the pack of pictures, and headed for the bathroom. I turned on the faucet, dumped the heap of bad memories into the sink, watched the remaining colors wash away, destroying physical pre-existence, then tossed the wad of wet paper into the trashcan, exhaled, and walked myself back to the bedroom.

The rest of the box contained select happy memories. I'd salvaged the little silver piggy bank Mom said I received at christening, along with the key chain I'd made in the special needs class in Arizona. I still had a box of letters and cards I'd kept from Luke, including the card that I'd taken from the trash when he sent me the two dozen yellow roses after my parents pulled that bullshit stunt. They'd tried to tell me that my grandfather had sent them to my mother. I hadn't really thought anything of it, but later that night as I cleaned dishes, I'd noticed a pretty card in the trash. Being nosy, I'd pulled the card from the trash, thinking it was from Papa to my mother. Instead, I inadvertently discovered the roses had been sent to me by Luke. Heartbreaking.

The bottom of the box was filled with notebooks from school and a little white box. My biology notebook, now a bit water damaged, was still special to me, as I'd carefully printed every word from my favorite Cat Stevens song, "Can't Keep It in," on the cover.

"And I can't keep it in, I can't keep it in
I've gotta let it out
I've gotta show the world, world's gotta see . . ."

I was the only one who knew what those words really meant to me. Maybe someday I'd be brave enough to share my secret. Maybe.

The little white box was my special box. It contained the things Luke had given me. A silver bracelet from when we'd first met, a silver chain with an Italian horn, and my favorite: a butterfly bracelet from Reed & Barton. Everything was in decent condition except for the butterfly bracelet. It had heat blisters from the fire, and the overcoating had peeled on the edges, but that didn't matter to me. I would have kept it even if it had melted into a ball.

More than a month after the fire, we were still at Uncle Jay's house. Mom and Dad were surprised to find out they weren't properly insured, so they opted to use some of the insurance money to keep paying the mortgage and put the property up for sale and use the rest for a down payment on a house in Hillsgrove. This was all planned for some time in July, which would place me in a new school in my senior year.

How was I going to make new friends in a school four times larger than Tomahawk? If I ever had kids, I swore I would never move in their senior year of high school. The last year was supposed to be the fun year. For me, though, I would feel like I did at every new school: a big, invisible nobody. At least I had prom to look forward to.

***

"I had a great time tonight," Ben said.

"Me too," I replied.

The foyer of our prom venue had been decorated in my school colors, green and white, with flowers and streamers everywhere, and the themes of photographs and memories, like the Jim Croce song, fit perfectly. Everyone looked so grown up, with the girls in sophisticated gowns and guys in tuxes instead of jeans and concert T-shirts. *This has been a perfect evening so far*, I thought to myself as we exited the venue.

"I love your dress," Ben said.

"Thank you." I blushed.

We left hand in hand and drove to our usual parking spot near Uncle Jay's house, where we'd be close when curfew time neared. Forestville's police department consisted of two cops and one police car, making the chances of getting caught parking slim. We drove up the barely visible, semisteep driveway to a former property of my uncle's, now empty and owned by the electric company.

Ben teased, "I look forward to your giant exhale when we reach the top of the hill and turn off the headlights."

"Yeah. I feel much safer once the lights are off." I sighed.

"What a beautiful night. Look at all those stars. Let's lie on the hood of the car. I'll grab the blanket out of the back?" he asked.

"That sounds great." I smiled. "I'll bet we look pretty ridiculous lying on the hood of a car in a gown and tux."

He laughed.

"So, is little Miss Level-headed going to have a beer with me tonight or not?"

"Little Miss Level-headed? Why do you always say that?" I snapped, and rolled onto my side to face him.

"You can't tell me you haven't noticed how sensible you are compared to the rest of the kids our age?" He was serious now.

"I don't mean to be. I'm not nerdy, am I?" I said.

"No! You're just so grown up most of the time. You're fun, but you never get into any trouble. Riley says you're the most level-headed teenager he's ever met!" Ben said.

"I guess it's because of my parents, mostly my dad. I get in trouble for things I don't do. I couldn't imagine if I actually did them," I answered as I shook my head.

"What's with your dad, anyway?" he asked.

"What do you mean?" I asked, feeling butterflies come alive in my stomach.

"Well, he's super nice to your brother Daniel, but he's weird with you, and it doesn't take a genius to notice he doesn't like me!" he said.

Somewhere during the past year, Danny had decided he would like to be referred to as Daniel instead of Danny because it sounded more mature.

"Daniel's definitely his favorite. My dad just doesn't like me. I'm not sure why. Maybe it's because I am not his biological kid? Or, more likely, it's because I'm not a loser like Daniel. It's so messed up. I think about it a lot, but I really don't understand it. My brother could go out and get a job just like me. No one is holding him back. They used to give him money just for getting Bs or Cs, but I am *expected* to get good grades, so no bribe money for me.

"My parents are kind of insane. Look at how many times we've moved! I want to be out on my own as soon as I turn eighteen. I need to be capable of taking care of myself. I *never* want to be like them! Especially *him*. He's a disgusting, lying pervert!" I said, realizing that the last comment had come out before I had a chance to stop it.

I looked up at Ben, staring right into my eyes. He'd been quiet, listening to every word. The stare was so intense I could see him thinking.

The few seconds of silence seemed like hours.

"Chris, he's never done anything fucked up to you, has he? Cuz if he has, I'll kill him!" he said, way more serious than a sixteen-year-old guy ever should be.

Oh, my God. No! This was the last thing I wanted. That was *my* business. People would think I was a freakin' wacko. This was *my* secret, *my* problem. No one else should have to deal with this. No one.

"No! He's just a jerk, that's all," I said as calmly as I was capable of at the moment.

Silence again.

"I love you a lot," he said.

"I love you too," I replied.

I'd gotten better at saying those words.

He pulled my body against him, my face inches from his, and I looked up to see his blue eyes sparkling in the moonlight.

My insides got fuzzy. I still had feelings for Luke, but different feelings, not like the ones I had now. I was incredibly attracted to Ben. He was different from the other guys I knew. He was very sure of himself yet still shy and polite in a cute kind of way.

"I'll never push you to do anything you're not ready for. Do you know that?" Ben said reassuringly.

"Yes, I know," I answered.

We'd been dating for eight months, and things were getting intense. Part of me wanted to do more than just kiss, but the level-headed part of me was saying, *No way*. But how much longer could I look into those eyes and stay sensible?

When his lips touched mine, my body tingled all over. What had been physically satisfying previously just wasn't enough tonight. Maybe it was from looking at him in a tux all night or being outdoors on a perfect moonlit night.

Our tongues touched and stopped just long enough to intensify the feelings between us. His hands were wrapped tightly around my waist. He stopped kissing me and whispered into my ear.

"Can I unzip your dress?" he asked.

"What if someone comes?" I whispered back.

"Well, then we'll just have to explain to the deer and raccoons that we don't go bothering them, so they shouldn't bother us," he joked, trying to lighten the mood.

"I'm scared!" I said.

"We come here almost every weekend, and no one has caught us yet. Right?" he asked. "I'll wrap my jacket around you, just in case."

Why was I so scared?

"I promise I won't go any further than that," he said as he looked directly into my eyes.

We didn't have much longer before I had to be home, and the moonlight was so beautiful, it made everything feel just right. Ben's chest felt warm and safe against mine. He was gentle and sweet. We kissed as the bare skin of our chests touched, and as he promised, he never asked for or tried anything else. I felt safe. It was nice—nothing like the nights at home.

1981 – sixteen years old

Chapter 18

I couldn't believe I was in another new house . . . another new room, with the same old *him* . . . about to enter another new school. Leaving Forestville, RI, was awful! My life had changed so much, and I missed Stephanie. I missed hanging out with my friends, and I even missed my teachers, as they, too, had become a part of my life.

Mom had to take us in to register us for school a few weeks prior to the first day. Northgate High School was so big, it took us almost a half hour to find the registration office. I was going to be the only girl in her senior year who couldn't find the school gymnasium. It was a quiet and depressing ride home from registration.

"Christina? Are you downstairs?" Mom yelled.

"Yup," I answered.

"Come upstairs. Your dad and I have something to tell you!" she said in one of her happy, guess-what-we're-up-to-now tones.

God only knows what I'm in for.

When I got upstairs, the boys were all sitting in the living room, as if waiting for my arrival.

"Guess what?" she said, almost singing.

I felt like I was three years old, but I'd play along.

"What?" I said.

"Dad and I just bought a diner!" she bragged.

"A what?"

"A diner!" Mom repeated.

"A diner? Like a fifties restaurant?" Zac asked.

"Yeah. Something like that, but it's right here in Hillsgrove," Dad said.

"The carpet-and-tile business is getting hard on Dad physically, and we're getting a great deal on the diner," Mom said happily.

"Are we going to get to cook and stuff?" Zac asked.

"Yes, and we can use all the help we can get. We're going to take another look at it tomorrow, and you're all coming," Mom said, and began to sing the "Rock Around the Clock" song.

Hmm. She's in a good mood.

"Mom, can I go to the mall to drop off my film from the last day of school?" I asked, knowing that she'd say yes.

"Yes. Don't be too long, though," Mom replied.

"Okay."

I preferred being back in Forestville, but living in Hillsgrove had its good points. The mall was only two miles away, and Uptown Camera was located in the mall. Unfortunately, I didn't have a job, so I had to count out my change jar to get my pictures developed.

The trip to the mall was productive, and it turned out Uptown was looking for help!

"Hey, Mom, I just came from the camera store in the mall, and they're looking for help. Is it okay if I apply?" I asked, so happy, I was tripping over my words.

"Well, what about school?" she asked.

"It won't be a problem. The guy said they are looking for people who want to work the hours I am available. I can still go to school and work. I've done it before," I said, almost pleading.

"What about the diner?" Dad asked.

"What about it?" I asked back.

"We're expecting your help there too. Can you handle all of it at once?" he asked, although his tone reflected that I would be able to.

Hmm. That was unusual. Dad usually didn't approve letting me do something that I was enthusiastic about.

"Yes. I think I can. And I won't be working every day, it'll just be part time. When I'm not working there, I can work at the diner. I know I can do it. Besides, I don't have the job yet. I have to go through the interview process. This is a real place," I explained.

"Well, if you think you can handle it," he said.

"Are you sure, Al?" Mom asked him.

"Yeah. Now that she'll have a job again, she can go back to providing for herself," Dad snapped.

Ahh, that explained it. He had something to gain in this.

"Okay," Mom agreed—of course.

"Great! I have to go back and see the manager after five. Okay?" I said.

"Okay," they both replied.

I didn't think five o'clock would ever come.

Okay, Christina. Act normal. Relax.

I waited for the woman behind the counter to finish assisting a customer.

"Hi," she said, and smiled. "Can I help you?"

Okay. Here goes.

"Yes. My name is Chris. I was in earlier today to drop off film. I heard you might be looking for help?"

Whew. I got it out without passing out.

"Yes, we are. Are you interested?" Sally asked.

She was pleasant, but you sure could tell that she was the boss. There was something authoritative about her. She reminded me of the girls that played field hockey in school, tough but still girly . . . the kind of girl you didn't mess with. She didn't look that old, maybe late twenties.

"Yes. I just moved to this area and would love a chance to work in a camera store," I replied, probably with a little more enthusiasm than I should have.

She laughed.

"Are you available to work nights and weekends, including Sundays?" she asked.

"Yes, I go to school during the day. Those hours would be perfect for me." I smiled.

"Well, our main office is in Wolfborough, Mass, so you'd have to go there for your interview, okay?" she asked.

"Yes," I answered.

I had no idea where Wolfborough was when I answered, but two interviews and a few weeks later, I was officially employed by Uptown Camera. Ben wasn't happy about my job, because he thought we wouldn't have enough time together between school, my diner responsibilities, and now this job. I promised him it wouldn't interfere.

Mom and Dad named the diner Grub 'n' Stuff, and it sat within the loop of one of the busiest rotaries in a small section of Hillsgrove only a few miles from our house.

I parked Dad's truck in front of the diner, wishing I still had my old car, but I'd sold it to pitch in after the house burned down.

Recently Dad had bought a new Ford F-150 pickup. I had no idea how we went from having no money to having a new house, a new business, and a new vehicle. But knowing Dad, I was sure he had some scam going. Lately he'd been hanging around with some guy from State Side Central Credit Union. I got a creepy feeling in my stomach when that guy and his friends were around our house. They dressed in expensive suits, but the sleazy vibe oozed out. Dad, of course, thought the guys were great.

"Wow. This place is sparkling!" I said, looking at the diner booths.

"Hey, Christina. Guess what?" Zac exclaimed.

"What?" I asked.

"Andy and I are going to be short-order cooks on the weekends. Mom and Dad are gonna open late night, and we're gonna get to make everything that comes off this grill!" Zac said as he flipped imaginary burgers on the grill with a shiny new spatula.

"That's cool, Zac, and you're definitely a perfect *short*-order cook," I teased.

"Hey. I'm not done growing!"

Mom came out from the back when she heard us joking.

"Christina, are you going to have time to help us out with your new job and all?" she asked. "We really could use your help. And . . . we *are* your parents."

Why did she always have to add the guilt?

"Yes, of course," I replied.

"Well, here's what your dad and I decided," she began. "The diner is going to open at five in the morning every day. We've hired a full-time cook and two waitresses, but the waitresses can't fill all the hours. Do you think you could fill some of the early-morning hours before school?" she asked.

"Yeah. I guess so," I replied.

How the hell was I going to fit all of this into my life?

"Okay. Good. The diner will open the week after school starts. Okay?" she asked rhetorically.

"Hey, what's Danny going to do?" I asked.

"Please call him Daniel. Daniel's too experienced for diner work. Dad says Daniel will find a better job," she said, as though it was no big deal.

I shook my head.

Amazing. I guess things will never change.

The rest of the summer quickly passed, and now three weeks into my senior high school year, as predicted, I hated it. My body was wrecked, but I wasn't about to complain. Mom and Dad would have made me quit working at the camera store before easing up on my diner hours. I'd met another high school senior who worked in different store in the mall and was in a work-study program where she'd go to school for a few hours a day and work full-time job too. So, she seemed to be pulling it all off and surviving okay.

All the kids at school talked about college. Back at Tomahawk, Stephanie and I had talked about colleges we could attend together. So much had changed since then; now I didn't even know how to find the guidance counselor's office, never mind who they were or how to apply for financial assistance. Stephanie's mom had helped her with her college applications, but my mom never offered, and when I'd brought it up, she reminded me of how busy she was. Since Dad made me pay for my own expenses and it was long distance to call Steph, we'd spoken less and less. As a result, I was pretty much on my own and had become used to it.

"Christina, are you downstairs?" Mom yelled from upstairs.

"Yeah," I answered.

"Can you come up here for a minute?" she asked, much nicer than usual.

Mom and Dad were sitting alone on the living room sofa.

"What's up?" I asked.

"We need your help," she said.

"With what?" I asked hesitantly.

"Well, we're doing our best to make things better for this family, and we've risked everything for this diner, but until it takes off, things are going to be tough," she said.

"Okay," I said, puzzled.

"We didn't expect money to be this tight when we bought the truck," she said, "We're wondering if you can take over the truck payments since you're the only one that has a job."

"But I've only been working for three weeks. How much is the monthly payment?" I nervously answered.

I wanted a nice car of my own someday, but not something forced upon me and definitely not an icky beige truck!

"Can't you sell it?" I asked.

"There's no time. We're behind on payments. If you take it over, it won't affect our credit. The bank won't even know that you're paying the loan. It's the least you can for your parents," Mom wheedled.

Wow, that was a bit of financial pressure! And what if he kept the money I gave them and they lost the truck anyway?

"What's the monthly payment?" I asked, afraid to hear the answer.

"$189," she said.

"You can afford that. You work enough," Dad said sarcastically.

My head was spinning. I made only $3.75 an hour, but if I didn't say yes, it'd be my fault they lost the truck.

"I could do it if I worked full time. And the only way for me to work full time is through a school work-study program, but that will mean no college for me next year," I said, amazed and disappointed at what had just come out of my mouth.

Not going to college had never been my intention; in fact, it had always been the opposite, but I had no financial means to get me there. Everything was a big mess. I'd spent the first three years of high school doubling up on math and science, working extra hard to get good grades with the goal of attending a good college. Now I found myself literally alone and lost, with my parents looking to me to be the financial backbone of the family. *How do kids escape bad environments without getting stuck inside? I can't become a statistic. I just can't.*

Mom and Dad looked at each other. Then Mom spoke.

"Well, I'm glad that you made that decision. Your father and I were going to ask you to wait anyway. We can't afford to send you to college, and we'd appreciate it if you stayed to help financially. Boy, Al. What a relief!" Mom smiled.

Had my parents just told me they were thrilled I couldn't afford college?

"So, you can take over the truck payments?" Mom asked again.

I felt there was no right answer.

"Okay, then it will be my truck, right?" I asked.

"Of course, but I'm sure you'll let us borrow it when we need to," she explained.

I took a deep breath and exhaled.

"Yeah, I guess so," I said, and then experience kicked in. "I know you guys are busy. Why don't I take the payment book and mail payments myself? That way you won't have to worry about it at all," I suggested.

Mom answered, "Okay. The book is in the top drawer of the dresser."

"Is that it?" I asked as I got up.

"Yes. Thanks for helping us out," Mom said sincerely.

"You're welcome," I said.

My good deed for the day was done. I walked down the hall to their bedroom to grab the payment book, proud of myself for keeping track of what I was doing and scared to death that I now had a legitimate financial responsibility.

1981 – seventeen years old

Chapter 19

It was an unusually frigid late-October morning. We—or to be honest, Ben—had just finished changing a flat tire, and the heater in his '57 Lincoln was barely working. As we drove farther north, the awe-inspiring view of the mountains created just enough magic to make the car temperature bearable and cancel out the broken heater. My family had traveled across the country and back, but I'd never been north of Boston, Massachusetts.

Ben laughed. "I still can't believe we're driving all the way to Vermont."

The thought of it was funny, but the reasoning wasn't. After countless conversations about it, we'd made the decision together.

"You know we're driving six hours north of your house just so you won't be paranoid that someone may walk in?" Ben teased.

"Yeah, I know, but I want this to be special. I don't want to be nervous about other people. You understand, right?" I whispered.

"Yeah. I'm just bummed my dad didn't build a cabin in Rhode Island instead of Vermont."

"Okay, okay. You've made your point."

"Just pointing out how much I love you, that's all." He smiled and pulled me toward him.

We had planned carefully. Ben had told his mom he was going skiing for the day, and I'd told my parents Ben and I were going to visit his relatives in Vermont. Mom had given me some hassle at first, but I'd promised we would be back in time for curfew.

"So, what exactly does this cabin look like?" I asked.

"From what I can remember, it's big and sits on top of a mountain all by itself. My dad had been working on it for about a year before he died. He wanted a place to escape to, probably from my mom more than anything!" He laughed.

"I haven't seen it since he began building, but my brother has. He said it has a huge fireplace right in the middle of the cabin, so you can see the fire from the kitchen and the living room. It's got two floors, but that's about all I know. I took plenty of blankets and pillows so we can stay warm till the fire kicks in. As long as my brother gave me the right directions, we'll be there in a few minutes."

Ben's brother was right. Minutes later, we came up over the top of the mountain upon which sat a beautiful Vermont cabin. The view was breathtaking.

"Well, I guess your brother was right," I said.

We got out of the car and stood side by side, looking over the mountaintop.

"Wow" was all I could say.

Ben replied with one word too. "Yeah."

It was below freezing, but the air was so crystal clear it didn't matter that my nose might crack right off my face. I couldn't stop looking at the scenery surrounding us. There were thousands of perfectly shaped, snow-topped evergreens. If Santa Claus existed, this could be his home.

"Your dad sure knew what he was doing when he picked out this spot!" I said, amazed.

"Yeah, too bad he never got a chance to enjoy it," Ben said sadly.

We were both quiet for a while before Ben spoke again.

"Ready to go inside?" he asked.

"Sure! Heat might be a good thing," I reasoned, lightening things up a bit.

We walked toward the front door.

"It looks like Grizzly Adams lives here," I joked.

As Ben opened the front door, it creaked, and I flinched.

"Will you *relax*!" he said, trying not to sound scared himself.

We both walked inside. Ben closed the door. Other than the creaking of the closing door, the lack of sound was almost awkward. He took my hand, and we wandered around in silence. We walked to the back of the cabin toward the kitchen area and made a circle right back to the spot where we'd started. I hadn't said a word or even taken a breath since we'd entered. I was in shock. And although he was trying to hide it, he was too.

I spoke first.

"Well, I guess your brother forgot to tell you a few things, huh?" I said, a bit bewildered.

He looked at me as if to apologize, hoping that I wasn't mad.

I needed to assure him that I wasn't. Actually, it was kind of funny.

"Well, it does have everything you said it did. That's where the kitchen was going to be, and there's definitely a second floor—there just isn't a staircase yet. Your dad sure as hell made sure there was a window everywhere humanly possible. Granted, it would probably be a bit warmer if he'd installed windows in those gigantic rectangular holes. But hey— the fireplace is just where you said it would be!" I smiled, reassuring him that this was still okay with me.

"I'm so sorry," he said.

"It's not your fault. I'm the one that needed to be far away from everyone to feel comfortable. I think this is totally cool and pretty romantic too. You must admit that this will be a place we'll definitely remember for the rest of our lives," I said.

"Yeah, you can say that again. I'll go get the blankets," Ben said.

"Okay."

I walked to the nearest window hole and admired the view. I was nervous, but not worried like I was doing the wrong thing. Ben and I had talked about this so many times. And he'd assured me that I had nothing to worry about. I'd explained to him that I wasn't taking any kind of birth control. I didn't like the idea of taking a drug every day to prevent . . . that. We did agree that he would use protection and we'd be careful as to when we did *it*. I'd read about when a woman was most likely fertile. To be a bit cautious, I'd planned our trip a few days before my period was due, as the last thing I wanted to be responsible for another human being.

I didn't understand why some of my friends were already talking about getting married and having babies. I couldn't even comprehend the responsibility of another human being. Yet here I was, about to have loving, consensual, voluntary, on-purpose sex for the first time. We had both talked about this, and we'd both come to this decision together.

Ben came back inside and dumped everything in a big pile next to the door.

"You want to lay out the blankets while I get the fire started?" he asked.

I could tell by the tone of his voice he was nervous. It made me smile.

A few minutes later blankets were layered in a heap beside a warm, glowing fire. Ben stood on one side of the blanket bed, and I stood on the other. Both of us waited for the other to make the first move.

He spoke, "I think we might be warmer under the blankets."

"Yeah, I think you're right," I replied.

He knelt to the floor, turned the first couple of layers down, and gestured for me to join him. I climbed in after him. Both of us were still fully clothed, shoes and all.

"Nervous?" he asked.

"Yeah. A little, but mostly freezing!" I replied.

"Me too. Maybe we should have brought a radio," Ben said, laughing a bit.

"Well, you were probably planning on the using the built-in stereo system by the lovely glass picture window?" I teased.

"Come here . . . ," he said as he opened his arms to let me in.

"What do we do now?" I asked.

"We stay warm! And just hold each other for a while, okay?" he said, pulling my body tight against his.

"What time is it anyway?" I asked.

"It's only 2:10. Relax, we have plenty of time," Ben said, rolling over on top of me.

I loved his blue eyes. Now inches from his face, I could see they were extra alive, almost electric.

We kissed. I let my hands unbutton his shirt, feeling his bare chest. Soon we were naked beneath the blankets; his body was warm against mine.

Wow! This was nothing like I'd imagined. I'd imagined it hurting. I'd imagined his touch feeling rough. But it was soft. Gentle. Caring. We were used to making out in the dark in the back of his car. This was nice.

I was in a dream of sporadic consciousness yet sensually aware of every move. I felt his body against mine. I heard the ripping of the condom wrapper and got vaguely curious as to how that thing actually went on, but I didn't look. I heard him ask me if everything was okay as he gently climbed back on top of me. I felt an incredible heat inside me, and the next thing I knew, we were lying side by side, quiet and close.

He whispered, just loud enough for me to hear, "I love you."

I rolled close to him. I felt good. "I love you too."

"Hey, don't get too close. I still have this thing on," he said.

Thing? What thing? Oh!

"Maybe you should do something with it?" I said, confused.

"Okay. I'm gonna get up and find someplace to throw it out. You want to get dressed to keep warm?" Ben asked.

Boy, was I glad he'd asked! It felt so weird being naked in partially built house.

"Yeah. Go ahead. I'll get dressed while you do that," I said, watching him get up.

Wow! This was the first time I'd seen a naked guy in the daylight. He looked nice. He was in great shape, like something out of a magazine.

It made me laugh.

"Hey! What are you laughing at? No peeking while I get dressed!" he yelled.

I was still laughing. I had a case of the giggles.

"How about you get up and get dressed too?" he shot back, smirking.

"Oh boy, no thanks! I'll turn right around so I can't see you! You go ahead, I'll be getting dressed under these covers!" I snapped, smirking.

"I thought that might stop you from teasing me." He laughed.

I heard him walk away. I began to dress under the covers. I checked my watch to make sure we still had plenty of time.

Wow! 2:20? I couldn't believe it. It had been 2:10 when I got under the blanket before I got undressed! That whole event had taken only ten minutes? I'd thought it was four o'clock or something. We had plenty of time.

We were both quiet and happy on the ride home. I fell asleep with my head on his lap for a while and woke to the radio playing Air Supply's "Girl, You're Every Woman in the World." While Ben sang along, I smiled and drifted back to sleep.

I got home way before my midnight curfew. Mom was watching TV in the living room when I got in.

"Did you have a good time today?" she asked, just for conversation.

"Yes, I'm exhausted, though. It was a long drive. Good night." I tried to be as chill as possible.

"Good night," she replied.

It took me a while before I felt sleepy. I was still all warm inside.

I wished I had my diary. I hadn't purchased a new one, as I still feared that someone would walk up to me one day and I'd know they knew everything was *not* normal about me.

Thinking about my diary made the lovely, warm feeling disappear. Every year, that man I had to call Dad gave me a reason to hate him more. I curled up in a ball as small as I could and grabbed on to the blankets with my hands gripped into tight fists. The clock said four when I looked at it last.

* * *

It was 4:30 a.m., and I needed to get myself out the door and to the diner in less than thirty minutes.

"Christina, are you going to be home after school today?" Mom asked.

"No. I gotta go to a seminar with my boss," I yelled, running to the truck.

I couldn't believe working two jobs *and* going to school hadn't exhausted me, but I felt fine. I'd managed to get the work-study program approved, but even though I had enough credits to graduate, English and gym were still mandatory.

I worked at the diner from five till seven, went to school for two classes, then headed straight to Uptown Camera in time to open the doors and some days work till 10 p.m. I only made tips at the diner, no hourly pay, but I used those for food and fun. The money from Uptown Camera was for bills, and the rest went to a savings account.

I loved working at Uptown Camera. Tonight, Canon Camera Company was introducing new camera models at a company dinner event in Wolfborough, Massachusetts.

"Next week is Thanksgiving, and that kicks off the Christmas season. Before we leave, I'd like each person to set a holiday season sales goal," Sally said.

"What do you mean?" I asked her.

"Well, how much commission do you think you can make between Turkey Day and December 24th?" she asked.

"I don't know," I answered, wondering to myself.

The rest of the crew guessed.

Sally guessed she would make $450, but she expected everyone else to guess higher, as she had manager responsibilities.

"I guess I could make $500. Is that counting my hourly?" I asked, thinking $500 was an awful lot of money just to make in commissions.

"That's not counting your hourly, and personally, I think you can do more." Sally laughed. "I'd like to see everyone crush their own goals. It makes me look good! Now let's go have a fun night." She smiled.

We pulled into the parking lot of the Wolfborough Sheraton-Tara hotel. The lobby looked expensive, like a hotel you'd see on TV. We found the directory for the event and followed Sally to our seminar room.

The room was packed. Sally made me feel welcome by introducing me to co-workers as we mingled. I tried not to look nervous and stood by patiently as she held conversations, using the time to check out the room because I'd never seen anything like it. There were so many tables, all set for dinner with linens and fancy silverware.

I knew I was one of the youngest employees at Uptown, but I thought there'd be a few other people my age too. But looking around, I saw everyone was much older. So many employees were guys, important ones in suits. They all sort of looked the same . . . except for one guy.

Who is that? He's gorgeous! Whoa! Just looking at him gives me butterflies!

I couldn't stop staring.

"Ready to go to the table, Chris?" Sally asked.

Huh? "Oh, yeah, sure."

I followed Sally to our table. We sat, and Sally introduced each person. She knew everybody. Just as she got done, Mr. Gorgeous plopped down—right next to me!

"Hey, what's your name?" he asked.

"Harry, this is Chris," she answered.

"Are you allowed to speak for yourself?" he joked.

"Ha, ha," Sally snapped.

"Hi" was all I managed to blurt out.

"So, you're the little girl from Hillsgrove we've all heard so much about," he said.

"What do you mean?" I said, thinking I was about to get teased for my young age.

"Rumor has it that you're some hotshot that's full of energy!" he shared.

I looked at Sally for help, but she was talking to someone else at the table.

"I'm just doing my job," I said.

"Yeah, yeah, yeah, that's what they all say," Harry teased.

"Yay, I'm sitting next to the company smart-ass," I snapped.

Wow! Where'd all the courage come from?

"Touché! Actually, I was kidding. Honestly, all I've heard is that you're a great employee and fantastic salesperson," he said apologetically.

By the time the seminar wrapped up, my sides hurt from laughing. I'd learned a lot about the new cameras and more about Harry. I was glad he worked in Boston. He was way too old for me to crush on, and besides, I had a boyfriend. Though lately, it admittedly seemed like we were stagnating. The more I worked and learned new things, the more I realized that Ben and I did not have as much in common as I'd thought. Or maybe I was just outgrowing him—I didn't know.

Christmas season came and went in the blink of an eye. By the end of January, the impact of school, early diner shifts, working overtime through the holiday, and finding time to see Ben was beginning to wear me down. I was expecting Sally to be back from her meeting any minute and couldn't wait to go home because I was wiped out.

"Wow! You look like shit!" Sally said, entering the store, full of smiles.

"Gee, thanks!" I answered.

"You feel okay?"

"Yeah, I'm just tired," I replied. "What are you so happy about, anyway?"

"Look at these," she said, tossing papers in front of me.

It was the Christmas commissions list with each employee's total noted separately under his or her store.

"Notice anything?" she asked, still smiling.

"Yeah, who's this Stanley guy? He made a bundle!" I asked.

"Who's that Stanley guy? Who's that Stanley guy?" she repeated in disbelief.

"Yeah. Who is he?" I asked again.

"Stanley Abraham's the best salesman in the company. Been here longer than anyone, been the best for as long as I can remember," she said, as if that meant something to me.

"Yeah? And looks like he's still number one," I answered, still confused.

"Who's number two, and by how much?"

"Hmm . . . Wow, that's me! He still beat me by fifty dollars, though Hillsgrove did pretty good all around. You must be proud!" I said.

"Yup! Now do you want the good news or the not-so-good news?" She sat down.

"Uh, I'll take the good news. Bad news sucks!" I said.

"Good News? Greg Randell, my boss, is coming to meet the kid, who works in one of the smallest stores in the chain, that almost beat Stanley, who works in one of the busiest stores in the chain. He's coming to give you a dollar-an-hour raise!" she proudly said.

"Nice!" I said. "So, what's the bad news?"

"Well, I'm not going to be your boss anymore. I got promoted to the Greenwood store," she said.

"Awww, that sucks! We're not going to get one of those nerdy guys that I met at the seminar, are we?" I said. "But I guess the move is good for you, huh?" I added, realizing she must be pretty happy inside.

"Yeah. It's the second-biggest store in the chain." She smiled.

"So, who's the nerd replacing you? Do you know yet?" I asked.

"Yep! It's that guy from the Harvard Square store, Harry. You met him at the Canon seminar." She smirked and walked into the office in the back.

Harry? Harry! Just the thought of him turned my insides into a loop-de-loop roller coaster.

I felt my forehead hit the countertop in disbelief.

1982 - seventeen years old

Chapter 20

The mall closed at ten o'clock. Ben and I, now the only car left, had been sitting in the parking lot for almost an hour, with the mall security truck making itself known by circling every ten minutes. The conversation had become uninspiring.

Someone should let the manager of Sears know that the S is out. The giant sign now reads "EARS." Geez. I must be really bored.

We'd become increasingly distant since I started working at Uptown. My life was consumed by work, and I liked it that way. Ben was a stereotypical seventeen-year-old guy. He played sports, got drunk, smoked pot, and stayed out late. We never used to run out of things to talk about, but now it seemed we had nothing in common. It was me that had changed, not Ben. I knew it, and he knew it, though he wouldn't admit it.

"I wish you didn't have to work so much. Just tell your boss that you need Saturday off. Everyone's bringing their girlfriend except me," Ben said.

"I can't, the schedule's already done. Besides, they're mostly your friends, and I don't drink or smoke. What fun will I be at a party?" I said, trying to convince him.

How did I get up the nerve to tell him how I felt? What was wrong with me? I was a wimp. Just thinking about breaking up brought back all the memories of that horrible experience with Luke. That feeling would never go away. I did that to someone, and no one should have to feel that way.

Why couldn't I just be happy with the way things were? Why did feelings change? And why was I so attracted to Harry? Sally had said Harry was twenty-eight years old—that was eleven years older than me! Did that even matter? There was no doubt there was an attraction there, but Harry aside, I got along with adults better than all kids my age. I had no interest in partying or hanging out doing nothing. The whole thing was confusing.

I needed to tell Ben that things weren't working, but I felt like a complete asshole. Plus, I'd have to face conflict; conflict sucked.

Then I looked over at him. He just wanted to have fun. He was a normal teenage guy. He needed a normal teenage girl, not me. I couldn't bring myself to sit in a backyard, letting loose with a bunch of teenagers I barely knew, aiming to get drunk and lose control. To me, there was nothing more terrifying.

"I think we've grown apart," I started.

"What do you mean?" Ben asked, voiced elevated.

"You don't feel it? Come on, admit it. I know you feel it too. I feel bad, but to be honest right now, if I had the choice of working or going to a party with friends, I'd choose work," I explained.

"It's because of your boss, huh?" Ben asked.

Before giving a knee-jerk, emotional reaction, adding fuel to an already growing fire, I stopped and took a deep breath.

"The reality is, even if I was working with all different people, I think I'd still choose work over hanging out and partying. And that's not fair to either of us."

"That's fucked up. It shouldn't be like this," Ben said.

Ben was right. It shouldn't be like that, but it was. Work had become my security blanket, and for now, I was okay with that.

He drove me home, both of us in silence. Before getting out of his car, we kissed as if mandatory and parted ways.

After Ben and I officially split, I continued to bury myself in work. My real friends were back in Forestville, living the lives of normal teenagers, bonding in shared experiences, enjoying their last year of high school. Meanwhile, I was living a bizarro version of a high school senior stuck in a larger-than-life, overpopulated city school, feeling more like a once-cherished, now-abandoned ragdoll.

***

"Mom, what in the world was Dad watching at three o'clock in the morning?"

"I don't know," she answered.

We were sitting on the sofa in silence, decompressing from Dad's emergency visit to the hospital. The sun was starting to rise.

"Well, wasn't the TV on when you went into the living room?"

"Christina, I wasn't concerned with whether the TV was on or not. Your father had passed out on the floor!"

A few hours prior, she had woken the entire house by screaming, "Al, Al, are you okay? Someone call 911!"

My father, after visiting my room, must have gone to the bathroom before heading back to his own room. Somewhere along the way, he'd collapsed, and my mother had heard a thud and then him softly crying her name.

Yes, she heard *that*.

"Well, I just think it's weird that he said he was watching TV and then turned it off just to go to the bathroom, that's all."

She looked at me like I was crazy.

"I don't even think about things like that. I'm more concerned about your father!"

Yeah. Tell me about it.

"Thank God he is going to be okay, but the doctor said his heart is stressed and he needs to relax more and eat better, or it will get worse."

I give up.

Nothing came of that incident except that we were all expected to be extra nice to Dad. Heart condition my ass—his heart was rotten to the core. His condition was guilt.

I was not sure how sick he actually was, but apparently not sick enough to stop hurting me.

I got home from work the next day and hadn't been home for more than a few minutes when the phone rang. It was Harry asking a quick work-related question. I answered, hung up the phone, and opened the fridge, looking for a snack.

"I don't want you going out with that man!" my mother yelled out of nowhere.

"Harry? What's wrong with Harry?" I yelled back.

"I can't believe you're doing something like this right after your father got out of the hospital! He gets all worked up just thinking about it! What was wrong with Ben? Why did you have to break up with him?"

How could I do this after my father just got out of the hospital? Seriously? Did she ever wonder why he'd ended up in the hospital in the first place? Maybe his conscience was catching up with him.

"You and Dad couldn't think of enough reasons for me to stay away from Ben and everyone else I've dated, for that matter. And now, all of a sudden, he's God? You're not doing this to me again!" I snapped.

"Listen, you little bitch! I brought you into this world! You owe me your life—you hear me?"

Wow! She was nuts! Was she listening to herself? Did she really believe that? Did she think that all kids owed their parents their life existence?

I stopped yelling.

"Look, Mom, I like him. We have a lot in common. He's not like the guys I go to school with. You've never listened to me long enough to actually know who I am. I'm a good kid. You can either deal with it or not. But you can't stop me this time." I turned, walked down the stairs, and left for work.

I didn't even look back to see if she was going to retaliate. I owed her my . . . life? *God, please don't let me turn out like her. Please.*

Instead of going home after work, I went to Harry's place. We were lying on his mattress on the floor, watching the Marx Brothers' *A Night at the Opera* on TV. Harry loved old movies, especially the Marx Brothers. His apartment was a typical bachelor pad: furniture, what there was of it, didn't match, and the few pictures hanging on the walls, taken by Harry, were of girls, some very exotic. The TV and stereo were in the bedroom, along with almost everything else he owned. His bedroom set was sort of antique looking and the only matching set in the apartment.

Sex with Harry was different from sex with Ben. It wasn't better or worse, just different.

Harry talked when we made love, and at first, it had made me feel a bit uncomfortable. He actually asked me questions during sex. Ben had never spoken during sex. Was that normal? Were we supposed to talk? Sex with Harry was intense and felt more grown up. Ben and I had never had a place to relax. We'd always been worried that someone might catch us. I felt safe at Harry's; we had a bed and privacy.

***

Today was graduation day!

"Mom, I'm ready. I'll see you there. Okay?" I yelled, rushing toward the door.

The boys, now dressed and watching TV, were leaving later with Mom and Nana. Daniel was at his girlfriend's house. He wasn't graduating. Mr. Know-it-all hadn't passed enough classes. Sometime during the past year, Daniel had realized that girls could be an asset and found himself a rich girl. The next thing we knew, he'd moved himself in with her and her family. And of course, that was fine with Mom and Dad, though it would have been the crime of the century if it had been me. So, he was not in school, and he was not working. God only knew what he was up to.

"Is that what you're wearing?" Mom asked in disbelief.

I was wearing a nice casual dress.

"Why? I look okay. People are only going to see my graduation gown, anyway," I said, confused.

"Is that what you're planning to wear to Aunt Janeeva's too?" she snapped, as if my dress wasn't good enough to wear in front of the snobs.

"Aunt Janeeva's? I'm not going to Aunt Janeeva's!"

"What do you mean you're *not going*?" she said as her voice increased in volume.

"I don't want to spend my graduation day at her house," I said, thinking there must have been a misunderstanding somewhere.

"Aunt Janeeva invited us. Your cousin is graduating today too. Aunt Janeeva expects to see you with me, so don't make me look like a disgrace in front of the whole family! I can't believe my own daughter doesn't have the decency to be with me on her graduation day!" she yelled.

"But Mom, it's *my* graduation! It's supposed to be *my* day. Everyone I know is going to parties with their friends! I hate it over there, she always finds a way to insult me!" I pleaded.

"You're still my daughter, and you still live under my roof. You're going to Aunt Janeeva's whether you like it or not, do you hear me?" she screeched.

"Yes," I answered.

After hours of grueling speeches, the ceremony was finally over. The class of 1982 began to file out; parents and families stood up and clapped as we exited the gym. Outside, seniors screamed in excitement, and caps went flying everywhere. Within minutes, the grounds were filled with parents and graduates, hugging and taking pictures. *Where's Mom?* I wondered.

I waited a couple of minutes more. Then I felt like the entire graduating class was looking at me, pointing and whispering.

Hey, look over there. That girl's parents didn't even come to see her!

I could feel their eyes laughing at me, and I wanted to cry. I continued to look, but no Mom. I acted as if I'd known she wasn't coming and walked toward the student parking lot.

After all the times she'd told me, "You are *my* daughter!" I felt humiliated.

I entered our house, still hurt but now mad too.

"Well, there she is," my grandmother said as I walked in.

"Mom, why didn't you meet me after the ceremony?" I asked.

"Why? I knew I'd see you here," she said, as if it wasn't a big deal.

"Every kid out there was greeted and congratulated by their parents. I waited, then just gave up," I said, defeated.

"Oh, c'mon, I didn't know I was supposed to do that. Settle down, and go get ready for Aunt Janeeva's," she said, as if I was making a big deal out of nothing.

1982 – eighteen years old

Chapter 21

"What do you mean you're moving back to Forestville? What about the diner?" I asked in disbelief.

"Your father isn't healthy enough to work this much anymore. We can't afford to hire someone full time, *and* I'm getting too old to handle all this stress," she said.

Too old? Early forties was old?

"Your father and I are going to lose this house anyway, so we've decided to let it go now and rebuild the house in Forestville, since that hasn't sold. We'll have a trailer delivered to the property and live in that while working on the house," she explained.

Moving again? Christ.

"God knows I can't take much more of this, and your father has finally realized that those fuckin' guys from State Side Credit Union are a bunch of lyin' thieves. They never had any intention of including him."

None of what she had just said made any sense to me at all, but I wasn't about to ask and open that can of worms.

"Mom, I have a full-time job now, and I can't afford to lose it. How in the world are we all going to fit in a trailer?" I asked, almost in tears.

"Well, your dad and I have an idea," she said.

This ought to be good.

"Daniel's living with his girlfriend and her family," she said.

Daniel's girlfriend was insane. We'd only met a few times, but she made about as much sense as a soup sandwich.

"We've spoken to Nana, and she'll let you move in with her and Papa until the house is done."

Nana lived in one of Uncle Jay's apartments.

"She's going to move upstairs from her apartment to the one that we stayed in after the fire, and she'd love to have your help," Mom explained.

This was amazing! I was being set free from him. Was I hearing that right??

"So . . . you want me to move in with Nana?" I asked, still in disbelief.

"Yes, would that be okay with you?" Mom asked.

Was she fucking kidding me? She was asking *me* if it was okay?

Am I okay with no longer living with your monster? Am I okay with the possibility of sleeping with both eyes closed? Am I okay with the possibility of finally being . . . okay?

My entire life had been a countdown to turning eighteen on September 24, 1982. And now my official get-out-of-jail date had an early-release option? Had I heard her correctly?

And I wouldn't have to figure out how I could afford to live on my own.

Am I okay with this, she asks.

My body had been locked inside hell's version of a pressure cooker, stewing in filth like a big slab of rotten meat for over a decade, and . . . now it was about to be set free, and she was wondering if this was *okay with me*?

I pictured myself busting out of that house, leaving a me-shaped hole in the side, like you saw on cartoons.

The absurdity of the question was almost hilarious. Almost.

But I proceeded with caution, because I'd lived with this woman long enough to know there might be a hitch—or four.

"Yeah, sure. But I can still keep my job, right?"

"Yes, you can keep your job, but you'll be expected to help Nana too. And when you're not working, we'll need your help at our house," she said.

My insides were celebrating like the Fourth of July of all Fourth of Julys, but still waiting for the hitch, I stood in silence.

She said nothing.

Then I said the only thing that I could get out of my mouth without going berserk with excitement.

"Okay," I replied, and secretly marched off.

***

"Nana, I won't be home right after work tonight. I'm going out afterward, okay?" I said, getting up from the kitchen table.

Living with Nana and Papa wasn't exactly the heaven I'd thought it would be, but it was *much* better than living at home.

I no longer lived under his roof, yet I still woke in the middle of the night, heart racing, terrified that I'd slept through something I shouldn't have.

I wasn't sure I'd ever sleep through the night. Only time would tell if those scars would eventually fade. Though now when I did wake up, the feeling of having finally escaped my own personal hell was euphoric.

One of my favorite things about living here was my Papa. He found a way to make me smile every morning before leaving for work. He might be deaf as a doorknob, but he knew when Nana was driving me nuts. He sat in front of the TV in his favorite chair, quietly laughing as if to say "Better you than me." Made ya wonder if he was actually deaf or just brilliant.

Nana didn't agree with, or understand, why I worked for a living. She'd accused my co-workers of being evil, because surely, they must be forcing me to work forty and fifty hours per week.

"They should understand that you're a girl. Girls shouldn't be working like that. You should be looking for a man that can support you. Working like this isn't ladylike!" she said.

This conversation had taken place so many times that I could lip-sync the words. I continued to tell her no one was forcing me and I enjoyed working.

But being the set-in-her-ways Italian grandmother that she was, she heard what she wanted to hear. Her closing argument would change, depending on the time of day when the conversation took place.

"Sit down, eat breakfast."

My grandmother believed food fixed everything.

"Going out? Why are you going out again? Are you going with that man? Your mother doesn't approve of him," she said, as if I'd suddenly come to my senses.

"Nana, we're just going to a movie. I'll be home by midnight," I said.

"You shouldn't be doing things against your mother's will! What kind of girl stays out till all hours of the night? I'll tell you what kind of girl . . . a whore. That's what kind—whores!" she yelled.

Had she really just called me a whore? Wow . . . just wow. There was no reasoning after that comment, so I zoned out and walked toward the door.

"Be careful out there tonight. Tomorrow's Halloween; there are all kinds of evil people out there," she said, as she genuinely believed there were real devil worshipers out this time of year.

"I'm not a whore," I whispered to no one as I walked out into the crisp October morning, tears running down my face.

The day went fine, but I never shook off the hurt from the morning with Nana, and by the time we got out of work, it was too late to catch a movie.

"Hey, is something wrong?" Harry asked as we exited the mall.

"You've been quiet all day, not even one smart-ass remark. What have you done with the real Chris?" He laughed, trying to lighten the mood up a bit.

"No, unfortunately it's the same old Chris in here," I said, trying to smile.

"You sure you're all right?" he asked, concerned. "Is this getting to be too much for you?"

"No! This and work are the only good things in my life!"

"I never want you to feel like I'm pushing you into this relationship. If it's making your life too crazy, I'd understand," he said.

"No, it's not you, it's my family. I'll be okay," I said, trying to reassure him.

"Okay, drive carefully. I love you," Harry said as he kissed me goodbye.

"I love you, too," I replied.

It was twenty past eleven when I left the parking lot.

I drove down Airport Road toward the highway just in time to see a plane taking off. The runway ran perpendicular to the road. It was an impressive sight when your car passed under a plane as it left the ground. That never got old.

By the time I pulled into the driveway, I was exhausted. I didn't even notice the other cars until I was out of my truck. My uncle must be having a party. Then I saw the police car and, behind that, an ambulance and looked up to Nana's apartment. Every single light in the house was on.

I ran up the stairs, through a curtain covering the entrance to the doorway, and yelled,

"Nana?"

Time briefly stopped while people I'd never seen stared at me as if *I* was a stranger in the house.

"Christina? Is that you?" a voice said.

It was Nana, but she sounded miles away.

"Yeah, it's me, Nana."

"In the kitchen. Please come here," Nana softly mumbled.

I walked toward the voice and found medics and a policeman surrounding Papa's high-backed, Medieval-looking, red-velvet-cushioned dark walnut dining chair. Only Papa sat in that chair. But tonight, a frail, lost-looking little old lady was sunken into it.

I baby-stepped to her.

"Nana?" I said again.

"Yes, Christina, come here . . . ," she whimpered.

I moved closer. Nana held her head low, crying and clutching a handkerchief.

"What happened?" I asked, and knelt to her.

"It's Papa. He got up to go to the bathroom and fell," she said.

I looked up to the medics.

They looked down, and I knew . . . Papa was gone.

"I heard him get up," she cried quietly.

"I heard him, but I didn't check on him. He always wakes up in the middle of the night. I hear him go to the bathroom. I don't have to check, I just know." She talked to the floor, but she wasn't finished.

I looked at the floor too, as if it would help me comprehend what she was saying, but the worn-out, olive-green Italian ceramic tile offered no condolences.

"I wait and I hear his bed creak, and I know he's back in bed. But the bed never creaked, so I got up and went downstairs. His bed was empty," she said, pausing for a moment.

"I went to check the bathroom, but the door wouldn't open all the way," she said, moving her arm as if opening the door.

"So, I yelled, 'Deardy! Deardy! Are you okay?' "

I never knew why she called him "Deardy." His name was Vincenzo, and we called him "Papa." It must've been an Italian thing.

"But he didn't answer. Then I knew. But they couldn't help him. They tried, but they couldn't help."

Tears filled my eyes as medics started asking questions about whom to call.

Over the next hour, the house filled with relatives while my Papa lay lifeless in the hall, surrounded by people in blue.

Through the years, Papa had made me smile and laugh. Every holiday, at one time or another, the family would play cards. Papa always sat next to me . . . and cheated, but that was okay. That was what Papa did. And he knew I'd catch him; he wanted me to. And when I did, he'd laugh and laugh till tears ran down his face. As I'd gotten older, I didn't see him much until I moved back in with him and Nana. Then I got to see him every day before leaving for work. If he wasn't sitting at the table eating a meal, he'd be in his favorite chair, watching *Let's Make a Deal* or *The Price Is Right* on TV. Sometimes Papa would stop me on the way out just so I could watch him guess the right price on things. When he answered correctly, he'd look at me as if to say "See? I told you so." I loved Papa.

***

"What do you mean you're moving to Raintree, MA?" Mom asked.

"Harry got promoted to the Raintree location, and there's an opening for a salesperson too. It's a great opportunity for me. And besides, traveling the backroads to Nana's at night can be dangerous, especially when it's foggy," I explained.

"But I thought you'd move back home. Our house is almost ready!" she said.

Mom and Nana were sitting at Nana's dining table, drinking coffee and eating pepper biscuits. They were going to visit a senior citizen apartment complex near the city because the commute was a bit much for Nana too and she battled with Uncle Jay constantly.

A few weeks ago, she and Uncle Jay had fought over some side business she started that involved selling crocheted G-strings to his topless dancers. How she could call *me* a whore, I'll never know. You'd think she'd notice the difference between me and those girls. Yes. It was definitely time for both of us to move.

"Mom, I don't want to move back to that house. I could never live there again."

They couldn't pay me to live there. No friggin' way!

"The house doesn't even look the same. How are you going to live on your own? Can you afford that?" she asked.

So, the insurance money from the house fire had been insufficient, yet somehow, they'd bought a new house and a diner, then lost that house and the diner, still owned the land from the dreadful fire, and now had money to rebuild the burnt house? None of it made sense.

I took a deep breath.

"I'm not going to live alone. Harry and I will share an apartment so we can save money," I said, counting slowly—from five, four, three—waiting for the forthcoming explosion.

"What did you say?" she yelled in shock.

"Mom, Harry and I are going to live together."

I could feel my heart beating.

"There is no Goddamn way my daughter is going to go live with some older guy! Do you hear me? I won't allow it!" Now screaming like a maniac.

My grandmother, still sitting at the table looking down into her coffee cup, lifted her head and softly spoke.

"No, no, Christina, you can't do that."

"Mom, I'm not asking permission," I said.

There was no way I was going back to that house.

"Who the fuck do you think you are? You are MY daughter, and you will return to our house and live with me until you are married! That's what decent girls do! Jesus Christ! What are people going to think of me? What kind of daughter did I raise? You don't tell me! You ASK me, do you hear me?" Now out of her mind.

"Mom, I don't need your permission. I'm eighteen, and legally, I can take care of myself. And thanks to Dad making me support myself since I was a child, I'm not worried. If you don't like it, I'm sorry, but I'm not changing my mind," I explained, tears in my eyes.

Though shaking like a leaf on the inside, I intended to stand by my decision.

"Christina, if you move in with that asshole, then you'll lose me. I raised you! I deserve more than this!" she continued to scream.

My grandmother spoke again.

"Paige, calm down. Relax. Please don't scream and swear. Let's go, you both need time to calm down."

Nana got up and headed for the doorway, hoping my mother would follow.

She did. Moments later, the house was quiet.

I sat down in the kitchen and waited for my body to stop shaking.

Christina, stay strong. You've done what she's wanted all your life. She wants to make you feel guilty! She wants you to live in that awful world with her because she's too weak to make her life better. If you stay, you'll end up being just like her.

***

The next three months went by without a word from Mom. I was sure she was waiting for my call, but I was in no rush. Part of me felt guilty for not calling her, but another part felt a freedom I'd previously only dreamt about.

Living with Harry wasn't at all the fairy tale that I had imagined. Some days he'd bring home a sentimental handwritten card, and other days he'd act as though we were strangers. We lived together, yet everything in the house was either his or mine; nothing was shared. Even the bills were split down the middle—except for rent, because his salary was substantially higher. I missed my old friends.

Stephanie wrote every now and then, mostly about how she was looking forward to college in the fall.

That evening, I lay in bed, unable to sleep, thinking about the move I'd made. I enjoyed working in a busy store, but once back home, it was lonely, like a visitor in someone else's world. It didn't escape me that this was the same way I'd felt every time I ended up in a new school and had to start over.

I woke early the next morning to a knock at the door. I was completely disoriented, unaware of the time and day. The clock read eight thirty. Who in the world would be knocking at this hour? I stumbled out of bed and meandered to the door.

For a moment I thought I might have been dreaming.

It was my mother, all smiles.

"Hi, Christina. Can I come in?"

Nope, not dreaming. It was real.

"Is Harry here?" she asked.

"No, he's already gone to work," I said.

She looked relieved.

"Why are you here?"

"Can I sit for a minute?"

"Yeah," I said, and pointed to the small drop-leaf table in the dining room.

We both sat down. I waited for her to speak.

"I've spent the last few months thinking, and I've realized that if I don't make the first move, I may never hear from you again," she said, stopping for a breath.

Ain't that the truth.

"You are my only daughter, and if I don't accept you as you are, then I may never see you again or my future grandchildren. So, I'm here to make amends," she said, and held out her arms as an invitational hug.

Grandchildren?

Is she being honest? Will she actually understand me for who I am, not who she wants me to be? It'd be nice, but at this point, is it even possible to have a mother-daughter relationship with her?

I reacted by doing what she expected. I hugged her.

We chatted for a while as she filled me in on things I'd missed. Zac and Andy, seniors now, were back in Tomahawk. Zac was dating Samantha Cortina, a girl he'd had a crush on since we'd first moved to Forestville. He'd always said he would marry her someday.

I didn't ask about Daniel nor did she mention him. Mikey had just started junior high. In my head, Mikey was always a baby or toddler, but in reality, he'd become a person I hardly knew. Dad was doing carpentry stuff, and for whatever reason, things appeared to be better money-wise. I hadn't realized how much I missed my younger brothers. We'd never been super close, but as warped as it sounded, this was my family, and though I *never* wanted to live there again, it was nice to know I could visit.

1984 – nineteen years old

Chapter 22

"You're going to need to stay in bed for a while. Mononucleosis is very contagious. It's essential to stay in bed for two to four weeks. According to our tests, you've had it for at least two weeks already. I can't believe that you've been working!" the doctor said.

By the time I walked out of the urgent care, it was 10 p.m. I had a boatload of meds, and I'd been poked and prodded more times than I could count. I just wanted to crawl into a ball and sleep for a million years.

At nineteen, I was proud to be Uptown Camera's youngest store manager, and I loved it, but the hour and a half drive to work each way, mixed with the emotional roller coaster of good and bad days with Harry, had taken its toll, and mono was the result.

I'd called Harry when I left work to let him know I was sick and would be driving to the hospital. He didn't even offer to join me. Something felt off about our relationship as of late, but I couldn't put my finger on it. Some days he was infatuated with me, and other days he was just the opposite. I wanted to fix it, but Harry never wanted to talk about it.

Why didn't he like me all the time? One second he'd tell me I was pretty, and the next he'd be outwardly flirting with the waitress at our dinner table. Did he expect me to get mad? I didn't get mad, I got hurt—well, I got angry too, but mostly hurt.

When I got home from the hospital, Harry was asleep. And when I woke up the next morning, he had already left.

When we first met, I'd thought he was the coolest, funniest guy. Now, years later, I realized that the cool, funny guy thing was an act. He said he loved me yet treated me like I was invisible. The effed-up thing was, even though my common sense knew it was wrong, it seemed to make me want him more. How could I still love him? Why couldn't I get the nerve to move out and live on my own? What was wrong with me?

I'd given up trying to talk to him about it. He'd either joke his way out of it or say I was nuts about whatever I was thinking. According to him, everything was excellent.

Was this a normal relationship? I'd thought it would be better than this, but this was real life. Why did everything on TV always seem so fantastic?

The next few weeks were spent in bed recovering, mostly by myself, watching way too much *Gilligan's Island* and *I Dream of Jeannie* and . . . thinking.

The workday had come and gone, and by the time Harry got home, it was eight o'clock. We made steaks in the broiler oven, cooked two boxes of chicken-flavored Rice-A-Roni, and settled in to watch TV.

"Our TV choices are 'An Evening with Billy Graham,' a repeat of *Moonlighting,* or some movie of the week starring Ted Danson. Wanna give it a shot?" he asked.

"Sure," I answered.

The movie began with an announcement.

"Tonight's movie contains mature subject matter that should be viewed with parental guidance. This program deals with incest and its painful consequences, and until tonight, it has been kept a quiet subject. We hope to make people more aware that there is a need to acknowledge and deal with issues of this nature. Please stay tuned for the world premiere of *Something About Amelia*, starring Ted Danson."

I felt as if all of my blood instantly drained from my entire body. Someone had actually had the guts to make it a movie about incest? Could I watch it? Harry didn't seem to have a problem with it, although I didn't think he was paying as much attention as he was busy looking up the value of his baseball cards and watching TV at the same time. I didn't say a word.

The next two hours went by as if I was in another world. Few words were spoken during the movie. I remembered Harry saying, "Wow, Ted is a great actor! That's a far cry from Sam Malone," and, "Why won't that mom admit she knows? Sure glad she's not my mom."

I nodded for fear that if I actually spoke, the reaction would be a never-ending scream.

But inside, I was yelling like a madwoman.

Stop hurting that little girl! She's too young. She's not there to make you feel better! What a stupid mom. He's the bad one, not Amelia! Why are they taking Amelia away?

Wow, I was glad I'd kept my secret. My mom was ten times worse than that mom. But I was impressed that someone had been brave enough to put that on TV.

When the movie was over, the news featured child abuse as the big subject of the night. Maybe it was a breakthrough. Maybe someone would make all the little girls of the future safe.

I wondered if Mom had watched it.

***

Hellish at best was the only way to describe Route 168 on weekdays, although today was a wonderful, sunny spring morning, so while the ride was mentally agonizing, the weather was visually pleasant.

Just before Exit 15, there was a hill that snuck up like a blind spot Mother Nature had intentionally installed as payback to humans dumb enough to drive on such an overpopulated section of earth. As I came up and over nature's revenge, all cars were stopped, leaving an ocean of brake lights as far as the eyes could see. I hit my brakes and veered to the left to avoid hitting a stickered bumper trying to solve the mystifying "Where's the beef?" conundrum. I intended to stop on the grass median; instead, I went airborne.

I spun aimlessly in midair as if trapped inside a soap bubble in the breeze.

This surreal ride began with a face-to-pavement tar motor oil tar experience followed by a slowly spinning, windswept snapshot of an endless pinwheel-shaped traffic jam fading away as I spun upward for a brief glimpse of puffy white clouds in a deep blue sky before I spiraled back toward the earth for a smashing touchdown; then everything went black.

A loud banging near my ear brought me back to reality.

"Are you okay?" a strange man yelled as he knocked on my truck window.

Who was he? Why was he asking me this?

I looked up from my seat.

Oh, my God!

I was on the median strip of Route 168. I had just crashed!

I sat still, assessing myself. I felt okay for the most part. My shoulder hurt, and my back felt stiff, but other than that, I felt okay. Then I touched my hand to my face.

My teeth! What happened to my teeth?

There was blood all over my hand. I couldn't see much outside, as my windshield looked like a big glass spiderweb.

"Miss?" the strange man asked again.

"Oh, yeah. Except for my mouth, I'm okay, I guess," I answered, no longer wondering or caring who the strange man was, as I was just happy someone was there.

By midafternoon, I was discharged with severe bruising and missing two front teeth, feeling like the little girl from that Christmas song. Good news? No broken bones.

I sat in the recovery room area, waiting for Harry. I had been scheduled to open the store alone. I wondered if anyone had ever arrived to open in my place?

Harry walked through the swinging doors of the waiting area.

"Hey, Crash! How ya feelin'?" he joked.

"I've been better. How's my truck? And is the store open?" I asked.

I loved my black Ford Ranger truck. It was the first time I'd been able to buy something expensive, and I felt like a real adult when the dealership approved *me* for a loan. At the time, I was pissed because my parents had just decided to take the truck back, making all the payments I'd made pretty much pointless to me. I felt deceived, but not surprised. Shame on me.

"Your truck was towed to a lot in Greenwood somewhere, and the store is open. I spoke to Greg. He knew what happened before I did," Harry explained.

"I didn't hurt anyone else, did I?"

"No, just you and your truck," he answered.

"How did Greg know before the hospital called you?" I asked, confused.

"Your mom called you at the store this morning and got no answer. Then she tried home and got no response. I think she panicked and eventually called Greg at the office, and he tracked you down.

"Well, you don't look too bad. I thought I was going to find black eyes and broken bones. By the way, nice teeth." He laughed.

"Gee, thanks. I'm hoping I don't get a black eye from getting hit in the face. My mouth hurts the most. I have a couple of bad bruises, but I think I'll be okay. The doctor told me I have to see a dentist about my teeth within the next twenty-four hours."

"I'll drive you down to your parents' house. I talked to your mom. She said she'd take care of you for the next couple of days," Harry explained.

Next couple of days? I didn't want to have to sleep there! What was he thinking? Why wouldn't he take care of me?

"Harry, the last place in the world I want to be is stuck at my parents' house!"

"I know, but I still have to work, and your mom said your doctors are all in Rhode Island. And as much as you hate to admit it, you *don't* have a truck."

"Yeah, I know," I answered, depressed.

The next few days were awful, though most of the time was spent at the dentist and the Ford dealership. More important to me than my teeth was a new truck. A new truck got me back on the road. I had to admit, I had severe anxiety about returning to the situation that I'd devoted my entire life trying to escape, but I found that as a visitor, the situation wasn't the same for whatever reason. I felt like an actual guest. Mom was overly nice, and Dad didn't bother me. Except when it came time to buy another truck. As it turned out, I didn't get much back from the insurance company because the truck had been too new when it happened, and my dad had talked me out of something called gap insurance. He said that was a scam. I couldn't afford another Ford Ranger. I ended up buying a lame, nothing-special car. But it was something to drive.

***

"Good morning. How are you feeling?" Greg asked as I sat down in the chair in front of his desk.

I had traveled to the corporate office for an early-morning meeting with my boss. Greg Randall was in charge of all of the managers and one of my favorite people at Uptown Camera. He was the one that had allowed me the opportunity to prove myself.

Greg looked like America's version of the all-around professional dad: tall, broad-shouldered, with an aura of dependability. He was the kind of boss that made you earn his respect and who you'd lean on for advice, but only after you had exhausted all other possibilities on your own.

"Okay, are you ready to talk?" he asked, sounding a bit mysterious.

"Sure," I answered, wondering what he was insinuating.

"First of all, let me say I'm glad you're okay. But if I'd known you weren't going to move to Danvers, I *never* would have given you that store. What were you thinking, traveling sixty-five miles each way? I know you're more than capable of running your own store, but you don't seem to understand there are *other* reasons I offered you a store that far away . . . ," he said, looking directly in my eyes, in an "I think you know what I am talking about" kind of way.

Boy! Not only did I get the point loud and clear, but I also had *not* been aware that our bosses knew of our relationship! Maybe he had a problem with our age gap? Perhaps it was something else, but whatever it was, message received.

I played it safe with a one-word answer.

"Yes."

"Okay, then. Let's move on."

And the meeting was back on course.

"It just so happens I have another opportunity I think you might be good for—and it's much closer to home." He smiled.

By the time the meeting was over, I had been transferred to a closer, higher-volume store in Rocktown, MA.

***

A few months later, I was comfortable and thoroughly enjoyed working in Rocktown, Massachusetts. The crew had learned to work well together, and we'd become friends.

Harry and I had amicably moved to different apartments, yet we were still sort-of dating. But instead of moving into a place of my own, I shared an apartment with a co-worker from the corporate office, Rosa, who'd recently split with her boyfriend. It ended up being convenient for both of us.

I couldn't understand why Harry and I kept breaking up yet still dated each other. As far as I could tell, he had the best of both worlds. I knew he was seeing another girl within the company, even younger than me, but when I tried talking to him about it, he got angry and acted like I was out of my mind. According to him, we weren't officially broken up, whatever that meant.

Hey! What happened to all the stuff on my desk? I panicked.

"Shannon?" I called into the front.

"Yeah, what's up?" she asked.

Shannon had transferred from Harry's store in Greenwood, Massachusetts, to Rocktown because it was closer to her home. Shannon was from a close-knit Jewish family, had a great sense of humor, and was always joking about her "Jewish schnoz." She didn't even have to work if she didn't want to; Shannon's family had plenty of money, so I admired her for her desire to work. We'd hit it off immediately.

I was in panic mode when she walked into the office.

"I had a bunch of papers here from yesterday, and I can't find them anywhere. Have you seen them?" I asked.

"Yeah. When I came in this morning, I stamped and mailed anything that was pending," Shannon explained, looking at me as though I was nuts.

My heart was beating like a drum.

"You mailed everything, even the envelope on top of the pile?" I asked, hoping that I had heard her wrong.

"Yeah. Why?" Shannon answered, still looking at me like I was nuts.

"I can't believe you mailed that!" I said, banging my head on my desk in disbelief.

"Why? What did I do?" Shannon sounded scared now.

"That wasn't a letter for work, it was personal."

"Uh-oh," she said as she pulled up a chair and smirked. "This ought to be good." She smiled. Shannon loved to gossip.

"Very funny," I replied.

"Well . . . ?" She waited.

"I wrote that letter last year to an old boyfriend when my relationship with Harry was a mess. Not that now is any better, but you know what I mean. Anyway, I chickened out and never mailed it. I came across it last week while cleaning out my briefcase. I couldn't bring myself to mail the letter or toss it out, so I stuck in on top of the rest of the crap on my desk. I don't even remember what I wrote. I can't believe you mailed it," I said, as if talking to myself.

Shannon didn't say anything. She just sat there and giggled.

"This is not funny!" I responded, trying not to laugh too.

"Oh, yes, it is!" she said. "So, who's this guy?"

I explained the Luke situation and what had happened with us and my parents.

"I wrote that letter when I was alone, feeling down, and admittedly stupid. I've always felt as though he deserved more explanation than I gave him back in high school, and I still think about him. I don't know if it's because Harry and I are a big mess or what, but I think I still have feelings for him. Or maybe it's because we never had closure? I don't know. But I live in Massachusetts, and I have no idea where he lives these days. It's been a long time.

"I didn't mail it because I have no idea what his current life is like and I should respect whatever life and relationship he may be in . . . and I didn't want to look like a total fool," I said.

"Well, it's too late now." She laughed and got up to go back to the front.

"Gee, thanks, you're a sport," I said.

"Nothing left to do now but wait." She smirked.

"Hmm. I don't think I told Luke where I live, so he doesn't know how to get in touch with me, anyway," I tried to convince myself.

"Or he could look up our phone number from the return label I put on the envelope," she sassed back. "All I have to say is if I were *you,* and knowing what *I* know about Harry, I'd go with the flow and just let the chips fall where they may."

She didn't have to say any more. I knew Shannon knew more than I did regarding whatever it was that Harry was doing behind my back, as she used to work with him, but I chose not to pry. I got her point.

Two weeks later, I stood in front of my bedroom mirror, cursing Shannon.

Luke had gotten the letter and quickly deduced how to contact me from the return label. We'd chatted just long enough on the phone to make plans to meet. Wondering if either one wanted to see the other didn't need to be mentioned, as it'd been obvious by the tones in our voices.

I couldn't believe I was going to go through with it! I was a bundle of nerves and had changed outfits more times than I could count. It'd been a month since I'd joined the local Richard Simmons gym, and I'd been going to exercise class almost every day since. Although I didn't look like I had in high school, for the first time in a long time, I felt pretty good about myself. I didn't know how it had happened, but I'd gained so much weight being with Harry. I didn't like myself anymore and felt like changing everything. Working out helped me feel better physically, but mentally, I needed a miracle.

We'd agreed to meet in the parking lot of Toys "R" Us at the mall in Hillsgrove, RI. By the time I exited the highway, it was dark. My stomach felt like the inside of a washing machine. I drove into the parking lot and turned at the Toys "R" Us sign, thinking the bright multicolored neon sign looked more like the entrance to a sci-fi drive-in than a kids' toy store. I was totally losing my mind.

I immediately spotted Luke's truck but acted as though I hadn't just in case he could see my face. I needed a second. I could feel my heart beating. Maybe I should turn around and go home?

Come on, Christina. You can do this.

I pulled up next to Luke and rolled my window down.

"Hey," he said.

"Hey," I replied, hoping he'd make the next move.

"Let's get in one vehicle, then we'll decide what to do," Luke suggested.

I got out, legs feeing more like noodles than functional walking appendages, and managed to get myself to the passenger's side of his truck. He opened the door, and I got in.

"Long time, no see," he said, and smiled.

"Yeah, huh?" exited my head.

"Okay, I'll start. What made you get up the nerve to write? Last I heard, you were living with some old dude from Boston," he asked.

Old dude? That made me laugh. I briefly explained my situation with Harry and somehow worked in that I'd often thought about him while staying a bit vague just to be safe.

I was afraid he'd met up with me to give me a piece of his mind and let me know that he couldn't care less and was now happily married with five kids.

I finished my ramblings of nothingness and looked at him.

"So, what's up with you?" I asked, feeling my heart sitting somewhere mid-throat.

"Hmm. Where should I start? Well, I was engaged for a while, but that ended before we tied the knot," he said.

"Yeah, I heard that but wasn't one-hundred-percent sure it was true. What happened?"

"Let's just say I woke up one day and decided it wasn't the best fit for me," he said.

I laughed.

"I'm in a relationship now, and she has three kids. We've been together for a few years. We live in Dales, Connecticut. Am I happy? I guess so, but mostly because I really like the kids," he explained, just as briefly as I'd shared my situation.

While swapping relationship stories, we simultaneously learned we had a lot in common. We were both unhappy yet continued to live in ruts, lacking the courage to make our individual lives better.

All in all, Luke hadn't changed much. He, too, had gained some weight, but he still smelled of Old Spice, and his eyes . . . still melted my insides. I tried to explain what had happened in school, way back when, but I couldn't justify it unless I shared the information about my dad, and I had no intention of ever telling anyone about that. I was aware that I sounded dumb, but he didn't really challenge it, as it was now water under the bridge.

We stopped talking about the old us and ended up sitting in his truck for hours, chatting about everything else. The attraction between us was undeniable, but we were well aware our lives were completely incompatible. I wanted to lean over and kiss him one more time, but I didn't. Even so, I felt like I'd be cheating on Harry.

It was at that very moment a typhoon of clarity rushed through my head, leaving me brutally aware I'd been holding on to Harry because I was just afraid to step out of my own damn comfort zone. It wasn't love at all; it was predictable, albeit sad, endless-nights-of-crying myself-to-sleep familiarity. This was ridiculous. I really needed to find myself.

All of a sudden, I felt I didn't belong in Luke's truck. I needed to leave. Luke didn't deserve to reunite with this me, a me that was even more messed up than the high school me. This was why I had never mailed that letter.

We sat in awkward silence for a few minutes, almost as if he could hear what I'd been thinking.

"I think I need to go," I said. Stopped and took a breath, then added, "I hope things work out with you and your girlfriend." Wishing, deep down inside, things could be different.

"Yeah, whatever," Luke replied.

I opened the door and said, "Bye."

"No, not 'bye.' Just 'see ya later.' Because I know I will someday," he said, very sure of himself.

I smiled back at him in acknowledgment.

"Okay," I said as I closed the door.

And just like that, without a kiss, the night was over.

The brief exchange reminded me of the Taxi song by Harry Chapin. My life wasn't ready for him, and my heart wasn't smart enough to control the situation. I had to leave.

Somehow, somewhere between the meeting with Luke and my ride home, I'd changed.

I drove home talking to myself. Vowing to be an emotionally healthier, more independent me. No more nights crying myself to sleep, wondering where and with whom Harry might be. The car ride home was a therapy session to me.

***

I pulled into our complex parking lot at 2:00 a.m., entered our apartment, and quietly tiptoed toward my room so as not wake Rosa. As I came upon my bedroom door, I noticed it was covered in Post-it notes. Covered. Each one said, "Harry Called." Each one noted the time of the call, and as times got later, the writing got bigger and bolder, and the word "Again" had been added numerous times. My stomach knotted.

Why? Why did I feel this way? I hadn't done anything wrong. And I *knew* Harry had been with other women, so why did I feel guilty?

I woke up just in time to take a shower and get to work. Rosa was already gone, so I couldn't get any information out of her. I was still a wreck, knowing I'd have to deal with Harry phoning at work. I got dressed and rushed down the hall stairs and opened the building exit door, and there was Harry, standing with arms crossed, looking angry as hell.

"Morning," he said, glaring at me.

"Morning," I replied.

"So, where you going?" he asked.

"To work. Where do you think I'm going at eight thirty in the morning?" I answered sarcastically, knowing that I shouldn't have.

"No, you're not. I called Shannon and told her you'd be late. She said she'd cover for you till you got in." Replying as if he'd just scored a victory point.

"Excuse me?" I asked. I couldn't believe he'd had the nerve to call one of *my* employees for something like this.

"Let's have a seat in my car and talk, shall we?" he insisted.

And just like that, the prior night's courageous self-therapy session vanished without a trace. "Okay," I said.

What was wrong with me? Was it conditioning? Or fear?

We got in and sat in silence for a while. I had been through enough of this ridiculousness with Harry to know every move and twitch he made *and* what each one meant. His pupils were very small, like tiny black dots. That meant things were about to get ugly.

"Where were you last night?" he demanded.

"Why?" I asked.

"Because I want to know," he replied, as if I was wasting *his* valuable time.

"I went for a ride," I said, not really lying. I hated lying.

"What do you mean, you 'went for a ride'?" he asked sarcastically.

"Just what I said. I went for a ride," I said.

"What kind of person goes for a ride and doesn't come back until after 2:00 a.m.?" he asked.

Okay, so I'll add stalking to his list of craziness.

I reminded myself of the conclusion I'd come to the prior evening.

Find that courage. You had it on the drive home.

"Someone just like *you*! How do you NOT know the answer to that question? *You* REGULARLY take rides into the wee hours of the night, so I figured I'd give it a shot," I nervously snapped, though proud of myself for doing so.

Okay! That felt good. I can do this!

"You're trying to tell me you just decided to go out for a ride, and next thing you knew, it was 2:00 a.m.? Are you out of your mind?"

"Well, I did have the intention of going to the mall. But when I got there, I just didn't feel like going in, so I kept driving . . . and thinking," I answered.

"About what?" he asked.

"About us. We're a mess. I don't like this anymore," I replied honestly.

He sat in silence for a few minutes. I couldn't tell what he was thinking, but he didn't look angry anymore. It was confusing. Then he said the last words I ever expected to hear.

"I want us to get married."

Was he out of his fucking mind? How in the world could he expect us to get married when we were like this? This was a side of Harry I'd never seen; this was insecurity.

I'd been waiting to hear those words for so long, but now it was too late. I wasn't in love with him anymore, though I wanted to be. And even with everything that had happened, I still felt responsible in some way.

"Don't you think we have problems?" I asked.

"Well, sure, but we can work our problems out, can't we?" Harry asked.

I was so confused. Was I supposed to try? We had spent so much time together already, but was this worth saving? I guessed I could try, but what if I couldn't make myself feel the way I used to feel about him? And . . . stupid me was back.

I answered—for him, not me. "I guess so."

"Good." He smiled, kissed me, then threw a ring into my lap.

The kiss didn't feel like anything. Neither did the ring.

1986 – twenty-one years old

Chapter 23

I opened the bathroom vanity drawer and reached down for my hairbrush.

"Oh, come on, really? My lost contacts have conveniently reappeared? Right after I bought new ones," I yelled from the bathroom. "This is absurd," I said, more to myself than him.

"What do you mean?" Harry asked calmly, as if I must be speaking to someone else.

"You don't think it's bit odd that my contacts mysteriously disappeared from the bathroom drawer? So, naturally I went back to wearing glasses. But I guess it didn't occur to you that I would order a new pair, huh? Now the day after my new pair arrives, my lost contacts reappear as if they'd never been missing?"

"I have no idea what you're talking about." Again, replying calmly.

"Is it because you think guys will find me less attractive with glasses? Do you know how asinine that sounds?" I asked.

"I really have no idea what you're talking about. I am sure you just didn't see the contacts in the drawer to begin with. Probably because you needed your glasses to see them!" he answered, trying to make a joke.

I was aware of what he'd done, and the absurdity of it was incomprehensible. But I'd learned my lesson time and time again. Arguing with Harry made things worse, not better. I counted to ten, exhaled, walked out the door, and went to work.

Eight hours later, I found myself sitting in bumper-to-bumper traffic, traveling at fifteen miles per hour, with not much to do except think.

Harry and I had moved back in together shortly after his less than romantic proposal, with our relationship worsening by the day. We'd been together for five years, with the latter years consisting of haphazardly living together and apart, neither of us facing reality head-on. And for the life of me, I couldn't come up with one decent reason for still being with him. What kind of girl allowed their so-called love to carelessly toss a ring into her lap as offhandedly as tossing a used Kleenex into a trashcan? What kind of girl allowed that same person to feel as if he'd done her a favor by doing so? Me, that was who.

I'd told myself that maybe I could get the old feelings back, but love didn't work that way. Harry had become a different man. In some ways, we'd reversed relationship roles, and he was now the insecure one. But his insecurity, unlike mine, was outwardly expressed via psychopathic, angry, and very jealous tendencies. I'd gone right back to being a coward and convinced myself that as long as I buried myself in work, I could ignore his craziness and survive.

But on this day, in bumper-to-bumper traffic with no end in sight . . . our relationship was, once again, weighing on me.

Was this morning's battle the final straw? How much more could I handle? Who did that kind of shit? But if I left, would he make my work life a living hell? I'd be lost without my job. Or was this all me, using my fear of being alone as a justification?

I pulled into the Oakdale Mall a little after 5:00 p.m. At twenty-one years old, my promotion to district manager was a considerable self-accomplishment, but with that came a crazy schedule and more insanity from Harry. As a store manager, he knew where to find me every day. District management put me on the road, visiting different locations every day, so tracking my movements had escalated his insanity.

"Hey, where have you been? You're on today's most-wanted list!" the store manager asked as I entered.

I frequently stopped by the Oakdale store last, as it was closest to home, and Carson, the manager, was one of my favorites. Other than routine maintenance, his store was managed well, and the visit was usually pleasant. Carson led a great team, and it made for a positive end to the day.

"Why? What's wrong?" I asked, assuming my boss was looking for me.

"Oh, nothing serious. Harry's trying to hunt you down. He's called other locations on your route too, so managers have called me to warn you."

"How embarrassing. I'm sorry. I should've been here an hour ago. Route 168 is a parking lot. I've spent most of the day sitting in traffic. I'm gonna use your phone before we go over the latest store updates," I explained as I walked into the back office.

I dreaded picking up the receiver, but if I didn't, he'd just call again. My stomach felt like a gurgling acid. I dialed and waited.

"Hi," I said.

"Where are you?" he asked sarcastically.

The gurgling worsened.

"I just got to Oakdale. Traffic was awful," I said.

"Yeah. Right," Harry said in disbelief.

"Oh, right. The truth? I stopped at a rest area, met a guy, screwed him, then zoomed right back to work, assuming you'd be none the wiser," I said, hoping he'd realize how insane he sounded.

"Very funny. Are you coming home or what?" he asked, a little calmer.

Sadly, I *was* going home. I had nowhere else to go. And I only had myself to blame.

I was on the path of making a lifetime career out of knowing what not to do yet still doing it. I'd done this with my parents, with Bobby, and with Luke. When people pushed, I gave in. I'd taught myself to allow hurt, as if there was no other choice, long ago.

"Yeah. I'll be home in about an hour," I replied, and we hung up and I left the office.

"You look worn out," Carson said.

"Thanks. I feel like last year's Easter egg," I answered, trying to joke it off.

"I was just going to get a cup of coffee when you walked in. Wanna talk business over a coffee?" Carson asked.

"Coffee sounds great."

We walked to the food court, ordered, and found a table away from the crowd.

As we sat in comfortable silence for a few moments, it occurred to me what a nice guy Carson was. I'd always known he was nice, but today, I took the time to really notice the nice guy I casually knew through work. He had a unique style, as if modeled from an official retail-manager action figure from the Barbie and Ken universe. His usual look was a white dress shirt—neatly ironed, with a right pocket for pens—dress pants, penny loafers, and a hint of sexy but not too sexy cologne. I think it was called Cool Water. I'd noticed it when we first met. But his overall look didn't quite fit his character. It was almost as if he was wearing someone else's outfit or abiding by a secret retail manager's fashion catalog. Carson was young for a store manager, maybe a year or two older than me, and not pompous like some of the know-it-all guys. In fact, he looked humbly unsure of himself. Maybe it was his boyish blonde haircut and soft brown eyes that gave him that "you can trust me" vibe. He was about five-foot-ten or so, not too broad, strong looking but lean. Carson came off as plain ol' nice.

"I know this is none of my business, and please let me know if I'm overstepping my bounds, but why do you deal with Harry's insanity?" Carson asked.

"That's a question I ask myself daily. I'm not really sure. I guess I'm afraid it will somehow jeopardize my job," I answered, as if talking to myself.

"Your job? Why?" he asked.

"I don't know. Maybe I'm afraid it will snowball into an embarrassing mess at work? I think that makes me a total wimp." I sighed.

"Well, I'm not sure I could handle it either. It's gotta make the job more intense," Carson replied.

I changed the subject, and we chatted for about a half hour, all work related.

"Well, I guess that's everything. I gotta get going. Thanks for your time," I said, getting up, gathering my notebooks and briefcase.

"See you later. Enjoy your weekend. I'll get the inventory list back to you by Monday," Carson said.

I waved as I walked away, thinking my thirty-minute drive home was the last half hour of peace I'd have today before facing Harry.

The conversation with Carson really had me thinking. Why the hell did I stay with Harry? Was it really my job that I was worried about? Deep down, I knew it was an excuse. Truth was, I had a horrible case of codependency, and I hated it, because the thought of spending every night all alone watching TV scared the hell out of me.

TV all alone . . . watching what I chose to watch, not what he made us watch.

Hmm . . . no more *Solid Gold* dancers shaking their asses in my face! No more comments on how great they moved or the shape they were in? On second thought, solitary life sounded like heaven!

I pulled into our driveway, inhaled a deep breath, and counted to three.

Ahh . . . home, sweet home. That was the dumbest phrase anyone had ever come up with.

After an hour of interrogation into my daily happenings, we settled in to watch TV, but I couldn't concentrate.

I picked up my briefcase, figuring I'd make a dent in paperwork. I reached in to grab my notebook and pulled out two. Carson's name was handwritten on the cover in pen. I must have inadvertently grabbed Carson's notebook along with mine from the table. *I wonder if he needs it.* I put it down just in case Harry noticed that it wasn't mine, as any little thing set him off on a tirade of stupid accusations.

By the time the TV show ended, I'd completed my work and placed my notebook back in my briefcase next to Carson's.

Curiosity was getting the best of me. What kind of notes did Carson keep?

"I'm going to take a shower," Harry said, getting up.

"Okay," I replied.

As soon as I heard the water start to run, I grabbed the book out of my case.

I opened it and was shocked to find that it wasn't a notebook after all. It was a journal of some kind! I quickly closed it and put it down.

Wow! A guy who kept a journal.

I would've never imagined Carson having something like that and was touched at the thought of his creative sensitivity. I laughed to myself, thinking Harry's psychotic bravado would never allow him to acknowledge feelings, much less write about them.

My first stop on Monday morning was Oakdale Mall. I knew Carson wasn't due in until late afternoon, so I stopped by and left the book on his desk along with a note:

Carson,
I found this in my briefcase this morning. Your name was on it. I assume it's your address book. I must've picked it up by accident on Friday.
Sorry.

Chris

I left as quietly as I'd entered, waving good-bye to employees busy with customers. I got in my car and headed north toward the Berlin Mall location. I used this location as my office.

"Your boss just called. He said call back when you get a chance," Maria told me as I entered the store.

Maria was the manager of the Berlin store. She'd become a good friend and repeatedly reminded me she thought Harry was a jackass.

"Okay," I replied, and headed for my office.

I returned the call to my boss and received the agenda for the week. I was instructed to take each manager in my district on a field trip to tour each other's locations, starting in Boston . . . with Carson.

Damn. I wasn't ready to look Carson in the eye, never mind spend an entire day with him!

I was leaning back in my chair, staring at the ceiling, when Maria entered the office.

"You're awfully quiet today," she said.

"Yeah."

"Okay, what's up?" Maria asked, knowing me all too well.

I had to tell someone, or I was going to burst. So, I spilled the beans about peeking at Carson's journal.

"Does this mean we can kill Harry?" she ribbed.

"Ha, ha, very funny," I said.

Maria wasn't your average girl. She was tough, tougher than most guys, standing almost six feet tall, with broad shoulders. She was Polish, with dark hair, light skin, and a round face with eyes that hinted at perpetual plotting of a devious prank.

"What does this have to do with Harry?" I asked.

"Isn't it obvious? This is the kick in the ass that we've been trying to give you!" she said, as if no explanation was necessary.

"I still don't follow," I said.

"Carson, you idiot! I can tell you like him. And if you don't, then you should!" she said.

I expected her to slap me upside the head.

"Even if I did, I think he'd have to like me too, smart-ass," I replied.

"Oh, details, details. At least it's a start," Maria said, as if she'd solved everything.

She'd been trying to find me a date since *she* decided Harry should be eliminated. Easy advice to give as opposed to accomplish, and I feared she meant "eliminated" literally.

"Well, I was instructed to spend the day in Boston tomorrow with Carson," I answered, and explained the assignment.

"See?" Maria smirked.

Was she right? Did I like Carson that way? I wasn't ready for this. This shouldn't happen with Harry around.

1986 – twenty-one years old

Chapter 24

Carson and I had planned to meet at the Raintree train station. We hadn't spoken since our coffee meeting.

Carson was standing at the terminal when I arrived.

"Hi," I said.

"Hi," he responded. "Hey, thanks for returning my notebook."

"Yeah, I must've grabbed it by accident," I answered nonchalantly.

"I wondered what happened to it. I couldn't replace that if I wanted to. So, what's up for today?" he asked as we got on the train.

We found two empty seats and sat, seemingly self-entertained as we watched others board. The Massachusetts train system, more commonly called the T, had a personality of its own. There was something distinctive about riding a train into any big city, each with its own concoction of smells and visuals. Unlike the eclectic artsy people found on the New York rail system, Boston transit was serious business. This portion of the T was an overbearing, testosterone-filled, "I'm cooler than you," cologne-scented colony of suits and briefcases sitting inside an iron tube on self-propelled track into the "Big City," aiming for "that one" life-altering promotion. I think joking was illegal while riding this train.

I shared an outline of the day with Carson, happy to have something on-point to talk about.

With work goals in place, the day proceeded stress free. Carson was a genuinely nice guy, unlike Harry, who only appeared to be a nice guy but in reality was a bit of a psycho.

We had just finished lunch and were walking to our next location. Out of the blue, Carson stopped, stood in front of me, grabbed my shoulders, and said, "I can't walk like this anymore."

"Like what?" I asked, totally confused.

"I can't walk with you on the outside side of the sidewalk. It's not polite," Carson explained.

"Why?" I asked, still confused.

His brown eyes echoed the sincerity of his words as he spoke.

"My dad always said when a man walks with a girl—any girl, even their own mother—it's the man's responsibility to walk on the outer edge of the sidewalk, nearest the street. Point is, if something happened, like a puddle splash or even an accident, the man would be harmed first. So, I have to ask you to walk on the inside, okay?"

I could barely speak. "Okay," I said, and moved over to the inside, feeling myself blush.

I spent the next few minutes rehashing it in my head. I almost laughed out loud a few times picturing Harry and me in the same situation. When Harry and I went out, he would place himself three feet in front of me. Nobody was aware we even knew each other, never mind being together. Harry wouldn't notice if I turned, left, or kept going. And if danger arose, he'd probably stick *me* on the outside.

By the end of the day, my head was mush. I had no idea how to deal with these new feelings. I hadn't felt this good in years, but what could I do about it? I was with Harry, and I had my job to think about. Besides, what if Carson didn't feel the same way?

We rode back on the train in comfortable silence. I was hesitant to say anything in fear of ruining a perfect day. We exited the train, and a feeling of mutual awkwardness arose as we both used obvious, unnecessary effort to locate our vehicles.

"There's my car," I said, sounding absurdly delighted.

"I see mine too," Carson replied.

"Well, it's been a great day. Thanks for a fun learning experience," I said, extending my hand to him.

"Right back at ya. I'll talk to you tomorrow," he replied, shaking my hand, looking in the opposite direction while answering.

Was he nervous, or was he in a hurry to get the hell out of here?

"Yeah, I should be by your store late afternoon sometime," I replied, back in work mode again.

"Okay," he said, and he got into his car and drove away.

I couldn't tell if he liked me or if I scared the hell out of him.

***

The next morning, I waited for Harry to walk out the front door, listened for his car to exit the driveway, then got out of bed. I stood in front of the bathroom mirror, staring into two puffy, swollen, bloodshot eyes. I felt terrible.

What an awful night! I'd tried to leave. I had tried, but I failed. His anger was debilitating. He'd thrown things, smashed things that were dear to me, and ended the night by slamming his fist through our bathroom door.

I got in the shower, turned the water temp to scorching, and stood there while it pummeled my back till the hot water ran cold. I robotically dressed myself for work as the night played through my head. I'd known I was in for a fight as soon as I'd walked in the door. His eyes . . . those little black pinhole pupils. A sure sign that it was fight time! Several hours into the same ridiculous accusations, my responses had become a broken record: "No, I am not sleeping with anyone else." I was drained.

What kind of boyfriend went through your checkbook to see if you shopped at certain stores too often? What kind of guy thought frequent shopping at the same store translated to sleeping with said store manager or owner?

Every time this ridiculous scenario arose, which was way too often, I thought back to that night I'd sat in a truck with Luke, not touching him because I hadn't wanted to feel guilty!

I went back to the bathroom mirror and looked at myself again. My eyes were still swollen. Not as bad as when I'd awoken, but it obviously not normal.

Look at me . . . . This was Christina. This was who I'd become. Hell, this was who I'd always been. This was not the Christina that I'd spent my childhood dreaming I'd become after moving out. What had happened to that little girl that wanted take control of her own life one day? Where was the Christina who had tolerated a horrible childhood so she could make it to adulthood and succeed on her own?

When I first met Harry, I'd been a size six. Now I was a size fourteen. Why didn't I care about myself anymore?

A few years ago, I'd even joined a gym and gotten thin enough to fit into my favorite black miniskirt for work. But before I'd left the house one day, Harry literally ripped it off my body. I'd cried and cried as he'd walked out the door that morning and gone to work as if everything was fine in his world because he'd gotten his way. Miniskirt ruined and a girlfriend too afraid to wear anything that might make her look "appealing," as he put it.

So, why bother being skinny? Less stressful this way, right?

I hated myself and my appearance. I wiped my eyes, inhaled a deep breath, and tucked it all away inside my head. It was time for work.

I skipped the visit to Carson's store to allow for traffic as I headed to a last-minute meeting with my boss in Wolfborough. I couldn't even imagine what it was about. I had worked above and beyond to earn the position of the only female district manager. I was proud of what I'd accomplished, and quite honestly, work was the only good thing I had.

I'd spent the day on pins and needles, figuring Harry would appear like Houdini at some point, but the day had run like business as usual.

I entered the receptionist's area and asked for Greg.

"He'll be right with you, Chris," she politely replied.

Moments later, Greg popped his head out of the door, smiled, and motioned for me to come in. I followed.

I was about to ask what was up when I saw Harry sitting there! What the hell was he doing at one of my meetings? Oh, damn.

"Sit down, Chris." Greg was now very serious.

Was it my imagination, or did he look angry?

"Well, I can't believe I'm actually sitting here wasting my time because of this situation," he said sternly.

This was not my imagination.

Had Harry done something I didn't know about? Was I going to lose my job?

"Both of you know how I feel about employees dating each other, right?" he asked.

We answered in unison, "Yes."

"It's been brought to my attention that this relationship is jeopardizing your jobs. I have issued you both a written warning. This is a professional company, not a high school. Do I need to elaborate?" he adamantly stated.

My job was a living hell thanks to Harry, but I hadn't thought anyone in the office knew! Had he initiated this? I'd never been issued a written warning, especially for something personal—how embarrassing!

I wanted to apologize and tell Greg it would stop immediately, but I'd be lying, as I'd been allowing Harry to control my life. This was my fault.

Harry spoke.

"No, Greg, you do not have to elaborate. We understand," he said, as if it was no big deal.

Harry got up and left before me. I rose to follow him.

"Chris, do you know what that was all about?" Greg asked.

I was humiliated.

"Yeah, I guess so. I'm sorry. I've been doing my best to not have it affect my work."

"The warning wasn't directed to you, but I had to give it to both of you. It was directed to Harry, and he knows it. You appear to be working unnecessarily overtime. Slow down; you can't fix things by burying yourself in work. Overcompensating in one area doesn't fix another," he said sincerely.

"I know, you're right," I said.

"Well, you'll think of something. You have a lot of friends here." He smiled.

"Thank you," I answered, trying to brush it off, and walked out of the office.

I couldn't believe I'd just gotten a written warning, and now I had to go home and face Harry.

I got in my car and headed for Route 95, but not north. South. It was time to go home. To the home I'd sworn I would never have to sleep in again . . . home to Mom and Dad, because my life had become so awful that living with them was better.

I felt like a complete failure.

***

My parents lived in a very Italian section of Providence known as Federal Hill. Providence, Rhode Island, was a small city with a big-city attitude.

The heart of Federal Hill was known as Atwells Avenue, a street with a red-white-and-green divider line painted down the middle instead of the conventional yellow everywhere else. Federal Hill had character.

A buffoon couldn't miss the obvious Italian heritage on Atwells Avenue. Generations of Italians had built a secluded, and legendary, village of restaurants, delis, bakeries, and retail specialty shops, some of which seemed conspicuously private, into the middle of a thriving city. I expected to see a little old lady hanging out a second-floor window, yelling for Antttt-onnnny!

All in all, the area made me feel good inside. Italian-colored streets might be tacky, but they reminded me of my Papa, and that was okay by me.

My parents lived in a typical three-story tenement on the corner of Day Street and Jury Avenue. They had purchased two houses, side by side, about a year after losing the rebuilt house in Forestville. Someone had learned of city loan program where you could buy rundown houses for dirt cheap, and in return, the city gave grant money to fix them up. Of course, my dad had found a way to forge receipts and make money on the grant money. His main focus in life, besides being a pedophile, was looking for the easy way out, figuring out how to cheat the system. He bought more hot stuff than anyone I had ever met.

The neighborhood of Federal Hill, aside from Atwells Ave, was just a bunch of triple-decker houses stacked side by side packed full of Italian folks. When my parents had purchased those two homes, six apartments in all, they'd convinced me to put the houses in my name legally. I hadn't quite understood what'd been going on at the time, but my parents said if I didn't agree to help, they might end up homeless, so I signed the paperwork. With my luck, Jimmy Hoffa was buried under one of them.

I pulled up to the front of the house, took a deep breath, and told myself I was doing the right thing.

"Hi, Mom," I said as I entered.

Mom looked concerned, as I never just popped in to visit.

"How are you?" she asked in an inquisitive, motherly tone.

"I'm okay, I guess," I answered, aware she knew I was lying.

I sat at the kitchen table. The kitchen was the biggest room in the house. They'd chosen to live in a little first-floor apartment in the larger house, with two bedrooms, both rather small, one for them and one for Mikey. The bedrooms had been cheaply remodeled, just enough to look present-day livable.

After losing the house in Forestville, they had very little money.

Over the course of the last year, my dad, now in his mid-forties, has had a minor heart attack and multiple seizures. According to what I'd been told, the doctor said he was unhealthy, should lose weight, eat better, and take it easy. So, he worked less and scammed more.

They'd recently become aware of a government-funded program that could deem my father one-hundred-percent disabled. If granted, he'd get a monthly income, and Dad wouldn't have to work. I was pretty sure the houses were in my name to hide any other signs of income.

I told her as little about my Harry situation as necessary. Even though she seemed sympathetic, I still feared the dreaded words "I told you so."

"Do you want to stay here?" she asked, knowing it had already crossed my mind.

"Maybe. I can't think of another solution. If I move out again, Harry will follow me and drive me crazy every night. I'm afraid I might lose my job. This is the only place I can think of where he won't bother me. I wouldn't have to stay here long, just long enough for this to blow over," I explained.

"You'll have to sleep on the couch," she said.

"That's the least of my problems." I laughed.

"Well, let's tell Dad when he gets home. You're staying for supper, right?" she asked.

"Yeah, I guess I am," I answered, not really having thought that far ahead.

"Mikey and Gabriella should be here soon too," she added.

Mikey had grown into a young adult with a deep voice, dark facial hair, and all the other normal guy stuff. Gabriella was Mikey's first girlfriend, and Mikey worshiped the ground she walked on. It had taken Mom almost a year to accept that Gabriella was not going anywhere.

Granted, Gabriella's tiny, five-foot-two Barbie-doll figure didn't match her Lucille Ball voice, Cyndi Lauper hair, or Tammy Fay Baker makeup job. She also wore super-high heels and smoked like a chimney. But Mikey liked her, so that was all that mattered. I didn't have an opinion of her either way yet, but she scared the daylights out of me.

Dinner went rather well. Dad didn't have a problem with me living at home—as long as I paid rent weekly. As it turned out, Gabriella had replaced me as the girl getting snide insults from Mom. However, from the faces she made behind Mom's back, Gabriella wasn't going anywhere without a fight. Gabriella was a lot tougher than I was. I decided I liked her after all.

After the kitchen was clean, we retired to the living room. It was still early, and I wasn't in any rush to get back home to Harry, so I stayed to watch TV.

I lay on the floor in front of the TV. Dad had the remote and was flipping through channels like a seal showing off at Sea World.

Mom sat on the couch next to him.

"What's on?" she asked.

"Not much," he answered, handing her the remote.

She stopped as the announcer said, "And now for the NBC movie of the week."

"Oh, these are always good . . . ," Mom said, and let it hang there.

My eyes were refocusing on the new channel as I heard a familiar announcement.

"Tonight's movie contains mature subject matter that might not be suited for all
viewers . . . ."

And there I was, watching *Something about Amelia* with my parents!

What were the fucking chances of this!? But I didn't want to leave. I didn't think I should have to go. As a matter of fact, I *wouldn't* leave, because if anyone should leave, it should be my father.

But he didn't move an inch. Was he actually that brazen? Or was it because he lied to himself even about that?

He just sat there . . . and so did Mom. No one said a word.

I took verbal shots at the guy Ted Danson played every chance I could. And I even took a few at the mom too. Each time, I sat and waited for a response from one of them . . . but nothing. Not a peep, other than Mom's occasional, "Oh, that's awful."

I kept it up:

"He should be shot!"

"Any guy like that is piece of human garbage."

"They should lock *him* up forever."

"Why don't they cut off his dick?"

"How does a mom NOT know or believe her child in a situation like this? That's impossible!" I was on a roll. Because I was saying all of these things about a fictional character, I found myself able to say all of the things I'd always wished I could say but never had. It was oddly empowering, and in some messed-up way, I was actually enjoying this!

The movie ended, and I got up as if nothing had happened.

"I've got to get going. It's late," I said.

Mom spoke. Dad still sat in silence.

"Okay, just let us know what you are going to do," she said. "Be careful driving home."

"Okay," I said, and walked out the door as if the last hour in that house had been just as normal as any other house on earth.

Was my current life really so bad that I had to go back into a house with that guy? Yep, it sure was.

I drove home as slowly as I could and was relieved to find that he wasn't home yet. It was like a burst of fresh air.

I walked into the house, put my things on the couch, and headed upstairs to change, feeling empty and numb, unaware my legs were moving back and forth, elevating to the second floor. Once at the top stair, I faced the fist-shaped hole in the bathroom door as a brutal reminder of my reality. I took a deep breath, exhaled, and walked to the bedroom.

I got changed, lay down on the bed, turned on the TV, and stared into space. Just the thought of moving back home, the place I'd spent my entire childhood plotting an escape from, made me nauseous. This was worse than a no-win situation. The only good thing about living with my parents was that Harry wouldn't follow me there because then people I knew would see the real Harry, and Harry didn't want anyone to see that, especially my parents.

1986 – twenty-two years old

Chapter 25

The alarm went off at 7:00 a.m. I got out of bed, trying my best not to wake Harry. I'd heard him come in at about one thirty, but I hadn't moved an inch in fear that I'd have to deal with him.

If I got ready quietly, hopefully he'd stay sleeping. I could feel my body shaking as I dressed and tiptoed around the apartment. Normally I didn't get up until after he did, but today, I was scheduled to visit our Cape Cod location. It was a long ride and a perfect excuse to leave early.

The drive was surprisingly soothing. Spring was in the air, and if the aroma had an expression, it'd be smiling. The trees along the route had started to bloom, making the bright new colors feel like a psychological reboot.

With an hour-plus ride to the cape, there was plenty of time to think about my screwed-up life. The more I thought about it, the better I felt about moving to Providence. As long as I kept working as much as possible, I'd hardly even be there. I only needed to be there to sleep. The irony that sleeping there was better than my current life wasn't lost on me.

The thought of that that fat, naked body positioned above me chilled my soul.

I'd learned to tuck that unforgettable black cloud of a memory away, but today the cloud was looming because I'd decided that going back to that monster was better than living with Harry.

Because Harry I could not control. The realization of knowing that my brain was better at handling my past than my present made me sick.

The plan was to visit Carson's store in Oakdale as my last stop, making it a long day on the road. Normally that'd be exhausting, but today it was therapy.

Since our day trip to Boston, things between Carson and me had felt awkward. I thought there was a mutual attraction, yet neither one of us had made the first move. Was my attraction to Carson legitimate, or was my brain simply looking for a way to validate a happier escape? My heart felt like it was legit. But even if Carson didn't have an ounce of feelings for me, he was a friend, and being around him made me feel better. Feeling better gave me strength. If there was one thing I needed, it was strength.

Why couldn't I be like the mighty Isis? Or maybe just borrow her magic wristbands?

I drove into the mall parking lot having convinced myself, once again, that I could be strong.

Carson was walking out of the mall as I was headed in. It took me by surprise, and I found it hard to speak.

"Hi, I was leaving," he stated, smiling.

"Hey."

"What's up? Anything we need to go back inside for?" he asked.

"No, not really. I was just stopping by to make my day longer," I said, more to myself than to him.

"Well, that's sad." He laughed at me.

"Yeah, I know, but true." I smiled back.

Walking toward our cars, I told him about the warning from Greg.

"I went to visit my parents last night, and they said it's okay with them if I stay there until it's safe," I explained.

"Wow! You've come a long way since our last conversation. Where's the courage coming from?" he asked.

"The combined fear of losing my job and anger at myself for allowing this to continue. But also help from a few good friends, namely Maria and you," I said as our eyes met and locked.

Something was definitely happening between us. We'd grown closer without even trying. Another intimate relationship was the last thing I needed right now, but I couldn't stop the feelings. For a second, I thought we were going to kiss, though suddenly aware of what might happen, we each backed away.

"Uh, I gotta get going," I said as I fumbled for the knob of my car door.

"Yeah, me too," Carson said with the same unsteadiness in his voice.

I got in and started the car, taking a minute to roll the window down before pulling away. I looked over to Carson and shouted, "Thanks for being you!"

Had that sounded stupid? I didn't know what I'd meant to say, but it sure hadn't been that!

I backed out of the parking space and put the car in drive. I felt like I was stuck in slow motion—*Drive, car. Drive!*

Then I felt a bang on my door. I jumped and looked.

It was Carson, and his hand was at my car door.

"Hey," was all he said.

The next thing I knew, Carson had popped his head through my car window, and we kissed. It happened so quickly!

"I know this isn't going to be easy, but ah, what the hell." He smiled.

I smiled back and drove away, thinking the same thing.

***

About a week had passed since Carson and I kissed. We'd both agreed that I needed to get my own life figured out before we could even consider being "we." So, as of now, Carson and I were friends that enjoyed time together.

I was leaving the mall exit by Carson's store when I spotted Harry's gray Nissan 300-ZX in the driving lane of the mall lot, stopped nose-to-nose with my car, blocking it in. He put it in park and exited the car. I could tell by the way he walked that he was mad as hell, and for the first time, I literally feared for my life.

"Hey! What's up?" he asked, smirking.

I was shaking inside.

Had he been inside? Had he seen me talking to Carson? But we'd only talked business. Maybe he'd noticed the spark between us. *Please don't show how scared you are. Control, Christina. Control!*

"I was just leaving to head home," I said.

"Do you know what time it is?" he asked, as if it was midnight, well past my curfew.

Noting his pinhead-sized pupils, I did my best to say what he needed to hear. Calming him down was top priority.

People were coming and going in the parking lot. I disliked seeing people fight in public and never wanted to be one of those people. I was so embarrassed; I just needed this to be over.

"It's six thirty; I'm just finishing my workday," I said, hoping that Harry might realize it really wasn't all that late.

"Six thirty! So, what have you been doing since five o'clock? You should have been here and gone by five! Tell me where you've been," he demanded.

But I didn't have answers he wanted to hear, because he didn't want the truth. My day had gone as usual—it'd just run a little longer for no particular reason. I didn't know what to say.

"Harry, I haven't even been here an hour," I said as calmly and quietly as possible.

By the lack of changed expression, I could see that it hadn't worked. Instead, he moved closer to me, pinning my legs up against the hood of the car. I sat on the hood, trapped. He put an arm on each side of my legs, and his face was inches from mine, glaring.

"Well, if you got here less than an hour ago, where were you before this? Visiting that little friend of yours at the vintage toy store? What's his name—Bob? Did the two of you have a cute little lunch date?"

He moved away from me and opened my car door as if to find millions of dollars in collectable vintage toys hidden under the seats.

Why on earth did he think I had something going with Bob? Sure, I'd purchased toys from his store, but how did that constitute a sexual relationship with the owner? I'd bought things for Harry at that store! I'd given him a Tom Corbett space gun so he'd see I shopped for him too.

But he didn't believe I was just a customer. We'd visited the small shop together once. Bob, the store owner, had smiled as we came in, said, "Hi, Chris," and gone about his business. Harry introduced himself before I could answer, initiated a chat about our personal lives, invented things we'd never done together, and concluded the ludicrous conversation by sharing a fictitious plan of us getting married and having children. Totally normal dialogue with a stranger after greeting hi.

I'd been mortified and never gone back!

"You are friggin' nuts, you know that?" I said, then jumped off the hood and got in my car. He was so amazed at what I'd said, he didn't try to stop me. But where was I going to go? He had me blocked in. I was stuck until *he* let me out.

He walked to my door and punched the window so hard I thought it'd break. Embarrassed that he was making a scene and genuinely terrified, I opened the window.

"Where do you think you're going?" He laughed sarcastically.

I was crying now.

"I don't know. I just want to get away from you. I'm tired of telling you the truth and you not believing it! No, I haven't been to the toy store! You fixed that so I can't go back there ever, it's too embarrassing! Please let me out!" I cried and begged.

"Come home with me," Harry softly said, a bit calmer than before.

I hated him so much, I wanted to be as far away as possible.

"I don't want to go home with you ever again! Let me go! Please?" I cried.

I looked up at him leaning into my window. His skin got white. He didn't say anything. He walked to his car and got in. Was he going to let me go? *Oh, thank you, God!*

He started his car, and I waited for him to back up, but he didn't.

I waited a few seconds longer, and then I got out and walked to his window.

"Are you going to back up or not?" I asked in a much louder voice than I expected.

"I'm not backing up till you get in this car and we go home," he said, as if there wasn't a problem. Or if there was, it must be me causing it.

I got back in my car, and he drove forward. His car was now pushing against the front of my car! *What a fuckin' nut!* I lost it.

I put my car in drive and began to go forward. I had a company car. He had a precious little "I'm over forty but can't admit it" sports car.

I could hear myself sobbing, mixed with screeching tires spinning and burning rubber. I didn't care if my car got scratched. But he didn't stop. Instead, he pushed harder.

Defeated, I shut my motor off, rolled up my window, and forced myself to walk back toward him. I opened his passenger's door and got in.

"I'm sorry. Let's go home," I said, still crying.

He didn't say anything. He backed up and drove home.

We spent the night in complete silence.

He watched TV, and I acted like I was watching TV.

But I was plotting my escape.

***

The plan was to take only what was absolutely necessary, basically clothes for work and my camera equipment. Not that my camera equipment was required, but it was small, easily packable, and worth a fair amount of money. Although heartbreaking, I knew I had to leave most of my toy collection. I had acquired an incredible array of vintage toys and collectibles dear to me, some irreplaceable. Most were displayed around our apartment, so packing anything prior would have made Harry suspicious. So, most things stayed.

Moving day was simply Carson and me carrying a handful of boxes into my parents' house.

I had taken the day off, and we'd planned carefully.

Carson had met my parents a week prior. My mom adored him instantly. Mostly because he was polite and twenty-five, not forty-something. My mother would have been happy to see me with anyone as long as it wasn't Harry.

Mom had asked about a thousand questions since we'd arrived at the house only moments before.

"When did you leave?"

"Are you sure he didn't see you?"

"I hope he isn't going to come here. I don't want a scene!" And so on.

Carson and I sat down at the table. Mom made us coffee, as we were both coffeeholics.

"Okay, Mom, here's the scoop," I began.

"I told him that you called me at work yesterday and asked me if I could take Nana to the doctor because you had to be somewhere else. I waited until after he left this morning to pack my things. I left so much stuff there." I sighed.

"Then I wrote him a note explaining this is the way it has to be. I said I was going home for a while and did not want any communication with him."

Carson shook his head in agreement with what had been said thus far.

"I also suggested he get professional help if he ever intends to be in another relationship. That's about it," I said, talking more to the tabletop than to anyone.

I was numb, drained, relieved, and a bit scared. Carson headed home after our coffee, and the rest of the evening was spent watching *Night Court* and *Newhart*.

After they went to bed, I sat on the sofa in my parents' house in complete darkness, reassuring myself this was still better than where I'd just escaped. I clicked the knob on the table lamp, giving me just enough light to make up the couch with sheets Mom had provided. I tucked the sheets tightly into the cushions, turned the light off, and sat back down.

It was time to get undressed, but I was too scared. What was I going to wear to bed? All those years with Harry, I'd only worn a long T-shirt and underwear, but I couldn't wear that now. That wouldn't be safe at all. I didn't even own a pair of sweatpants. Holding back tears, I frantically looked for something, anything, to wear on the bottom. I'd wear my jeans if I had to. The light from the street filled the room with furniture-shaped shadows. I could turn the light back on, but I didn't want anyone to wake up and see me sitting on the floor, crying. Finally, at the bottom of a box, I found a pair of jean shorts and sighed at the small victory. I tiptoed to the bathroom, shorts and T-shirt in hand, quietly closed the door, and changed into my safe clothes, then went back to the couch, hoping I'd be able to sleep, as my body and brain were completely exhausted.

"Christina. Christina, it's time to get up," Mom said.

I answered immediately, as I'd woken on the hour throughout the entire night. Between the slim chance of Harry bursting in and the higher chance my father would pay me a visit, I'd hardly slept at all. I was glad it was morning.

I was showered, dressed, and out of the house within an hour.

By the end of the week, I was toast. Although work seemed to be going fine, I was not. Harry assumed this ridiculousness would clear itself up. So, my days often ended with meetups in various parking lots, trying to calmly reiterate to him that this was a permanent situation.

Carson and I met up outside his store and headed for coffee.

It had been a hot day, and the sun was finally melting into the horizon, far away from where we sat in silence, watching it go. I turned to Carson and saw little red dots dancing around his face.

"You missed Harry by minutes," he said.

"How could that be? I just left him at Berlin Mall!"

"Well, he was here. For a good long time too, and it was his second appearance of the day!" he said.

"This is all so exhausting. I don't know what else to do," I said.

He jumped up, as if, all of a sudden, he had the solution. He put his hand in his pocket and pulled out a sheet of paper.

"We do this," he said, smiling as he handed me the paper.

I looked at it and read.

"What's this?" I asked, smiling.

"That's our quiet, uninterrupted weekend in which I am going to make you forget this world exists."

I laughed and responded, "Am I supposed to make you forget this world too?"

"Of course. You're the one who's responsible!" Carson teased back.

1986 – twenty-two years old

Chapter 26

We arrived at the Newport Sherwood just before 9:00 p.m.

Part of me wanted to tear off Carson's clothes as soon as we got into the hotel room, and another part of me was hoping we wouldn't sleep together at all, because the thought of him seeing my fat body was terrifying.

What if he didn't want to touch me? At 190 pounds, this was the heaviest I'd ever been. A far cry from the 128 pounds I'd been when Harry and I met.

"Here's your key, Mr. Stone. You're in room number 132," the desk clerk said.

"Thanks," Carson said, taking the key and pointing us in the right direction.

I followed quietly.

It was the longest, prettiest hallway I'd ever seen. The hotel room doors were trimmed in beautiful gold flake and matched perfectly with the elaborately designed carpet lining the halls, featuring rows and rows of gold diamonds laid out like Russian nesting dolls. The detail was incredible. It must have cost a fortune to build this place. Finally, Carson stopped in front of the entrance to our hotel room, door 132.

He motioned for me to walk in first, and I did. The door closed behind us, making a vacuum-packed sound. I heard him click the lock on the knob, then the deadbolt.

He walked up and whispered in my ear.

"Okay, now we're safe from all evil. How does it feel?" I could tell he was smiling.

I turned, put my arms around his neck, kissed him, and said, "It feels nice."

"There's only one problem," he said.

Oh, no! What could it be? Were we supposed to have two rooms?

"What?" I asked, my heart pounding.

"Well, the restaurant closes at ten, so if we want dinner at all tonight, we'll have to go now. Is that okay?" Carson asked, as if it was some kind of big deal.

Was that okay? That was terrific, as far as I was concerned. That just meant less time for me to worry about what might happen in this room.

"That's fine with me, I don't mind at all," I said, probably a little happier than expected.

The restaurant was in the same building as the hotel, and dinner was fantastic.

We shared a bottle of wine over dinner. Out of embarrassment, I opted not to tell Carson that at twenty-four years old, it was the first bottle I had ever shared with anyone. So, after a few glasses, I felt good—a bit loopy perhaps, but I was less nervous and way more relaxed.

Carson paid our check, then quietly asked, "Are you ready to settle in?"

Images flashed through my head when I heard "settle in." An hour earlier, those images would have sent my stomach into a frenzy, but now everything felt fine.

I smiled. "Yes, I'm ready."

We walked hand in hand back to the room, and once inside, I felt calm . . . with a just hint of nervousness.

Carson walked to the TV, turned it on, and sat on the bed—the only bed.

Okay, Christina, you probably look pretty stupid standing in the corner of the room, so get your butt over to that bed.

We lay together and watched *Top Gun* on one of the cable stations. I had no idea what was going on in the movie. I sat, appearing to comprehend whatever was on TV, far too busy thinking about when *it* was going to happen.

We hadn't kissed since we'd gotten back to the room.

Maybe we weren't going to kiss? Perhaps we were just going to sleep in the same bed. *Oh, come on, Chris, you know that's not what's about to happen here.* But why hadn't we kissed? Was I supposed to make the first move? Was it the girl's job now? It'd been so long. I'd been with Harry for six years. And before that, there was Ben, but I wasn't sure how much weight a ten-minute experience in a freezing-cold cabin and teenage backseat experiences held.

Wine or no wine, I had no idea what to do. I looked at the TV screen just in time to see Tom Cruise kissing someone in a low-lit bedroom.

Oh, great! Let's make this just a little more uncomfortable!

"So, what would you like to do tomorrow?" Carson awkwardly asked, trying to avoid sitting through the nerve-wracking sex scene.

"Oh, I don't know, maybe take a nice long walk on the ocean," I replied.

"Have you ever been here? Newport, I mean?" he asked.

"A few times, but I don't know the area. I just know there's a special walkway along the cliffs," I answered honestly.

I looked at him for an opinion, but he didn't say anything. Now eye to eye, staring intensely at each other, I wanted to kiss him so badly, but I was a bit woozy, and I think my body was frozen.

And then it happened. Carson kissed me for a long time. And the nervous feeling in my stomach disappeared, and after what appeared to be hours later, our lips parted.

"Hang on a second . . . ," Carson whispered, and got up.

"Okay," I replied, and watched him get up and turn off the light next to the TV.

Now I could only see his shadow. I thought he was going to lie back down, but he stopped when he got to his side of the bed. What was he doing?

"You okay?" he asked softly.

"Yeah, why?" I replied, confused.

I wondered if he was having second thoughts.

"You're not sorry you're here, are you? You're happy, right?" he asked sincerely.

"Yes, and I've had a great time so far," I answered, thinking how nice it was of him to ask.

I honestly thought that if I had said, "No, take me home," Carson would have.

"Okay, I just wanted to make sure." He smiled.

But he didn't lie back on the bed. He was still standing there, looking down at me in the shadow light of the TV.

I stared and waited.

Then I heard movement, but I couldn't see what he was doing. I squinted. *Oh, that's nice.* I smiled. *He's taking his shirt off; he must be comfortable.* I noticed his chest and how surprisingly aroused I was, but I didn't even see what he did next until it was done, and then he was standing there naked.

He didn't say a word. He slowly took the covers down and got into bed.

Am I supposed to get up and do the same thing? I hope not! Because I'm pretty sure my legs are paralyzed!

So, there we were. Carson stark naked under the covers. Me, fully clothed in my work shirt and skirt, on top of the covers, paralyzed from the waist down . . . and the neck up.

He'd better make the next move, or we'll still be like this at sunrise.

He did.

He kissed me. And again, my nervousness faded.

He stopped and whispered to me, "I want to make love to you."

I could only utter, "I know."

"May I?" he asked.

"Yes," I barely uttered back. *Dear God, yes. Please.* "Let me take my clothes off."

And again, he asked, "May I?"

Wow! This was already so different from being with Harry. Harry had never asked anything; he'd just done it.

"Yes."

He began to unbutton my blouse, and before I knew it, we were both naked under the covers. We lay on our sides, facing each other.

"As much as I want this to happen, you know it doesn't have to be right now. Right?" Carson explained.

"Yes," I answered, still in total disbelief of his sincerity.

This time, I kissed him. Even his kiss was nothing like Harry's. It was softer, warmer, and, at the same time, more intense. Until then, I hadn't realized the lack of passion in my past relationship. Even in the beginning, this kind of passion had never existed between Harry and me. This felt warm and intimate.

What happened next made me lose all sense of time and place.

Our bodies together was like nothing I had ever experienced. We were touching and feeling with a slowness that made time stand still. And then there was something I hadn't expected—a surprise. I quickly learned that every man didn't feel the same inside. For six years, my body had gotten used to "it." But this was different. A different size, a different shape, a different movement, a different man. This different man was soft and gentle. This man whispered. This man . . . just poured something warm and wet on my body!

I jumped and stopped kissing him, wondering what was dripping all over me.

"It's okay," he whispered. "Just relax, trust me."

He was smothering our naked bodies in warm oil, and he wanted me to trust him?

"Okay," I whispered back.

Apparently, my voice trusted him.

During the next hour or so, my life was a chapter from a hot and steamy romance novel.

And all these years, I'd thought those authors made that stuff up. I didn't care what anyone said; all men were not created equal, and baby oil wasn't just for babies! *Thank you, God.*

We lay in silence for a while, both gathering our thoughts. I was in a trance until I heard Carson move. I listened to the rustle of papers and then a click followed by a glow of light about three inches from his face.

I laughed out loud, because it seemed so movie-like to me. Carson was lying in bed, post-sex, actually smoking a cigarette.

"What's so funny?" he asked, and though it was dark, I could tell by the tone of his voice he was smiling.

"I can't help it. It's your cigarette. It's like you're following some movie script or something. I didn't know this actually happened in real life." I giggled.

"Well, it does." He smiled. "Does it bother you?"

I didn't like smoking, but it really wasn't bothering me. Actually, in its own weird way, it was flattering.

We spent the rest of the night talking to each other about ourselves. He told me all about the old him and his former girlfriend, and he even cried about how he missed his dad.

"Now that you know all my deep, dark secrets, how about you? Did you leave anything out?" he teased.

Did I leave anything out? I had told him a lot about me, more than I had shared with Harry, but not that. *That* was my secret and mine only. That was something no one would ever know.

"No. I didn't leave anything out," I answered.

1987 – twenty-three years old

Chapter 27

I heard the floors creaking above and the pipes echoing from inside the walls as someone flushed the toilet upstairs.

I didn't think anything of it; I just acknowledged it in my head.

Instead of getting an apartment together, my parents had convinced Carson and me to build a room in the basement—or two bedrooms, as it turned out, because that would benefit both them and us. Some things never changed. The idea was presented with perfect timing after a surprise, late-night visit from Harry, which had left us both in chills.

Over the past six months, Harry had been dating his therapist and at least two other girls at work. It didn't bother me at all. In fact, I felt sorry for the new victims that had fallen for his whole funny-guy facade.

The two new rooms downstairs had been built for Mikey and me, with a couch in my room for Carson if he happened to crash there, as I still wasn't allowed boys in my bed. That was a rule only my father could break.

At 1:00 a.m., I was unable to sleep, while Carson was slept soundly on the couch next to my bed, snoring, probably loud enough to be heard upstairs. Mikey had arrived home about an hour before. Now he, too, was snoring in the adjacent room. We had nicknamed the two rooms, divided by paper-thin walls, "the barracks."

In some ways, sleeping on the couch in the living room had been comforting and safe. Dad had never tried to visit me there, but I'd never gotten a full night's sleep either. Sleeping downstairs felt safer with Mikey in an adjoining room.

The footsteps were now wandering the kitchen.

I'd thought getting older and me moving away might have calmed my father a bit, but rotten was rotten. He looked at Gabriella like he would love to get his hands where they didn't belong. His disgusting comments, which my mother always laughed off, made me want to vomit. Gabriella was tough and would sass right back, but I wondered if she thought he was out of line.

The footsteps above stopped. When we'd added rooms to the basement, I'd gotten the bigger of the two rooms, but there was one drawback: a spiral staircase that went from upstairs directly into my room, as it was the only space where the transition allowed.

The footsteps above moved again, and a shadow of feet and ankles from the staircase entrance above projected down onto my bedroom wall.

Are you fucking kidding me?! Please, it can't be! Please, God. No!

I closed my eyes, hoping the shadow would go away. I stared at the top of that black spiral case, and my heart sank. Two fat, flat, furry feet were standing as still as night.

No! How could he? How could he with Carson AND Mikey so close? Where does his nerve come from?

Tears ran down my face. It was the first time I couldn't stop the tears. The shadows of his legs on my wall made him look like the real-life monster he actually was.

What if he came down and Carson woke up? I couldn't bear for that to happen. What would Carson think?

My entire body was shaking. I had to wake up Carson, but what would I say?

Who cares, Christina! Just wake him up before those feet move!

I got out of bed as quietly as I could. Carson, only a few feet away, was on his side, facing the wall, his back to me. I reached over just far enough to shake him, but I was so nervous I inadvertently punched him. I jumped back in bed fast and looked at the feet. They hadn't moved, and Carson didn't wake up but instead rolled over onto his stomach.

The feet are still there. He's going to come down here! I didn't stop him!

I closed my eyes as if it would all go away, while my entire body shook.

Then Carson rolled over again and started coughing—loudly. I looked back up at the feet, and they disappeared. Carson rolled back onto his side, snoring. For the first time in my life, I thanked God for cigarettes. I disliked his awful cigarette cough, and tomorrow I probably would again, but tonight, that sound was a lifesaver.

I made it through the workday with a feeling like I'd narrowly escaped an oncoming freight train the night before. After dinner, I started organizing for the next day. I reminded myself to grab Missy's money and put it in my purse so I wouldn't forget it in the morning.

Missy, one of our store managers, was having trouble saving money. She had asked me to hold on to $400 she'd saved until she had another $200 for a deposit on a car. I was reluctant, but she'd finally worn me down and put her $400 in an old metal box under my bed, and now she was ready to purchase the car. It felt good to have helped.

I crawled under the bed, pulled out the metal box, opened it, and . . . almost had a heart attack. The money was gone! Out of panic, I crawled back under the bed and looked everywhere. I knew it hadn't jumped out of the box by itself.

"Mom? Mom!" I called upstairs.

"What? Why are you yelling?" she snapped.

"Have you been down here recently?" I yelled again, ignoring her question.

"I was down there yesterday getting Mikey's dirty clothes. Why? What's wrong?"

I zoomed up those narrow, slippery, winding stairs as if I could fly.

"Because I am missing $400! And it's not mine!"

I was shaking my head like I was in denial. *This can't be happening!*

"Are you sure? Did you misplace it?" she asked calmly, precisely what I didn't want to hear.

"Yes, I'm sure! I put the money in a metal box under my bed! It was $400, all in twenty-dollar bills! It wasn't mine!" I yelled, as if that would make a difference.

"Sit down, relax," Mom said.

I sat and explained the story in detail, hoping she would have the answer, but she didn't. A half hour later, after tearing my room apart, we were both sitting at the kitchen table in silence. If Mikey, Gabriella, and Dad hadn't walked in, we probably would have sat there till midnight. I went through the entire story again. And answered all the same questions again.

"I don't know what to say, Chris," Mikey said, sadly looking at me.

Gabriella agreed. "Yeah, me neither."

Dad sat down at the table with us.

"Maybe Carson took it?" he said.

How could he even say that? What nerve! I wasn't accusing anyone; I just wanted to know where it was!

I looked up at him, and a strange feeling came over me. What if *he'd* taken it? *He* was the only one who would do something like that. He'd have no problem stealing from his daughter. He hated that I'd actually done okay for myself. He'd never said, "You're doing a good job." He just saw me as a resource for when he needed something. It was time for me to get out of that kitchen.

"All I know is that I had $400 in what was supposed to be a safe place, and now it's gone! I'm going to bed." I didn't even look back to see his face.

He was guilty. I could feel it in my bones.

I read a few chapters of my latest mystery novel, had a long phone conversation with Carson, and fell asleep. The morning seemed to come moments later.

Mikey was already gone, and I could hear Mom upstairs coughing her brains out from years of smoking. She was coming out of the bathroom when I got to the kitchen.

"Good morning," she said.

"Morning," I answered.

"I'll probably be gone when you get out of the shower. I have to pick up Dad," she said.

I didn't ask where Dad was.

I was still upset about what had happened, so much so that I surprised myself.

"Mom, I think Dad took that money," I said, proud of myself.

She stood quietly for a moment. Maybe she knew something? Maybe, for once, she wasn't going to protect him.

"I really don't think he would do something like that," she said softly, but not so reassuringly.

"Well, I do. Especially to me," I said, now very annoyed.

Where had she been all these years? Didn't she see or hear anything?

Her only response before she walked into her room and closed the door was, "Well, I hope he didn't."

She was gone before I finished showering. Was she ever going to deal with reality?

Before I left for work, I checked their bedroom.

I just knew he'd taken it. I didn't know what I intended to prove in there, but it was worth a shot. If he had it, did she know it?

They each had their own bureau, and I knew from many countless moves that the top drawers of each dresser were referred to as the junk drawers.

His bureau had two little top drawers. I opened the one on the right first. I sifted through various items: cuff links, old carpenters' pencils, lots of receipts, and a pile of condoms—I closed the drawer in disgust.

"Eww," I said aloud.

I shook my hands back and forth as if I had touched something grotesque.

I opened the left drawer.

There was more of the same. Receipts, a small folding ruler, pencils, change, an oversized old coin . . . but not $400! I folded my arms over the open drawer and rested my chin on top in disappointment. I stood there for a few minutes, gazing into the drawer. Then, for no reason at all, I pushed my fingers through the mess of stuff again. I opened up an old receipt. It was dated 1980 from some carpet place. I put it down. Then I picked up one of the carpenter pencils. I'd always thought they were cool because of the flat rectangular shape. I wondered why carpenters had special pencils and why they were flat instead of round like all other pencils—*why the hell do I care right now?* I put it down on top of a little pile of change next to that big coin. Actually, it was a big old penny. *Hey! Wait a minute!*

I looked down again, and there it was: *my* old penny, the one I had hidden in the back of my diary! But Bobby had taken my diary . . . . What was it doing here? I picked it up and held it tightly, and visions of my soot-filled bedroom came back to me. Memories so vivid, I could smell the soot again, right there in that room as if it was happening now. The room went dark. Tears dropped uncontrollably from my eyes as I realized what I should have realized so many years ago.

The penny had been in the diary. If he had the penny, then he'd taken the diary, not Bobby. And if *he'd* taken the diary . . . oh, Jesus, fuck. *All these years, that bastard knew. He knows that I know—HE FUCKING KNOWS THAT I KNOW!*

That was why he was so mean to me now. He knew I knew, and he knew what I thought of him. That terrible excuse of a human being had sat through that movie with his daughter right there . . . and hadn't said a fucking word. Why did God make people like that? Was there even a God at all? There had to be a more powerful word than "hate."

I was crying uncontrollably as I felt a tidal wave of stupidity rush through my body, laughing at me like a parade of horror-movie clowns.

Then everything started to lose focus . . . .

The next thing I remembered was being at work. I didn't recall the drive at all.

I got home just before dinner. No one else was home yet. It had been a long day. I walked down to my room, took off my shoes, and dropped onto my bed. It'd cost me $400 out of my pocket, but Missy was on her way to buy a new car. I didn't let her know what had happened; that wouldn't have solved anything. I looked around at the sight of my messy room, wishing it would mysteriously start cleaning itself up, but no such luck. I had turned the place upside down the night before.

Clothes had to be put back into drawers, books had to be organized again, and the little metal box had to go back under my bed so I'd never have to see it again. But when I picked it up, it made a noise. There was something inside.

I sat back down on the bed and opened the box.

I couldn't help but laugh!

There in the box was a wad of money.

I counted out $400 and laughed even harder. The $400 that just yesterday had been crisp, new twenties had somehow become a pile of worn fives, tens, and twenties. Was he that stupid? Or was he just so arrogant that he knew he could get away with it?

Carson arrived at the house before my parents got home. I explained the little mishap to him, leaving out the penny episode, of course.

"Chris, no matter what his reason might be, you really need to get out of here," he said.

"I know," I agreed.

Dinner went pretty much as we expected. Mom and Dad said I must have not seen it the night before, even though all of us had seen the empty box. And there was no comment whatsoever as to how it had reappeared in different denominations.

Before going to bed that night, I cornered Mom.

"He took the money, you know," I said.

Her only reply was "I know."

Nothing else was ever said.

***

Route 95 South is quite possibly the most boring road in the world, but it allowed for plenty of thinking.

We were driving to South Florida for Thanksgiving to visit my parents, who now spent their winters living in a mobile home retirement park. As the mile markers ticked by with Carson asleep in the passenger's seat, I thought about how hectic the past six months had been. My life was better, but I had a little bug inside that said something was still off. I felt as if I'd stepped off one roller coaster right onto another.

Somehow over the past year or so, my parents had gone from dirt-poor to having enough money to buy a second home, albeit a mobile home, in Florida. I had always referred to them as trailer parks, but I had to admit, from the photos, it looked much nicer than expected. The park was a cute little retirement area neatly landscaped with fresh-cut grass. Kind of like nice camping, if camping was actually nice.

We arrived on Thanksgiving morning.

The majority of the residents were elderly. I could never understand why my parents, who were still in their forties, wanted to jump right to retirement age. It was probably for discounts and benefits. My dad had finally convinced the government he was totally disabled and could no longer work, so now the government *paid* my dad to exist. Meanwhile, Mom had a job at a bank in Providence that allowed her to take winters off. With only Mikey at home to provide for, they were, as far as they were concerned, living large.

Dinner was excellent. And we enjoyed listening to Uncle Jay, who had a charming double trailer in the park next door, tell funny stories about the goings-on in his club. Uncle Jay, who'd spent countless days on our couch feeling sorry for himself after his divorce, was now the owner of a lucrative strip joint. How someone went from being a blacksmith to that, I'd never know, but by the time dinner was over, everyone was stuffed and hurting from laughter.

A few hours later, Carson and I went for a drive to get some ice cream. We stopped at a parking lot on the beach. The sun had set, the night was clear, and the sound of the ocean was soothing.

"Is there an ice cream place on the beach?" I asked.

"I think so from what Mikey said, but let's go for a walk first," Carson suggested as we exited the car. I agreed and followed him, and we walked hand in hand to the beach sand.

The Florida beaches were different from Rhode Island's. The sand was more delicate and whiter than home's but still smelled of salt air and freedom. It was a beautiful night. We took off our shoes and walked the line where the waves would occasionally make their way up and tickle our feet. The stars above twinkled brightly over the tips of the ocean waves. It was so calming I hadn't noticed we'd been walking in silence for quite some time.

Carson stopped and pulled me close to his body. We stood face-to-face, inches apart.

"I'm glad we're finally alone," he whispered.

"Me too," I answered.

I noticed his hand was shaking.

"Are you cold?" I asked.

"No, just nervous," he said, and looked down at the sand.

At that very second, it hit me!

Oh, my God! Oh, my God! This isn't happening! What am I going to do? I haven't really thought about this! He's going to do it! He's going to ask me!

My heart was pounding, and my tongue was dry as a bone. I couldn't speak; I had lost control of my tongue, so I looked at him and waited. Usually, we stood almost eye to eye, but my feet had unconsciously dug a hole in the sand, leaving me eye level with his neck.

"You know how much I love you, right?" he asked as he lifted my chin to his eyes.

"Yes." *Stick with the one-word answers, Chris.*

"And you love me too, right?" he asked.

At this point in our lives, that should have been a rhetorical question.

Unless I wanted to be responsible for crushing someone's emotional confidence, this was no time to answer with "Kind of" or "Yes, but . . . ."

Why would that even cross my mind now? Of course I loved him! I did love him! But marriage? This was serious.

Did I have any justifiable reason to respond with a "No"?

So, why did I feel like Jiminy Cricket was on my shoulder, making me hesitate? It was probably just a bad case of nerves. Carson was more than any girl could ever want. He was cute, sweet, predictable, and dependable. There was no reason to say no.

"Yes. I love you very much," I answered.

"I've been a nervous wreck carrying this thing around all night," he said, pulling a ring out of his pocket.

"Will you marry me?" he whispered.

As the moonlight sparkled onto the swooshing waves, we stood facing each other, barefoot in soft beach sand, with a perfect Florida breeze cooling our warm bodies, and I knew the only plausible answer in this scenario, doubts or not, was yes.

"Yes," I answered, and he kissed me.

Most girls only dreamed about proposals like this. Why? *Why, God, do I not feel like this is heaven?*

Walking off the beach together, he shared how he'd partnered up with my friend Maria to help get the ring and how everyone else at dinner was also in the know.

I didn't remember the ride back to Mom and Dad's or even what I said when I got there. I only remembered waking up the next morning and looking at the ring that was my future.

1988 – twenty-three years old

Chapter 28

I walked out of our corporate office with a load on my mind. Most of my fellow colleagues had been laid off in recent weeks. Uptown had recently been purchased by a much larger chain of camera stores. Granted, I was definitely bored with what I was doing, but not knowing what would become of my future was admittedly unsettling.

I was one of five district managers in the company. District managers were also known as middle management, the easiest ones to do without. The new company had plans to bring in some of its own people, so recently promoted managers had been laid off along with most of the corporate office staff. Harry had been one of the first to go. I had to admit it'd felt a bit satisfying to hear that. Unfortunately, Maria, Missy, and Carson, my future husband, had been laid off too. I wasn't worried about Carson. He was so white collar he wouldn't have any problem finding a job.

Willard had been hired by the new owners to clean the place up. "Reorganize" was how they'd put it. He was strict, direct, vague when he needed to be, and heartless at times. Still, I sort of liked him. He was dressed in an expensive dark blue pin-striped suit, crisp white shirt, tie with tiny polka dots, and newly polished, tasseled penny loafers. And the glasses—what a stylish touch. Clever, even. If there was a perfect businessman catalog, he'd be the cover model.

The meeting was not unexpected, and I'd prepared myself to be axed, so to speak.

"Hi, Chris, sit down," he'd said.

We'd met in one of the larger conference rooms. Dark oval table, light-gray walls decorated with posters about success and determination. We'd sat facing each other. It hadn't been quite as intense as I'd anticipated.

He'd spoken first.

"I'm sure you know why you're here," he said.

I'd assumed I was losing my job, so I nodded in agreement.

"I like you. You're smart," he said, and stopped.

I sat, anticipating what I knew was the next word.

But.

"But I have a terrible job ahead of me." Again, he'd paused.

I spoke, "Yes."

"Just between you and me, I want you to know that out of the five district managers, I think you have the most potential, and given more time, I think you'd blow the other guys away. You have something that can't be taught. You have drive."

And again, I'd waited for the "but."

"But you're the only female district manager, you're single, you don't have any children, and you're a good ten years younger than the four remaining guys. Logically, you have to be the first to go."

I'd been shocked. I couldn't believe the reasoning.

"Logically?" I snapped.

"Hang on. I'm not done, and I'm being honest, but there's more. If the decision was up to me and I was one of the men who was going to run this new company, then you would stay right where you are and most likely move right up the corporate ladder. But I'm not. These new people don't know you. They see you as a number on paper. Young, female—you have plenty of time to begin again. It won't be so easy for others."

I'd interrupted him.

"You're serious, aren't you? What you're saying is I am losing my job because you think I can afford to, not because I'm not doing a good job? Did I really hear you correctly?" I'd been amazed.

"Calm down for a minute. I didn't have to tell you this. I could have lied, but I felt you deserved to know the truth, and I think I have a solution. I really put some thought into this." He'd sounded sincere, and I'd decided to hear him out.

"Okay," I said, waiting.

"The owners of Uptown Camera are keeping two stores. Two big ones, Greenwood and Oakdale, Massachusetts."

"Okay. Get to the point, Willard," I said sternly, but smiling.

"I would like to offer you a management position in either one of those stores. Your salary will stay the same as will your benefits. The only thing you'll lose is your company car." He'd paused, waiting for me to speak.

Part of me had been flattered, and part of me had wanted to tell him to shove it up his ass. I'd kept my cool.

"Do I have to decide this right now?" I asked.

He'd smiled. "No. Being that it's Friday afternoon, I suppose I could wait until Monday," he said.

"Thanks," I answered.

"I think I was right in being honest with you," he said sincerely.

"You were, and you didn't tell me anything I didn't really know deep down, but it's still mind-boggling to hear," I said, shaking my head.

"I'm sure it is. Whatever you decide, keep one thing in mind: never put yourself in a position where you can't go somewhere else and make more money. Please call if you have any questions. Unfortunately, I'll be here all weekend," he said, getting up, walking me to the door.

I hadn't quite known what that last comment meant, but I'd said, "Okay," anyway and left the office in a daze.

Women in the corporate world. Only there when they couldn't find another unqualified man to do the job. Nice.

I got in my car and turned the radio on for background noise. It was a twenty-minute drive from Wolfborough to Providence, and I had about twenty hours of thinking to do.

Achieving a district manager position was undoubtedly a fulfilling career goal, but it'd become dull and unchallenging. Did I want to be a store manager again? Financially, it might be a wise decision, but was that the direction I'd like my life to go? At twenty-four years old, maybe it was time for something more challenging. Something exciting.

By the time I arrived home, I had a thought, albeit far-fetched, but it was a thought.

Carson was there when I arrived.

"Hi. So, what's up, do you still work at Uptown?" he asked, anxiously awaiting answers.

I explained what had transpired.

"Do you want to be a store manager again?"

"No. Been there, done that. I want to work for my Uncle Jay in his club," I answered.

"You want to do *what*?"

"Remember on Thanksgiving when he shared stories about projects and aspirations he has for the club?"

"Yeah?" Carson answered, still in amazement.

"Well, maybe he has something for me to do. Like work in the office or something until I figure out what I really want to do with my life. I want a creative and exciting job," I said, knowing it made absolutely no sense at all.

"Um, okay, but isn't your uncle in Florida right now?"

"Yep! And if we fly there tomorrow, we can be back by Monday to give Willard my answer."

He didn't say anything for a second, then smiled, shook his head, and said, "Okay, this is totally absurd, but when do we leave?"

"Tomorrow afternoon. I have just enough money in my savings account to buy the tickets. This better work," I said.

I called my uncle shortly after Carson and I had spoken. Coincidentally, he was looking to make some changes in the club, so my timing was good.

Less than twenty-four hours later, we arrived at Uncle Jay's.

Walking into his trailer was a bit shocking. This wasn't a trailer! It might have looked like one on the outside, but it sure didn't on the inside. I wasn't even sure how he pulled it off, but this looked like a nice, full-sized home. Newly painted white walls, with a chandelier in the dining area, mixed with a touch of traditional southwestern cowboy here and there.

"Let's chat in the sunroom," he suggested, leading the way through a sliding glass door to a small screen-enclosed outdoor area.

A pitcher of iced tea sat on a glass-topped white metal coffee table. As he poured the tea, I noticed that he looked much bigger today for some reason. At six foot five, he was big enough, but he had grown wider too, and the authoritative tone in his voice made him bigger than life itself. Uncle Jay was like E. F. Hutton: when he spoke, you listened.

He smiled and sat back, running his hand through his curly brown hair. I didn't know a whole lot about Uncle Jay, but I did know one of his habits was unconsciously massaging his scalp.

After a moment's silence, he spoke.

"So, you want to be in the nightclub business?" He snickered and smirked.

"Yep," I answered, trying to sound totally in control.

I briefly reiterated what we had already discussed on the phone about my past at Uptown Camera.

"I want something new. I want to learn about your business. I'm willing to start anywhere," I said, reassuring him I wasn't expecting anything more.

Uncle Jay was the guy people went to when they needed financial help. Over the years, I had seen family members—including my parents—take advantage of him for money and material things. I never wanted to be that person.

"I think I've grown as much as I can with Uptown, and although they've offered me a new position and financial stability, I'm bored out of my mind. I'm not asking you to put me in an important position, I'm just asking you to let me work in some facet until I figure out what I am going to do with my life." I waited for his response.

"Well, I've been thinking about it since you called last night." He paused.

By the look on his face, he was more than a few steps ahead of me.

He continued. "I am having issues in a couple of areas, and I'd like to make changes. The image I have of The Diamond Mine is much more than it is now. As you heard on Thanksgiving, my partners don't exactly have the same vision as me.

"There's Terry. He's a good guy and a mathematical genius, but he's crazy. He doesn't want to know anything about what's going to happen, but he trusts me. All he needs each week is his paycheck. But then there's Earl. Earl's the stubborn one. Don't get me wrong, he's great, and he's my partner, but our ideas are different. He just doesn't understand. Now that I spend my winters in Florida, I'm away too long, but I don't want to be there all the time anymore either. That club's full of crazy girls!" He stopped just long enough to laugh.

"Twenty-five crazy girls with twenty-five hundred different problems they love to share with whomever will listen. I don't want to deal with that anymore." He paused again.

Carson and I sat there in silence, just listening. So far, it definitely sounded different from anything I had ever experienced. I was curious to know how I'd fit in.

"I have two big problems. One, I'm pretty sure one of my bartenders is stealing. I can't prove it, and he's a friend of Terry's, so it's hard to approach, but I've come up with a plan. I'm flying back home Monday morning. We have a meeting on Tuesday, and I'll tell them I need to do my niece a favor. I'll explain your work situation and tell them you are going to bartend for the bachelor parties. This way, you're not taking away anyone's shifts, and it will get you in the door. Eventually, I want you to take over Joey's shifts. Bartending shifts pay $50 each plus tips. We have at least three bachelor parties a week, and most of the time, more. How does that sound?"

Bartending?

"Uncle Jay, I don't know a thing about tending bar. Forget mixing a drink—I wouldn't even know how to pour beer!"

He smiled.

"Christina, you're only twenty-four years old, and you're the district manager of a major company. Most of my bartenders never finished high school. It'll be a piece of cake. I'll have Enzo teach you."

What was I getting myself into? A strip joint? Working for my uncle? With guys named Enzo? Was I out of my mind?

"When do I start?" I asked.

I could feel Carson's laser stare beaming into the side of my head.

"We have a party Wednesday night. Why don't you meet me there at noon, and I'll show you around," Jay said.

"Okay," I answered.

"Now for problem number two," he said.

Oh, no. Now what?

"Carson," he said in a direct sort of tone.

Carson?

"What about me?" Carson responded, trying to sound harsh.

"Well, I have an opportunity for you too." He laughed.

"Me?" Carson said, shocked.

And so was I.

"You're also out of a job, correct?" Uncle Jay asked.

"Yes?" Carson uncertainly answered.

"Well, the second problem I have is Greg. Greg manages the girls, but he's leaving in a few weeks. That's where I think I could use someone like you." He paused.

Carson? He wanted Carson to manage a bunch of strippers?

Carson laughed out loud.

"You can't be serious! Why me?" he asked.

Yeah. Why him? I wondered.

"Well, I know you have a business background, and you're supposed to be pretty good at what you do. After all, my niece was your boss." He smiled.

"I want people that I can train, people who know what *I* want The Diamond Mine to be. Educated people who haven't been in nightclubs their whole lives." He stopped, but I could tell he wasn't finished.

"Okay—I need a guy who doesn't want to sleep with the girls or do drugs with them. I need a guy who isn't going to let them run him. Do you think you can do it?" he asked very seriously.

There was a moment of silence.

Our lives were changing overnight.

"Jay, you just hit me with a ton of bricks!" Carson said, smoking his fifth cigarette since we'd arrived.

"Well, you've got to be better than the current manager. You have experience. You don't do drugs, and you're engaged to my niece, so if you sleep with any of those girls, I'd have to break both your legs," he half joked, trying to lighten the moment.

We both laughed, but I knew he scared the hell out of Carson.

"God, Jay, I don't know . . . ." Carson was still a little hesitant.

"Well, how about this," Uncle Jay said, looking at him as if he had left the best part for last. "The job pays $150 a shift, and you'd be working a minimum of eight shifts a week."

Holy cow! That was way more than he was making now!

Carson's expression changed dramatically. Again, he laughed out loud.

"I'd have to be a moron to turn down an offer like that. When do I start?" He smiled, holding out his hand to shake my uncle's.

"Well, I still have to talk to my partners, but I call all the shots when I have to. Greg's away for a week. Let's plan on Sunday, a week from tomorrow," Uncle Jay said, shaking his hand.

"Okay. I'll wait to hear," Carson said.

We got back on that plane, knowing that both of our lives would never be the same.

1989 – twenty-four years old

Chapter 29

I returned to Wolfborough on Monday morning, thanked Willard for the generous job offer, and respectfully declined. Carson followed me in his car and waited in the parking lot while I returned my keys, company credit cards, and, unfortunately, my company car.

No matter what was happening, I would always be grateful for this job. Who'd have guessed that this little company would've provided me a more real and in-depth education in business and functional life than any college education ever could?

I walked out of the home office and closed the door, leaving behind a place that'd been my home and security blanket for the last eight years. My insides were an emotional smorgasbord of sadness, emptiness, anticipation, and a big dose of fear because I'd just traded a secure, sensible career for a strip-joint bartending gig.

The club was not in the best section of Providence. I followed the directions precisely, exited the highway into an area of old, rundown triple-decker houses that used litter as front yard decor. The giant sign, painted with shadowed figures of sexy girls, appeared both out of place and yet appropriate in the ghetto-feeling neighborhood. The Diamond Mine, home of the 24-Karat Dancers.

I pulled into the parking lot of a concrete building with no windows. If it weren't for an old, worn-out Diamond Mine awning above the unmarked black door, the building could have easily been mistaken for a fallout shelter. There were a few cars in the lot; I assumed they belonged to office-type people.

Well, here goes. At least my uncle was meeting me at noon instead of nighttime when the place was open.

I opened the door, and everything went black while my eyes adjusted from the sun. When vision reappeared, I saw a man sitting just inside the entrance. He had dark hair, deep-set eyes, and a giant face and was wearing a silk button-down shirt, unbuttoned almost to his belly button, showing off his bulbous, hairy torso. He looked like he was wearing someone else's shirt.

"You Jay's niece?" he asked in a gruff voice while openly chewing parts of a meatball sandwich.

"Yes" was all I could muster up.

He took another bite of his sandwich and again answered with his mouth full. "Go down doze stairs." He pointed to a set of stairs to the right. "He's waitin' fo' ya." Then he returned his attention back to the meatball sandwich.

"Doze?" And people thought the Massachusetts people had weird accents!

I glanced at him just long enough to notice the sauce from his sandwich dripping down his arm. I didn't wait to see what he was going to do about it.

I turned to walk toward the stairway. So far, all of the walls were painted black and had begun flaking in several areas. In between the meatball guy and the stairwell was the smallest bar I had ever seen. Not that I'd seen a lot of bars, but this one was barely big enough for someone to stand behind. It leaned a bit to the right, was also painted black, and looked more like a depressing lemonade stand than a functioning bar. As I headed down the musty-smelling old carpeted stairs, the carpet stuck to the soles of my shoes, and I chose not to think about why. The only light I had as guidance was a dirty, yellow-tinged overhead bulb, probably from the dust and cigarette smoke. No fixture, just the bulb.

Should I turn back and forget about this insane idea? Nope, this was still less scary than passing the meatball guy again.

I came upon a long hallway that led to the left, so I turned and followed as if I was in one of those old, walk-through carnival haunted houses. The hall was narrow enough for me to touch each side with my hands to help lead that way. I slowly crept forward a few more feet and stopped near a closed door with lots of noise coming from the opposite side.

Should I go through this door? Gut instinct was yelling "No way!" I stood still for a second, noting an odd smell. It wasn't an everyday smell. My first impression was cheap sex, but how would I know what cheap sex smelled like? I decided not to open that door, instead focusing on another door straight ahead that was open just a few inches.

I stopped just shy of the slightly ajar door.

Well, it's either open the door all the way or stand there until someone notices you.

I gave the door a soft push. It opened to a woman standing on the other side. She looked like she might have been ready to leave.

"You must be Christina! Come on in, your uncle's in here too," she shouted.

I was relieved to find someone that seemed normal. My heart, which had been beating at the speed of light, began to slow back to normal. She was older than me, about forty or so, broad shouldered and tall, like Bea Arthur, but with short brownish-red hair.

"Hi," I said.

"I'm Lynette, your uncle's bookkeeper," she said.

"Nice to meet you," I answered.

I heard my uncle from around the corner.

"Christina, come on in."

He was sitting next to Lynette's books and paper-scattered desk.

"So, ready to tend bar tonight?" He smiled.

"I hope so." I tried to sound confident.

"I'll show you around, and then Lynette will have you fill out paperwork, okay?" he asked, getting up from his chair.

"Okay," I answered, and followed him out the door.

We walked back down the hall and stopped halfway at the door with all the noise behind it.

He pointed to the door but didn't open it.

"That's the dancers' dressing room," he said.

I guessed that explained all the noise, but I wondered why they were here so early. Did it take all day to get ready?

When we got to the end of the hall, he stopped and turned on a light. It looked like someone's basement that had been remodeled for college parties. There were tacky orange vinyl-wrapped metal banquet chairs around little black tables surrounding a beat-up large round stage of some sort. Off in the corner was a small room that appeared to be a bar, blocked with a bank-teller type window so no one could actually speak to the bartender. Weird.

"This is the bachelor-party room, where you'll be tonight," Uncle Jay began.

"The stage in the middle is where the dancers perform. They'll come out in pairs and dance a twenty-minute set, rotating through the four-hour party. Tonight, there are two parties, one right after the other. It's St. Patrick's Day, so it should be busy with all the commotion at the Civic Center."

"What's going on at the Civic Center?" I asked.

"It's the Final Four. College basketball playoffs; we'll be mobbed afterward. The second event is just a bunch of guys that wanted some privacy after the game. It's gonna to be like sah-dines upstairs," he said, walking over to the bar.

My speeding heartbeat returned. Maybe this wasn't a good idea.

"This is your bar tonight. Enzo is going to help you, but I don't think you're gonna have any problems. It's mostly Budweiser and shots. The waitresses will help too," he said, like it was no big deal.

Hadn't he heard me when I'd told him I had never been to a bar in my life?

I answered as if he was right. "Okay."

"Don't worry, you only have to serve the waitresses at this bar. I don't allow customers in our bar areas. That's why there's Plexiglass—it's a service bar only. I like my bartenders tending bar, not chatting with the customers. Time is money. The customers come here to see entertainers, and I want to keep it that way."

He sounded so no-nonsense. And why did he call everything his? Didn't this place belong to his partners too?

"Let's go upstairs," he said.

When we got to the top of the stairs, we were facing the little bar I'd seen upon entering the club. I assumed the messy dark-haired guy with wild-looking eyes in the dirty red T-shirt standing behind the bar was the bartender.

What was he doing here so early? And why was the music blaring? It was only a little past noon.

He glanced over, just long enough to notice us.

"Hey, Jay," he said, and quickly returned to his work.

Uncle Jay gave a quick wave to the guy and motioned me to follow him.

If it wasn't for the light from two pinball machines squeezed into an area on the right, I wouldn't have been able to see a thing.

We stopped at a big stage against another black wall.

I popped my head up when he started talking. I hadn't looked up until now because I'd been too busy focusing on where I was walking. It was so damn dark in here!

"This is my main stage, where the entertainers perform their shows."

When I turned to acknowledge what he'd said, I realized why it was so noisy.

The place was open—at noon—and there were heads all around the stage area.

As my eyes adjusted to the darkness, I noticed the heads had bodies.

This place was insane.

The stage was tightly surrounded with guys sitting in chairs, some eating lunch on the edge of the stage while watching the girls. I saw a girl on stage surrounded by randomly swinging arms waving dollar bills in the air as if feeding Milk Bones to a dog, all while they ate their lunches. This place was freakin' weird.

I glanced back at the stage just in time to see a little girl with big, floppy breasts backflip across the stage and finish with a split, just inches from some guy's face and meatball sandwich. He looked up, smiled, and shoved a dollar bill into a string around her waist. She smiled, made a squeaky noise, jumped back up, and bounced her way to the other side. Ironically, "Sweet Child O' Mine" was blaring while all of this went on.

What in the world had I gotten myself into?

I continued following my uncle, mostly for fear I'd be left behind.

"We have a free buffet Monday through Friday from noon to three. That's why we're busy. We've been featured in the *Rhode Island Gazette* for having the best lunch in town!" he said as he pointed to an article framed and hanging above the buffet.

Then he proudly continued with, "No frozen food here, and all of our dishes are made from scratch by our on-site chef."

My brain was internally hemorrhaging, so when he looked at me for confirmation, I just nodded, wondering what type of people wrote articles on a strip-joint food buffet. He led the way, though I lagged a few feet behind, momentarily distracted by a little old man at the buffet, spooning meatballs, sauce and all, into his pants pockets.

The thought of eating lunch in the dark, listening to blaring rock music while naked girls did splits in your face, was a little beyond my comprehension. Most of the men were drinking beer, but at this point, that was trivial.

We stopped at what looked like another stage, with a tall rectangular, phone-booth-style plexiglass structure in the middle. Just as my uncle began to speak, a bleached blonde snuck up behind him, said, "Hey," kissed him on the cheek, and jumped into the plexiglass contraption.

"This is the small stage. It also has a shower," Uncle Jay shared, like I knew what that was all about.

I stood still right next to him and watched as if this was a normal day.

The bleached blonde, wearing a skintight neon-pink dress, turned the water on and began dancing outside the shower stall while the water heated, creating steam and fogging up the walls. By the time the plexiglass room had filled with steam, the dancer was naked with the exception of a teeny triangle cloth covering her personal front area secured in place by a kite string tucked into her butt crack. I guessed that was considered covering your privates.

Once in the shower, she took the handle off the holder and proceeded to hose off the steam of one wall, smiling at the mesmerized guys watching her. If it wasn't so dark, I'd bet I'd have seen drool running down their chins. I almost laughed out loud.

Bizarre as it looked, she was funny, entertaining, completely aware of what she was doing, and doing it well. By the time she finished, I'd seen unimaginable things done with a showerhead. She was now thoroughly clean.

On the wall at the far end of the stage was a big sign that read "A new, bigger Diamond Mine coming soon."

We stopped at a room with a one-way glass window that allowed the person inside to see out, but no one could see in. Uncle Jay opened the door.

"This is Aaron; he's the DJ. Aaron, this is my niece, Christina. She's going to tend bar."

Aaron was nothing like I had imagined a DJ would be.

He looked like a complete nerd. Skinny, innocent looking, with a clean, never-been-shaved face.

"Hi, nice to meet you. Welcome to The Diamond Mine!" he squeaked as he extended his hand.

Wow, and his voice was so high. He seemed polite. I instantly liked him.

"Aaron and another DJ spin on the day shifts. With some training, Aaron will make a great DJ someday," Uncle Jay said, as if that meant anything to me.

He led the way back to the little office downstairs, past the noisy, sex-filled dressing room.

The office was now full of people.

"Christina, I'd like you to meet my partners," Uncle Jay said. "This guy over here, the one in a hurry to leave, is Terry." He laughed.

Terry wasn't anything like I had expected. Terry looked like a homeless guy, except cleaner and happier. He was wearing old powder-blue polyester pants made to look like jeans, a faded blue-and-white-striped pullover shirt, and a worn, tattered checkered linen baseball hat.

He spoke to the others as he left.

"Bye guys, I gotta get the fuck outta here. I'll call you from Florida."

As he passed me, he stopped and put out his hand for me to shake.

I extended mine.

"Hi, Christina. Any relative of Jay's is a friend of mine. Do you believe my kids are putting me on a fucking plane? Do good, okay?" he said, rushing out the door.

My uncle was right. He was crazy.

I looked up at him in disbelief, but he didn't say anything. Lynette, his bookkeeper, did.

"Don't mind him. He's nuts, but he's harmless." She laughed as if this type of thing was a regular occurrence.

"We'll see him back here by midnight. He's not getting on that plane. He's the only guy I know that tells the pilot to hold on when he gets out of a plane. He thinks it's a taxi, ya know," my uncle said to the others in the room, all laughing at the comment.

I smiled, but I really didn't understand.

When they calmed down, my uncle continued.

"This is Earl. Earl takes care of all the financial stuff around here."

He wasn't like any of the others.

"Hey, Christine, how-a-ya, kid, welcome to the family," he said, not looking directly at me.

I didn't like him. And it wasn't because he hadn't gotten my name right, even though I hated that. It was something more rooted than that . . . something not good. He wore a tacky, salesman-like tweed jacket with matching pants that would have turned anyone off. Maybe it was his squinty, beady little eyes or the blatantly fake kindness in the tone of his voice or that he didn't look me in the eye when talking.

I responded out of politeness. "Thank you."

As I attempted to get a grip on remembering names, another walked in.

He was almost as tall as my uncle and looked very tired and ragged, like Sasquatch after four days of not sleeping or bathing. But when he spoke, he sounded more like Mike Tyson.

"Earl, the bank's all set, okay? I'll be back tonight," he said after dropping a few slips of paper onto the table by Earl.

"Okay, Matthew, thanks, kid. Hey, Matt, this is Christine, Jay's niece. Enzo's going to work with her in the bachelor-party-room bar tonight," he said, pointing to me.

Matthew smiled. I felt terrible that he had to take what little effort he must have had left to say "Hi."

"Hi," I said quietly.

"If you have any questions tonight, you ask Matthew, okay?" Earl said to me. "He'll be back tonight."

When Matthew was gone, I waited for an explanation of why he looked so worn and tattered, but no one said anything. It was as if they hadn't noticed.

I spent the next half hour with Lynette. She explained what I had to wear and what I needed to bring with me and so forth. My brain was pretty full by the time I was done.

She was accommodating, and she seemed to get along with everyone. I got the feeling she kept them all together.

"Well, I guess you're all set," she said.

I guessed I didn't respond quick enough, as she followed with, "This place is a zoo." Lynette smiled. "Do you smoke?" she asked.

"No," I replied.

"Do you drink?"

"No," I replied.

"You don't do drugs, do ya?" she asked, concerned.

"No, never!" I answered.

"Well, with all the craziness around here, you'll be doing at least one of 'em by the end of the year," she said, as if it was a law.

Walking out of that office, I made a promise to myself that she was as far from right as she could be.

I left the building feeling like I'd walked out of the *Twilight Zone.*

Although I really hadn't known what to expect, the club wasn't exactly what I'd imagined. But I did know one thing: I might be entirely out of my element, but for whatever reason, I wasn't sorry I'd left my career behind. I was out of a real job, driving my fiancé's car, and mixing drinks for a bunch of hard-up guys, and for some reason, it was kind of okay with me. Maybe I was cracking up.

1989 – twenty-four years old

Chapter 30

I pulled back into the parking lot at six o'clock. The lot was full, and a few girls, who I assumed worked there, were carrying big bags into the club. A cab pulled up as I got out of my car.

"Thanks, Abe," a girl said, getting out of the cab.

I glanced over to see what kind of person knew a cab driver by name.

"You Jay's niece?" the girl from the cab asked in a raspy but friendly voice.

I turned to answer, but the shock of what she looked like silenced my ability to speak.

She was wearing a pair of outdated, skintight black satin pants, zippers up both sides, with creatively torn holes everywhere, though maybe not intentional. Up top, she had on an insanely wrinkled aqua-blue sweatshirt hanging off one shoulder. Probably wouldn't have looked nearly as disastrous if it had been washed recently. And that was only the beginning.

She looked as though she'd used an entire stick of eyeliner on her deep-set, teardrop-shaped brown eyes. Above the eyeliner on each eye was an uneven wad of metallic blue eye shadow. And I think she had keg of blood-red lipstick caked on her lips like kindergarten paste.

I had no idea how they didn't stick together when she spoke.

Her head looked like a failed attempt at a Make Me Pretty Barbie doll head that children put makeup on. Maybe she didn't have a mirror at home? I probably should've been afraid, but oddly enough, I wasn't.

"This is your first night, huh?" she asked.

She smiled, and almost everything disastrous out the outside disappeared . . . sort of.

Underneath all that garbage, she had an innocence about her that made me feel sorry for her. I looked past that awful makeup and saw a faint sparkle in her eyes, and as she smiled, her head tilted, like a dog who'd heard a kissing noise.

"Yeah, I'm working in the bachelor-party room," I answered, feeling pleasantly pleased I wasn't walking in alone.

"My name's Becky. What's yours?" she asked.

She was sweet, not mean like I had expected.

"Christina," I answered.

"That's a nice name." She nodded, thinking about it.

"Thanks."

Inside the door sat the same guy from earlier, still eating.

"Hey, Lenny," she said, having a tough time getting her heavy bag through the door.

He didn't even attempt to help her.

"Get down the stairs, ya lazy fucking tramp. Youz is all late tonight. Fuckin' figures," he said, making a kicking motion with his leg.

I followed Becky down the stairs, shocked at what I had heard.

"Who is that guy? And what's his problem?" I asked.

"Oh, that's Lenny. He watches the door. He's always like that, just ignore him," she answered, waving her hand in the air as if it was no big deal.

As she headed to the dressing room, she said, "Hey, good luck tonight. I'll come by and say hi, okay?"

"Thanks." I waved, heading to the bar to meet Enzo.

Enzo was behind the bar, cutting limes into little slices.

He looked to be a little younger than me, with dark, short, perfectly combed hair and dark eyes, and he was very physically fit. In short, he looked Italian.

He looked up and smiled.

Geez! Dimples too.

"Hey, how you doin'? Yaw Christina, right?" he asked.

"Good. And yes," I replied.

"This yaw first time in dis joint? Or did Jay show ya around first?" he asked.

He didn't exactly sound like I had pictured him, but he'd been polite so far.

"I was here this morning. Jay showed me around a little. Did he tell you I haven't got a clue about tending bar?" I asked, hoping he would still be nice after this.

"Ayyy, don't worry about it. Most of dese fools drink beer, and da ones that don't are so whacked out over dese girls day wouldn't even know if ya screwed up." He chuckled.

That wasn't the answer I had expected, but my nerves did relax a bit.

"So, did ya meet any of dese fuckin' nut-balls today?" He snorted.

The bizarre thing about him was that he was smiling through all of this. He wasn't being mean in any way. He made me giggle.

"Well, I met the owners and Lynette," I answered, with a little question in my voice.

He laughed out loud.

"Hah! Ya met da head nut-balls. Come on back hea', I'll show ya how to slice up dese friggin' fruits," he said.

I ducked under the counter and joined him.

We went over liquor names, how to pour beer, and several other things I forgot by the time the conversation finished.

"Hey, don't look so nervous. By the end of the night, it will be a piece of cake. Dis is the easy part. Dealing wit dose douchebags, that's the hah'd part," Enzo said, pointing to an almost naked girl heading our way.

Coming toward us was one of the oddest-looking girls I'd ever seen. Granted, until this moment, I hadn't seen a hell of a lot of almost-naked girls—but this?

She was about five feet tall. As she got closer, her short, bowed legs scampered faster than her head, while a ridiculously large chest jiggled and balanced precariously on top of the presentation. She literally walked like an ape.

She entered the bar as if Enzo was her best friend.

"Enzo!" she exclaimed in a high-pitched, insanely loud voice. "How ya been?" She held her arms out, waiting for a hug.

This itsy-bitsy girl in a miniscule bikini sure was friendly. Each boob, bigger than her head, hung almost to her belly button! Between the weight of her boobs and the absurd amount of gaudy gold she wore, I couldn't understand how on earth she was standing upright. Her body, tan everywhere that I could see, was like a tiny, thin, well-endowed monkey's. Very puzzling. But her face was pretty, like she was wearing someone else's head. The head had flawlessly applied makeup, high cheekbones, and a beautiful smile with perfect white teeth. The head looked rich.

Enzo didn't respond with the same enthusiasm, but he answered her, smiling and laughing.

"Ivy, ya big pig! Whaddya want?"

She kept up her "so glad to see you" look.

247

"Aww, stop teasin'. I just came over to say hi," Ivy insisted.

"Okay. Hi," Enzo answered, still waiting.

"Hey, how 'bout a shot of Dewers before I gotta go upstairs?"

Enzo snickered.

"How 'bout five bucks first?" Enzo snapped back, holding out his hand.

"Aww, come on. I haven't even been on stage yet! I'll give it to you later," she said, with a sad and innocent—though failing—puppy-dog look.

"How 'bout ya go and find that Jaguar-driving seventy-year-old sugar daddy of yaws, jerk him off for a few minutes, then come back wit da five dollars, and I'll trade ya a shot of Dewers," he said, very proud of himself.

She smiled and laughed as if it was just a joke, but I could tell there was some truth in it. She answered as she left the bar area, still laughing. "Fuck you, Enzo. I'll be back latah."

"Yeah. Ya do that." He laughed back, getting in the last word, which I imagined was something Enzo did often.

He looked at me again.

"That was Ivy. She's runnin' for president douchebag. Against dis one here," he said, pointing to a list on the wall of the bar.

The list consisted of names I'd never heard of like Chardonnay, Mercedes, Lady Rio, Black Widow, Chantel, and others. Some had been crossed out.

But the name he was pointing to was Bebe.

As vulgar as Enzo was, I still couldn't help but laugh at him.

"Who's Bebe?"

"Bebe is a perpetual pig. That girl does things that even dese sluts don't do. But da guys love her, and so does yaw uncle, so da rest of us deal wit her. Dis is da no-drinking list. Bebe on her own is bad enough, but Bebe mixed wit alcohol is fucking insane!" he answered quite seriously.

"A no-drinking list?" I asked.

"Oh, yeah. Dese' broads need to be watched constantly. Day're like X-rated kids, a breed of their own. And believe *me*, whatever ya do, don't let one of them talk ya into giving them a drink if day're on dis list. No mattah how much day offer ya."

Damn, they were worse than Gremlins.

"Okay," I answered.

"A few are on da list because day're under twenty-one, but most are dere because day're nuts," he explained.

"Not twenty-one yet?" I asked, wondering how someone that young could be in here.

"Oh, yeah! I think some of dese girls have been doing dis shit since day was in diapers. Don't let da age fool ya!" He shook his head.

He stopped talking long enough to look at his watch.

"Uh-oh, it's time for pigs on parade. You're in for a treat!" Enzo said, turning to a switch on the back wall of the bar.

Minutes later, a herd of guys stormed down the stairs, shouting vulgar things, sounding like they had already had a few. One guy even had a real bowling ball chained to his ankle. His T-shirt read "One last fling."

"Nice, huh?" Enzo said.

"Oh, yeah," I agreed.

A tall, thin girl came into the bar and handed Enzo a tape.

He took the tape and placed it into a deck on a shelf behind the bar.

"Oh, yeah. Did Jay tell ya that ya gotta be da DJ too?" he said.

"Huh?"

The girl spoke.

"Thanks, Enzo," she said, and then turned to me. "Hi, I'm Celena. You the new bartender?" she asked politely.

She wasn't at all like Ivy. In fact, if she wasn't standing in front of me in a silk robe, I'd have guessed she was a librarian.

She had the look of Upper East Side wealth, and she seemed a bit older than the other girls. She had long, long legs that made her look even taller than she really was. She wore an ankle-length opalescent silk robe, loosely tied in the front, covering up a beautiful piece of dark-green lingerie. She had a sense of class that the other girls didn't. Maybe because she didn't have massive fake boobs? In fact, she didn't have much on top at all. Celena was intriguing, with an educated, rich-sounding voice that conveyed "I am the classy one."

"Yes, I'm Christina. Tonight's my first night," I answered.

"She's already met Ivy," Enzo said.

Celena laughed as she walked toward the stage. "Ohhh, we're not all like that. The world couldn't take it," Celena said, as if reassuring us.

As the music began, Celena slowly climbed the stage stairs.

The song was called "Fever," and it was sexy.

"She's one of da nice ones," Enzo said. "I call her da human ostrich. Watch." He looked up to the stage.

I watched for a few moments and couldn't help but laugh. Enzo was right. It was her legs and the way she walked! She walked just like an ostrich! One long leg slowly extended out and stopped for a moment, and then the other slowly followed. Her toe hit the ground, and then she dragged herself to meet the other . . . and it started all over again. It was hysterical.

"She's nice, so I don't tease her 'bout it," Enzo said, sounding a bit human for the first time.

She was accompanied, a song later, by a very peculiar bag-ladyish-looking short dance partner. She obviously had spent little to no time on makeup or attire and had the smallest inset eyes I'd ever seen. I wasn't sure if they were actually open.

Why didn't someone tell her to comb that matted bleached-blonde hair? Enzo must have seen my amazement, as he put in his two cents.

"That—and notice that I said 'that'—is called Ezmay. It's amazing what years of acid can do. I don't go near her. I'm serious! If she's supposed to bring me a tape, I send her right back in that dressing room, tell her to get someone else! She's a walking friggin' disease," Enzo said, making a disgusted noise and expression.

I really couldn't blame him.

Somewhere during that last song, a waitress had entered the bar, but it didn't completely register in my head because even though my eyes had seen her enter, my brain was still on . . . whatever it was on stage.

At one point, Ezmay bent down to touch the floor, trying to—what one could only assume—look sexy. But she got stuck!

She stayed in the stuck position for a while, hands touching toes, as though the position was intentional. Finally, due to gravity, her legs bent, and her butt hit the floor. She smiled, spun around, and proceeded to gather money from guys who didn't care what she was doing as long as she was topless.

When that little episode was over, the waitress placed her order.

"I'll take seven Buds, three Lights, and a Jack 'n Coke," she rattled off.

I noticed that she hadn't written any of it down; it was all from memory.

"I would have ordered earlier, but that was just too funny," she said, pointing to Ezmay.

Just before Ezmay got off stage, a vampire-looking girl wearing a floor-length black-and-red-cape draped over a skimpy, skintight black dress, wrist bound with a boa-constrictor-sized leather whip, entered the bar. She handed Enzo a tape and walked toward the stage.

Once on stage, she snapped the whip on the floor. The room went completely silent, then all the guys instinctively howled like dogs and waved fists in the air as if there'd been a Christmas miracle.

I looked at Enzo with curiosity.

He held out his arms and smiled. "Welcome to Da Diamond Mine."

1989 – twenty-five years old

Chapter 31

I was making over a thousand dollars a week tending bar, and I'd saved more money in the past three months than I'd ever been able to at Uptown Camera.

I was really enjoying my new pseudo career, but Carson wasn't having as much fun. He said trying to handle a bunch of strippers was harder than house-training a hundred puppies. Carson and Enzo both thought the girls were a bunch of pigs. In some ways, they might be right, but the girls were also naive, human, funny, and not nearly as complicated as Carson thought.

I'd been working a few night shifts upstairs on the main level bar because Uncle Jay had fired the daytime bartender for stealing. Friday nights were my favorite because they were crazy!

The dancers' night shift started at six thirty, bartenders' at six, so I'd see them all file in.

One by one, I was getting to know each dancer and learning more than I'd ever imagined whether I wanted to or not. The dancers and I, possibly because I was the only other female working in the club that wasn't a dancer or a cocktail waitress, were forming a unique bond. The cocktail waitresses and dancers did not mix, like it was an underground stripper law or something.

Ivy usually arrived late and left, via sneaking out the side door, just before last call. If it was a slow shift, she either got a headache or an emergency call, causing her to conveniently have to leave early. She was a piece of work, to say the least.

Ezmay only worked day shifts or bachelor party nights and didn't drink alcohol. Instead, she opted for drugs. Like, all of the drugs. At once.

Elise, a beautiful dancer, should have been on Broadway, not in a strip joint. She danced to old classic tunes with the grace of an Olympic ice dancer. She stood about four feet ten with a perfect Barbie-doll body, long, thick golden hair, and a sweet personality . . . unless she was drunk. Elise was on the no-drinking list.

Tonight was Friday, so almost everyone worked.

Cherry and Bebe entered the club, duffle bags dragging behind.

"Fuck off, Lenny! I hope y'all's dick falls off next time you hafta touch it!" Bebe screamed as she walked in the door.

Bebe and Cherry were best friends and danced as a pair. Both had long bleached-blonde hair. I was pretty sure Cherry had never attended high school. She stood about five feet seven and weighed about a hundred pounds, most of it boobs. The guys called her "Tits on a Stick."

Bebe was a horse of a different color altogether. She was Ivy's nemesis. Prior to Bebe's arrival, Ivy had been top girl. Bebe was a Texan with a strong Southern drawl. The energy in the club changed when Bebe got on stage. She stood about five feet, six inches and had an average chest size with a perfect, naturally curvy body and an ass like God had created just that one. Bebe was double-jointed and, when younger, had practiced gymnastics. Her stage act consisted of backflips, contortionist moves, and zero morals. As far as the guys were concerned, Bebe was perfect!

But unlike Ivy, Bebe was likable, and when she wasn't drunk, she was sincere. Ivy danced because Ivy was greedy and it was an easy way to make lots of cash. I wasn't sure why Bebe danced, but I didn't think it was because she wanted to be rich.

"Ch-riiii-sssss?" Bebe asked as she came up to the bar.

I had no idea how she could make my name sound like it was three syllables.

"Yeah, Bebe?"

She looked horrible, like she'd been up for days, with matted, uncombed hair and not an ounce of makeup. I'd have thought someone had beat her up, but she didn't have any visible marks.

"Where's Jay?" she asked.

"I have no idea. I haven't seen him yet tonight," I replied, still wondering what she wanted or needed.

Before she could say anything else, another dancer approached the bar. The bar was a parade of half-naked girls during shift change.

I'd seen this dancer a few times before but didn't know who she was.

She pushed Bebe aside with her elbow.

"Give me a Seagram's and tonic, and don't put a lemon on it. I hate that shit," she insisted.

She'd never introduced herself and was always, for some unknown reason, in a bad mood. She was an itty-bitty cross between an evil Billy Idol and a pissed-off David Bowie. Needle-spiked bleached-white-blonde hair, extremely sharp cheekbones, lots of eye makeup, a ton of blush, and always fashionably dressed. She paid for her drink and left. Sometimes she tipped, and sometimes she didn't.

As she was leaving, Bebe put her two cents in. "Have a nice night, Lizard."

"Lizard?" I asked.

"Yeah. That's what we call her. She's just a bitch, don't mind her. Got some damn stick up her ass or somethin'. Ch-ri-ssss, can you ask yer uncle to take me off the no-drinking list? I can't dance if I don't drink," she said, almost in tears, leaning on the bar as if it was literally the only thing holding her up.

"I'm not sure where he is, Bebe, but you seemed happy when you were on stage."

She looked at me and snickered before she whispered back to me.

"That's cuz I keep a bottle of vodka in my locker. Shhhhh. Don't y'all go tellin' yer boyfriend, though! But I didn't have no money today, so I couldn't buy one on my way in, and the fuckin' cab driver wouldn't even lend it to me. Bastard. I've given him so much money for all them rides. I even offered to blow him, and he told me to go to hell. Asshole." She sighed.

I didn't know how to respond to that, so I didn't. I was relieved to see a waitress with a drink order and hoped Bebe would disappear when she figured I was too busy for this little scene.

"I'll have a Jack and Coke, three Alabama slammas, a slow comfortable screw up against the wall, thirteen Buds, and five Lights." She rattled it off and stood there, not even acknowledging Bebe.

I made the drinks, laughing to myself, thinking not only was there a drink called a slow comfortable screw up against the wall, but I also actually knew how to make it. The things ya learn.

The waitress paid and left. Bebe remained.

"Yer boyfriend doesn't like us, Ch-ri-ssss. He makes me feel bad," she said.

"Why do you say that, Bebe?" I asked.

"Cuzzz he treats us different. And when we all go near him, he swats us away like we're flies or somethin'. He barks orders at us and doesn't even listen to our problems," she said with such sincerity in her voice she made me feel bad.

She went on talking. "I tried to buy drugs off of him, and he didn't have none—not even pot. Asshole!" She laughed. "And he won't take bribes for anything! I've tried paying him to miss my set and go home early, and I got nothin'! I know he's just doin' his job, but he really doesn't like us. We have feelings, ya know."

I didn't know what she wanted me to say or do. I knew Carson didn't like the dancers, and I even liked that about him. But I felt for her.

I'd only been there a short time, and it didn't take a genius to figure out that dancers weren't exactly regular folk, but they weren't exactly what they appeared to be either. In fact, they were the epitome of the phrase "don't judge a book by its cover," and most went out of their way to be kind. The majority of the dancers overcompensated in search of acceptance, just hoping for a sincere response. It was difficult and sad to watch it in action.

This building was a world within itself, encompassing two completely different ongoing, coexisting reality shows. One occurring outside the dressing rooms, featuring girls looking to be ogled at by guys needing to ogle them as if their lives depended on it. And then other, occurring backstage with the day-to-day uncensored lives of those featured stage girls.

I enjoyed working here. In fact, I loved it.

I was learning, albeit a bit more up close and personal than I would have chosen, why these girls had ended up where they were today.

They didn't all become strippers because they abused drugs or alcohol. In fact, it was the other way around. They abused drugs and alcohol as an escape from whatever they couldn't deal with in everyday life, and as a result, stripping seemed like a feasible financial option.

In some ways, it was a harsh reality check of what might have become of me if I had lacked inner strength and the ability to compartmentalize.

Once home from work, I tried to explain to Carson what Bebe had shared with me and how she felt about him, but I couldn't get my point across without going into my own horrible personal experience. I wondered why I hadn't shared *that* with

Carson. He was to be my future husband, my life partner, yet I still couldn't bring myself to tell him.

If I thought about it, I'd probably be more comfortable sharing my secret with a stripper than with Carson.

I was beginning to sound like a crazy person.

The day shifts were much calmer than the night shifts. The daytime clientele was a quirky conglomeration of construction workers, suit-and-tie businessmen, and a bunch of what I referred to as the "others." The others consisted of physically or mentally disabled guys and a few real freaks, though in all honesty, the creepiest and scariest bunch, by far, was the suit-and-tie businessmen. Most of them made my skin crawl.

The construction workers were best described as "what you see is what you get." They were boisterously loud but relatively harmless.

There were a few mentally disabled daily regulars. Today was Dicky's regular day. Dicky was mentally impaired, and it was visually obvious as soon as he made contact, but he was always happy and quite comical. Some of the others were hard to identify.

Dicky was big, round, and somewhat misshapen and dressed the same every day. Tan polyester pants pulled up too high, leaving a wide gap between the hemline of his pants and his sneakers, seemingly to show off his white tube socks.

He exuded a perpetual high-level jolliness, like one of Santa's helpers who had gotten lost, now looking to reform a new gang. What was left of his gray hair was always disheveled, and he never left home without his late-seventies satin Red Sox jacket. He wore that jacket through hot and dry, cold and wet, snow and sleet. It didn't matter, as the jacket and Dicky, along with his 1970s-style, high-top Keds sneakers, had become one.

Dicky was precariously heading toward the bar, arms waving in the air with the excitement of a first-place marathon runner about to cross the finish line: running, sweating profusely, yelling, and expelling spit like a lawn sprinkler.

"Where's Saphire? Where's Saphire?"

I wiped the spit off the bar, choked back a gag, and answered, "Dicky, we just opened. Saphire is probably in the dressing room."

"Can you get her? Can you get her? I hafta give her my present! She's my girlfriend. Nobody else's. Just mine! Can you get Saphire now? She's my girlfriend. I hafta talk to her."

The man was clearly on a mission.

Carson was heading toward us, and I motioned to him from the bar. He saw Dicky and started to laugh.

As soon as Dicky spotted Carson, he ran, explaining his issue all over again. Dicky knew everyone's name and job responsibility and was well aware that Carson was his direct contact to Saphire. Dicky knew the important stuff.

Minutes later, Saphire appeared from the dressing room, acting as though she'd spent the entire morning thinking about Dicky. His eyes lit up as if he was experiencing a miracle. Saphire hugged him, kissed him on the cheek, and sat at table with him. He was in heaven.

Dicky and Saphire had a strange relationship. His entire life revolved around her. He lived in a group home paid for by the state. He received a biweekly paycheck from a job he did within the home, and upon each payday, he'd come running into the bar with a gift for Saphire. Sometimes he brought his paycheck, and Saphire would cash it for him with tips she'd made on her shift, and then Dicky would fork over that money, dollar by dollar, right back to her on stage.

Saphire wasn't overly pretty nor ugly. She was stocky, mixed with a subtle dose of femininity, and like many other dancers, bleached-blonde hair. She lived in Newport with her real boyfriend, whom she complained about daily. Saphire's parents were from Greece. Her mom had passed away when she was young, and she had grown up with a strict father that hadn't allowed her to date until she was twenty-one. Her dad believed she was a waitress at a fine-dining restaurant in Providence. If he only knew.

Saphire walked up to the bar with a pair of earrings in one hand and Dicky's check in the other.

"Hey, Chris, can I get a Long Island iced tea?" she asked in her usual raspy voice.

I noticed the earrings were the clip-on type you saw at the ninety-nine-cent store.

"Sweet!" I said, and smiled, knowing we both knew what I meant.

"It's the thought that counts!" she answered back with a sarcastic smirk.

"And you're nice enough to cash his check too! What a fine girlfriend you are."

Saphire had a great sense of humor—dry and very witty.

"Nice enough? Hah! Fuck that. This check is for a hundred bucks, and I'm gonna give him eighty. Then he's gonna spend the next few hours buying me drinks and giving me tips. This is work, honey. It ain't supposed to be nice."

Before I had a chance to respond, she dropped me a ten-dollar tip for a six-dollar drink, backed away from the bar, posed to show off her microscopic bikini, lifted her glass as if to toast, and said, "It ain't easy bein' sleazy!," then waved good-bye and headed back to the dressing room.

I shook my head in indecision. Was she doing a bad thing or a good thing? Saphire was happy taking Dicky's money, and Dicky was happy because Saphire showed him the affection he would never otherwise see.

I laughed to myself, thinking, *Dear God, I think she's right.*

1989 – twenty-five years old

Chapter 32

Construction workers celebrated rainy days much in the same way that children celebrated school cancelations. But instead of parking themselves on the sofa to watch cartoons, they headed to The Diamond Mine.

By 1:30 p.m., the club was filled with hundreds of lively guys celebrating as if on holiday. Regular customers and businessmen tended to sit at the bar or a table and wait for a cocktail waitress. Construction workers entered as if debarking a plane for spring break, but despite a room full of scantily clad girls and buckets of booze, they made a beeline for the buffet. Food first, then fun.

The pace of a rainy day was like working retail at Christmastime: fast and profitable. I was trying to catch up and wash glasses as another large group of construction guys loudly piled in, expressing their appreciation of a bonus day off. I smiled, watching them find their way to the food, organizing themselves in single file as if buffet-line etiquette was internally programmed.

I looked up and did a double take. Then I closed my eyes and inhaled. I reopened them, hoping I'd just imagined I'd seen that damn high school sweetheart that kept spontaneously dropping into my life. But nope, no such luck.

What in the world was Luke doing in this place?

He was the last person I wanted to see here. Or maybe it was the last place I wanted Luke to see *me* in. So much had happened since we'd sat in his truck, swapping life stories.

Maybe if I squatted my body down just shy of the bar top, he wouldn't see me.

"I need a gin and tonic, a seven and seven, and four Buds," a cocktail server ordered.

I tried to keep myself hidden as I prepared her order.

She pointed over her shoulder as she spoke, "Hey, that guy over there keeps asking me questions about you. Do you want me to answer him or just tell him to fuck off? He's kind of cute."

I answered, attempting to sound nonchalant, "Tell him if he has any questions, he can ask me himself."

Snapping her gum, she nodded and walked away.

I watched her give him the info. He smiled, got up, and headed toward me.

Oh, crap.

He was like a bad penny. Or was he a good penny? I didn't know anymore.

"Well, you're the last person I thought I'd ever see in a place like this!" Luke said, smiling and laughing.

I looked at him and replied, "Ditto."

Luke continued, "I had no choice. I'm not driving today, and this is where the guys wanted to have lunch. Who am I to complain? The food's great!"

Out of the corner of my eye, I saw my uncle approach the bar. He laughed when he saw Luke. Uncle Jay knew most of our history and loved to tease.

He also knew Luke and his dad, as they had done all of the club's excavation work. My guess was Uncle Jay probably knew more than I was aware of.

"Luke! How's everything?" Uncle Jay asked.

"Good, Jay. Where'd you find her?" Luke asked, pointing toward me.

"Ahh, I stole her," he said teasingly, looking at me. "You want a short break? I'll hang around and watch the bar for a few minutes."

"Um, okay," I replied.

My legs were wobbling like a newborn colt's. I thought I was going to faint. Why did Luke make me so nervous?

Those unsteady legs walked me outside to the parking lot, and I leaned myself against one of the dancers' cars, face-to-face with Luke.

He started. "Okay. I gotta ask. How in the world did you end up here? And I hear congratulations are in order too?" Luke said, smirking, referring to my engagement.

I took a deep breath and answered.

"Well, I don't really know where to begin. Uptown Camera got bought out, and everything was changing. I was bored with my job anyway, so I had the bright idea to call my uncle. Next thing I know, I'm tending bar at a strip joint. So far, I like it here, and I'm making a lot more money. Go figure." I paused, looking up at him, subconsciously remembering how easily those blue eyes made my insides melt.

"And?" he asked, eyes sparkling as he smirked.

I knew what he meant. I hadn't mentioned Carson or the engagement. I'd been hoping he would let it slide, but Luke was having too much fun with this situation.

"And . . . thanks for the congratulations?" I answered, smiling.

Before he could say anything else, I started again.

"Hey, did you see my new truck?" I asked, pointing to the white Ford Ranger in the lot.

I walked toward it, sharing every detail about the truck I could come up with, including a few things I was pretty sure I made up along the way to keep the deflection going.

He didn't say a word. He just kept smiling at me, almost laughing. He was thoroughly enjoying every second.

We walked back to the club entrance in silence. Just before we got to the door, Luke put his hand on my shoulder and stopped me.

My heart was in my throat.

"Thanks for the chat about the truck. Rumor has it you're getting married in April next year. I'll plan on seeing you shortly after your divorce, and we'll take it from there, because we both know we're going to end up together," he said with a bit of arrogance and a lot of conviction.

"Well, that's all kind of presumptuous! What makes you so sure of yourself, Mr. Moretti? Divorced? You don't even know the guy. A bit rude, don't you think?" I snapped at him.

"Rude, maybe. Presumptuous? Not really. In fact, I would say there's a ninety-nine-percent chance that I'm correct. I just sat through a ten-minute conversation about your truck. Not even one word about your future husband. If I were you, I'd do a little more thinking about *that* situation."

He looked directly at me when he spoke.

"Trust me, I'll see you soon." He stopped talking, kissed me on the forehead, turned, and walked inside.

I followed a few feet behind, mumbling words under my breath as I entered the club.

Who did he think he was! Definitely more outgoing and way more confident than I remembered. He made me so mad!

I spent the rest of the afternoon angrily replaying the conversation in my head again and again. But the more I thought about it, the more my anger faded, only to be replaced with fear. And fear was worse than anger.

Dear God, Luke was right! I hadn't mentioned Carson or the wedding, but I didn't think it was because of Luke. Come to think of it, I never really thought about the wedding at all.

I laughed at myself.

Even when we spoke of the wedding, I referred to it as "it." Mom and Carson had driven me crazy about setting a date. They were so excited that I didn't have a chance to say much of anything. Before I knew it, April 7, 1990, would be here. I was less than one year away from being married. Married.

I *had* to be in love, right? I couldn't believe I was actually having this conversation with myself! Why did seeing that man get me all messed up?

My uncle interrupted my thinking.

"How are you doing?" Uncle Jay asked as he leaned against the bar.

I could tell he was on some sort of mission, because his eyes twinkled when he had something up his sleeve.

"How's Luke?" he asked.

Oh, boy. Here we go.

"Fine," I answered simply.

"That's all? Just fine?" Uncle Jay asked, prodding for information.

"Yes. That's all," I answered, keeping it simple.

"You sure?" he asked, still smiling but looking concerned.

Huh. I'd never really had someone, or at least someone related to me, sincerely care about how I felt. It threw me off guard a bit.

"Yes. I'm sure," I answered, thinking I was probably lying to myself.

"I have an idea . . . ," Uncle Jay said.

"About what?" I asked, having no clue where he was headed.

"Your job," he answered.

Oh, no! Was I not doing a good job?

"What about my job?"

"Well, I've been watching you and Carson for the last few months, and I think I made a mistake," Uncle Jay shared.

Oh, great, we were both getting fired!

"And . . . ?" I whispered, more to myself than to him.

"I think you should switch jobs. I'll have Carson tend bar and you manage the girls and a few other things," he said, as though it was no big deal.

"What?" I replied.

"I've already spoken to Carson. He seems relieved," Uncle Jay said with a laugh.

I smiled. I knew Carson didn't really like working with the girls. It just wasn't for him.

"What exactly do you need me to do?" I asked.

"Well, as you know, it's managing the girls, so basically scheduling and making sure they're behaving . . . although I'm not sure anyone's capable of that." Uncle Jay laughed.

"I never thought I'd consider putting a girl in charge of the dancers, but now that I've seen your work ethic, I'm pretty sure you're capable of that and handling the advertising and marketing end of this business. I'm juggling too much, with all of the construction and whatnot. I need someone I can rely on when I'm not here. You know, keep an eye on things, make sure everything is running smoothly. There are some things a manager can do that an owner can't, if you get my drift. And you don't take any shit from anyone—including me!" Uncle Jay laughed again, assuming I was taking all of this in without hesitation.

It was a lot of information to comprehend at once. I wasn't even sure I could do the job. In fact, I had no idea why *he* thought I could do it, but he seemed fine with his decision.

"So, what do you think?" Uncle Jay asked after an awkward moment of silence.

"Who's going to be my boss?" I asked, wondering if I had to work with Earl, the partner who made me feel uncomfortable.

"Well, technically all four of the owners, but in reality, just me. I'm the only one who has the wherewithal to develop this into an A-level entertainment complex. Plus, if you don't listen to me, I'll tell your mother!" he teased, trying to lighten the moment.

I laughed too. Uncle Jay had a way of making me feel at ease, and I was gaining respect for him as our relationship continued to develop.

1989 – twenty-five years old

Chapter 33

I parked my truck and said good-bye to the beautiful summer morning, as that'd be the last glimpse of sun I'd see till tomorrow. Once inside, it was pretty much a fallout shelter.

There could be a hurricane outside, and everyone inside The Diamond Mine would be oblivious, nor would most care.

The dancers' dressing room, roughly ten feet by fifteen feet, was more like a large walk-in closet. The walls, covered in decades of peeling paint, had been touched up with countless layers of vulgar, sexually graphic graffiti I'd thought only existed in men's bathrooms. The room had the ambiance of grade school recess, though instead of children, we had colorfully profane, lewd naked women.

Calmly gathering twelve overly vocal alpha-female girls, carrying twelve bags of clothes and twelve makeup cases into a cramped space at ten in the morning, went about as smooth as tossing a fork in a blender.

"Any of you bitches got a tampon?" I heard one of them yell.

"Tampon! Hah! If I had a pussy like yours, I'd be looking for a dryer hose!" Saphire responded jokingly.

"Fuck you with my brother's dick," Randy yelled back.

Emerald, petite, polite, and beautiful, like she'd popped off the cover of *Cosmopolitan* magazine, handed Randy a tampon.

At nineteen, Randy could easily pass for a twenty-five-year-old. Randy was an original package. She stood about five feet ten, bleached-blonde hair and a knockout body—and she could literally knock you out! I had never met a girl that could punch like Randy. I'd come to the conclusion that she'd been raised by wolves. She lived with her dad, and I wasn't sure there'd ever been a mom in her life. She drove a 1968 metallic-blue Corvette Sting Ray. Randy never possessed a legal driver's license. She said there was no need to go through that "bullshit" because in her town of Fall River, Massachusetts, most of the cops knew her anyway and any problem could be fixed with a blow job. She had a vulgar vocabulary, zero manners, and fewer morals than the Devil himself. As crazy as it was, that aside, a naive little girl occasionally surfaced and made you feel for her. I liked her—a lot.

There was so much commotion, the girls hadn't noticed I'd walked into the room.

"Morning, ladies," I said.

And then a different type of chatter began.

"Chris, Randy's being a pig!" someone shouted.

"I ain't being no pig, I just needed help, was all," Randy responded.

"Somebody stole my red G-string, and they better give it back!" Cherry whined.

Brandy, who'd just arrived, still disheveled, bags in hand, shouted, "Girls, I gotta tell you about the sex I had last night!" Because, obviously, everyone would be interested.

Bebe pointed at Brandy and shouted, "There's y'all's damn G-string, stickin' right the hell outta Brandy's bag, oiled up and all."

"What the fuck! Brandy, why ya always gotta be greasin' everythin' up with that damn baby oil?" Cherry grabbed the red G-string out of Brandy's bag.

Brandy just laughed and responded, "That's cuz I'm one slick mutha fucka!" She slapped her own ass as if a visual was needed.

I was about to put a halt to the more than usual chaos when Ezmay tumbled in the door and silenced the entire room.

It was evident that she had not looked into a mirror in days. One side of her short, uneven, straw-like bleached-blonde hair was bedhead-matted down, and the other looked as though she'd stuck her finger in an electrical socket. She was wearing an outfit that appeared borrowed, as nothing properly fit at all, with 1960s-style leather sandals, unbuckled and on the wrong feet. Behind her dragged a wet, overstuffed old work bag full of God-knew-what.

Ezmay stopped and looked up at us as though she had done something wrong.

"Sorry I'm late. I got raped again last night," she said, as if that was a typical excuse for tardiness.

She wasn't even late; her appearance was so mind-boggling it had stopped time itself.

Before I responded, I looked back at the girls in the dressing room, and the reaction was priceless. No one had the same expression. I saw Brandy slap herself on her face and fake a fainting spell on a chair. Saphire got out a small notepad as if she was a detective about to take down full details. Celena didn't react all at. She just went about getting ready as if Ezmay didn't exist.

Ivy responded with, "Damn drugged-out hippie."

Then Bebe spoke and made everyone laugh, but I didn't get the joke.

"Ezmay, you get fuckin' raped every night. Either git used to it or git over it."

"Bebe!" I yelled, as if I was scolding a two-year-old. "Be nice!"

"Chris, y'all don't understand. We all're used to it. She says that at least once a week. We all used to feel bad, and then one night we followed her and found out she's just a crazy, hallucinating druggie. We ain't being mean or nothin'," Bebe explained.

I looked at the girls for their reaction, and all of their expressions agreed with Bebe.

Ezmay had listened to the whole conversation and acted as if she hadn't heard a word, carefully putting the contents of her bag into her locker as if each piece had been professionally dry-cleaned.

"Morning, girls," my uncle said, popping his head in.

Everyone responded as if their favorite teacher had entered the room.

"Christina, can I come in late on Saturday?" Desi asked, knowing that Jay was still in the doorway and obviously looking for him to grant her the exception.

There was something about Desi that I did not like at all. She had a fakeness about her that superseded her adorableness. She was petite, looked like the innocent girl next door who always did what Mommy and Daddy asked of her, with big brown eyes, curly, silky dark-brown hair, and a cute, smooth little body. Whenever Desi asked a question, she'd bat her eyelashes as if there was no way in hell anyone would let *her* sweetness down. Behind those eyes was a clear message saying if she did not get her way, she would do everything in her power to make you regret it.

"Desi, why do you need to come in late?" I asked politely.

"Well, I have to get up early and go to the bank, then I have to go shopping, then I have to get an abortion, and then I have to go back to the bank again. But I don't want to miss an entire day, so I want to come in late," Desi explained, as if the request was commonplace.

I looked up at my uncle staring blankly into my eyes, waiting for my response.

I had no idea what to say, so I answered as if this insane conversation was typical. "What time can you come in?"

"I can be here by 2:00 p.m.," Desi answered, smiling, knowing she had just gotten her way, and that was all that mattered.

"Okay. I'll make a note on the schedule," I answered.

Just as I finished the sentence, I felt my uncle kiss me on the head and whisper, "You're gonna do just fine." He smiled and left the room.

I must have looked baffled, because Celena looked at me and responded as if I'd asked her a question. "Don't worry. We're not all like that."

"Fuck, no! I've had nine abortions, and there's no way you'd see me here the same day!" Randy snapped, lying on her back, lifting her legs over her head and into a G-string like she was getting dressed in a room all by herself.

"This is The Diamond Mine, Christina. We might not be normal, but we sure aren't dull." Celena shook her head.

"You can't make this shit up. No one would believe it." I smiled.

"Aww, come on. Admit it. You like us!" Saphire said.

I looked up, realizing I'd said that last sentence aloud, and smiled.

"We like you too. We like having a girl for a boss. We don't need a guy in here tellin' us what to do. We wanna make money and git the hell out of here," Bebe said, sounding more mature than expected.

All of the other girls spoke at once, agreeing with Bebe. On my way out of the dressing room, I posted the daily dance schedule on the wall, but not before someone got in one last remark.

"Hey, Chris. You're looking pretty happy today. Did you get some last night?"

And the teasing began, coming from all directions. I didn't even look back to see who was saying what.

"Hey, that means Carson got some, too."

"Hey, boss lady, we want full details!"

"Hey, how is Carson in bed?"

"Screw that! I want to know how you are!" someone screamed.

I just waved my hand as I closed the door, listening to a room full of laughter. Naked or clothed, girls would always be girls.

And I liked these girls. I felt I could relate to them even more than my former co-workers at Uptown Camera. Here in this club was a sense of raw honesty that hadn't existed at my other jobs. Or even in the outside world in general. Sometimes, society taught us all the wrong things.

***

"Christina, you really need to start looking for a wedding dress. Christmas is just around the corner. April 7, 1990, isn't far away," Mom said impatiently.

"I think she's gonna wait until the week of the wedding. It's not all that important," Carson said sarcastically.

Carson and I, along with Mikey and Gabriella, were visiting my parents for dinner. We had moved shortly after the missing-money incident into a townhouse in Smithfield, RI, not too far from the city. It was a quiet country town, completely opposite of the chaos of Federal Hill.

Wedding planning was overwhelming, and I'd found the best way to deal with it was procrastination. I'd rather stick kabob skewers in my eyes than spend days doing girlie wedding things with my mother and grandmother. I knew I was not capable of sharing my fear of marriage with my mother or Carson. As far as I was concerned, going through with the wedding was the lesser of two evils, even though the lesser of two evils was still an evil.

I had to be a complete idiot for not wanting to marry Carson. There was absolutely nothing wrong with him! He was good looking, kind, and incredibly thoughtful, and I'd never have to worry about bills or financial security. Carson was Mr. Organized. If he could, he'd reorganize the word "organize" so it'd be spelled in alphabetical order. Carson was nothing like me.

This wedding had everyone operating at an unacceptable level of excitement, like all humans in my inner circle had absorbed the persona of Odie, the dog from the Garfield cartoon. No one should have to live in that world. No one!

My mother was in wedding-planning heaven. I, on the other hand, was having an internal emotional meltdown. If I didn't agree with her wedding plans, she'd rephrase the same idea in a sweet-as-pie, see-through fake way, hoping to steer me toward whatever she thought was best. It was all so ridiculous.

She'd taken charge of all event planning and become the self-appointed center of attention. She was aiming for a new personal high at self-absorption.

"I think we should go dress shopping on Wednesday. There's a shop in North Providence where they have beautiful dresses for under $500," Mom said, as if it was front-page breaking news.

There wasn't any fighting this battle. Sooner or later, I needed to follow through with the dreaded dress-shopping day. Dad had agreed to let Mom pay for my dress. I didn't know how that decision had come about. As far as he was concerned, I made enough money to take care of everything myself, but somehow Mom had talked him into springing for the dress and the caterer.

My guess was it was more about showing off so Mom could brag to everyone that she was paying for those things. I was positive that this meant I would have zero say in what type of dress I was going to wear or what food our guests would be eating.

"As this all gets closer, it's going to get really ugly," I mumbled, not realizing I had spoken aloud.

"What!" Mom snapped.

"Nothing, I was just talking to myself," I said, not looking up. But Carson had heard me and was laughing under his breath, enjoying it all.

I'd learned Gabriella's tough-girl attitude was far from tough. In fact, she was pretty compassionate for a wise-cracking Providence girl. Gabriella and Mikey had started working in the club too, which added a bit of normalcy to the insanity of that environment.

Mikey, who'd grown up to be a good-looking young man, had left his job as a telemarketer at the phone company and was now a full-time DJ at the club. At first, it'd been like pulling teeth to get him to speak on the mic, but he'd eventually gotten the hang of it and had an incredible speaking voice. Maybe he'd end up branching out when he got older to a bigger career from his experience at the club.

Gabriella had kept her full-time job at the phone company and worked part time as a souvenir girl, selling drunk guys souvenirs from the "now-famous"—as the items boldly stated—Diamond Mine. Gabriella and I had battled over what would be a mutually acceptable sexy uniform. When all dressed up, she looked like a slightly classier version of Peg Bundy from *Married . . . with Children*, with her red hair piled high on her head, black high heels, sexy black stockings, a skintight black leotard, a fitted tux jacket with tails, and a cute little black-and-white bow tie, neatly clasped around her bare neck. She topped the ensemble off by chewing and snapping a fat wad of gum. She did a fantastic job, and she sold more than anyone had anticipated, but in the back room, she was Peg Bundy, loud and clear.

1989 – twenty-five years old

Chapter 34

I was on my way to the office to give Lynette information on upcoming advertising for the annual Diamond Mine Christmas party. Christmastime in a strip joint was a bit different than I was used to, but even so, Christmas made people warm and fuzzy inside. I laughed to myself, imagining my uncle as the club's Santa Claus.

But when I opened the office door, the warm and fuzzy feelings were instantly replaced with sheer terror. Was someone trying to kill Santa Claus?

My brain was having a hard time comprehending the pieces of life happening in front of my eyes. My ears heard an angry voice. My eyes saw a hand attached to a gun. I followed the hand to the end of the barrel of the gun, and I found my uncle's face. It didn't make any sense. Then I followed the gun barrel back to the hand holding the gun to my uncle's face and realized that hand belonged to Earl, my uncle's partner! Holy shit.

"Close the fucking door!" Uncle Jay yelled.

Out of instinct and fear, I slammed the door shut, feeling a breeze of ice-cold air narrowly escape.

What had I just witnessed? Why the Christ was Earl pointing a gun at his own partner? They hadn't always gotten along, but a gun?

I'd amazed myself at how easily I'd become accustomed to this mobster porno circus freakshow from hell, but this was a bit much. And yet my only reaction had been to close the door and carry on as if office gun fights were as common as buttered bread. This was nuts.

The club had remarkably excelled over the last year and was gaining success and notoriety daily. But its achievements had become harmful to the relationships between the partners. I had never seen greed so drastically change an individual's personality and priorities. It was the success that had poisoned them.

I walked back down the hall for no other reason than it was away from what I'd just seen. I continued up the stairs into the dark, music-filled room and sat in the new VIP table-dance area, where I wouldn't be noticed. The new seats, designed to be like puffy, very comfortable first-class airline seats, each faced a small, knee-high round table. This was the new first-class section at The Diamond Mine. "First class" meant men were treated like royalty while viewing female body parts up close and personal, one-on-one. With typical first-class status came first-class pricing, and these seats were usually full on a busy night, but early in the day, with the exception of the occasional businessman, it was typically empty. I sat down, hoping that what I'd caught a glimpse of downstairs had been my imagination, but I knew that wasn't the case. I had no idea what the outcome would be, but the club music was deafening, so if there was a gunshot, I probably wouldn't hear it.

I sat alone, vaguely listening to one rock song after another, when the DJ announced an upcoming T-shirt-and-shot special. I smiled at myself, thinking, *My uncle is a smart man . . . with partners that own guns.*

As the special concluded, my uncle surfaced, saw me sitting alone, and came to sit beside me. He sat and said nothing while rubbing his hand on the top of my head to teasingly mess up my hair. That was his way of showing affection. At six feet four, it wasn't a big stretch to rub anyone's head, but I sometimes felt like a puppy who'd just learned a new trick.

I could tell he was thinking about what to say and how to say it, so I broke the ice.

"Good to see you're still alive," I sassed.

"Yeah, well, it's good to *be* alive," Uncle Jay said, laughing but only half joking.

"What the hell was going on down there? Is Tuesday now Shoot Your Partner day?" I asked.

He sighed.

"Christina, this place has run the same way for the past ten years. I've always wanted to improve, advertise, market, etcetera, but Earl had a hard time comprehending that. Now that I have you helping me and we're pulling it off, he sees it as some kind of blow to his ego, and today it came to blows," Uncle Jay explained.

"Blows? Jesus Christ, I thought someone was going to end up dead!"

I still didn't understand how anyone could rationalize what I'd seen.

We sat in silence a while longer, both of us watching the club run like clockwork. Sitting next to him in complete silence, it all seemed a bit surreal, like we were watching a late-night movie. I sank deeper into the oversized, first-class, comfy chair and thought about the last nine months and how this had become my actual life.

Uncle Jay took another shot at explaining.

"Earl was angry because he thinks we've spent too much money on advertising, but I knew that wasn't what was really eating at him, and eventually, one thing led to another. Then he said something about you that wasn't very nice, and I shouted some things back at him. Then he shoved a gun in my face. It really wasn't a big deal. The bottom line is the club is doing great, and we are growing beyond expectations. You gotta understand, this isn't your normal bunch of guys in here."

He paused, inhaled, and continued.

"Earl will always dislike you because you're my niece and you helped me follow through with ideas when no one else would. So, every new promotion just adds fuel to the fire. This all started when we kicked off Legs 'n' Eggs, remember?" he asked.

"*Remember?* How could I forget? Christ . . . I thought I was going to die that day!"

My uncle had thought the club was leaving money on the table by not offering anything special for third-shift workers, so he wanted to open for breakfast at six in the morning, and I, just to be funny, had jokingly said, "Like . . . Legs 'n' Eggs?"

The next thing we knew, we'd kicked off the Legs 'n' Eggs breakfast debut at our annual Christmas bash with a live broadcast from the rock radio station hosted by DJ Dr. Metal.

Unfortunately, the idea of a new promotion had pissed off Earl, and he'd taken his frustration out on me. The day before the kickoff, I'd found myself with my back literally pressed against the wall, squeezed into an eighteen-inch opening between the bar and a closet, inches from Earl's screaming face.

"Mark my words, we're not gonna have more than twenty people in this club that early in the morning. This is a stupid promotion."

He'd been so angry I'd felt every spit-pronounced syllable as he screamed it out.

"You are wasting *our* money because you think you're a fuckin' big shot. You're never going to be able to keep this pace up, you're gonna fail, and I'm gonna watch it happen."

Inside, I'd been terrified the promotion wouldn't be a success, so I worked extra hard in hopes it would not fail. I'd even brought fifteen dancers to our townhouse the night before for a slumber party just to ensure they'd all actually get up early enough and be on time. We'd opened the doors that morning to a line halfway around the building, the girls made a shitload of cash, the guys had a blast, and Earl despised me for having to eat his words.

"Ha ha, yeah, I thought you were gonna die that day too," my uncle answered, and continued.

"We all have different backgrounds and different hang-ups. Sometimes things get ugly, but we're still partners, so ya have to overlook stuff from time to time," Uncle Jay said, leading me to believe that may not have been the first gun episode.

"Why does Earl get madder as the club gets more successful? You'd think he'd be happy." I paused.

We sat in silence for a few minutes.

"You've taught me a lot," I said to him.

He snickered before he answered.

"You've taught me a lot too. I would have never believed it, but it's true." Uncle Jay looked at me, reached up, and twisted my hair.

That was the nicest thing that anyone had ever said to me.

I hadn't realized until then just how much of an impact he'd had on me. I didn't know if it was seeing him almost die or the from statement he had just made.

I admired him, respected him, learned from him, and loved him. I'd never felt this way about my own parents, but I imagined this was the kind of sincere love a child had for a parent. This was a deep emotional love. And though it frightened me a bit too, I felt I'd acquired a piece to a puzzle that'd been missing for a long time.

***

A few months later, things had calmed down, and thankfully there hadn't been any more gun scenes.

"Morning, Lynette," I said, entering the office.

"Morning, Christina. You seen Jay yet?" she said without looking up from her bookkeeping.

"No. Why, is he mad at something? Should I go and hide?" I half-seriously teased.

I loved my uncle a lot, but when he got mad—watch out! There was no question he and my mother were related. There was a crazy gene that ran through that family. But even at his maddest, which was way scarier than Mom's, I still cared for him deeply.

"He's looking for you. He said he had something to talk about," Lynette answered.

"Any hints?"

Lynette usually knew everything that went on, as if "must know all" was written into her job description.

"No, sorry, he just poked his head in here, looking for you. Let me see if he's in the dressing room," Lynette said, turning to the intercom. "He said he'll be right down. Grab a cup of coffee, have a seat."

"Okay," I said, wondering what he wanted to talk about.

Maybe it was the incident with Bebe? She was his favorite, but she was wildly out of control. All the guys loved Bebe. All the girls tolerated her. It wasn't that she was a terrible person, but she made it impossible for the other dancers to make it through a day without trouble. Bebe simply felt the need to break every rule in the house.

This club had become known as one of the best-run and most respected topless clubs in the country and had been the Featured Dancers favorite club in the USA.

Featured dancers were basically either porn stars or regular dancers with a little business sense and an unusual talent or other marketable physical attributes. Sometimes, features were centerfold girls of the month who were under contract to walk on stage and *slightly* dance while collecting buckets of cash from guys that weren't allowed to get anywhere near them. Then they'd sit in the VIP section for hours, charging ten dollars a pop for a Polaroid photo with them.

In the process of balancing all of this, I'd inadvertently become a mother figure to some. It seemed there was always a dancer staying with Carson and me for a few nights here and there, and Bebe was a regular member of Christina's inner-group home. There was just something about Bebe that made me want to help her. Deep inside, she didn't want to be what she had become. But everyone in her world, my uncle included, benefited greatly from the mixed-up, drugged-up, drunken Bebe, so they weren't quite as quick to jump to her aid. My uncle acted as if he sincerely cared by sending her back home to Texas once in a while to get her life in order. But he knew she'd just end up right back at the club as the same old Bebe.

Managing Bebe was like babysitting a criminally insane, naked, drunken toddler. Impossible. I'd had enough of Bebe the night I found her screwing some guy between two pinball machines. I pulled her away. She'd yelled, punched, and stormed off. Minutes later, I'd found myself in an ugly, angry tug-of-war with Bebe and a nearly empty bottle of rubbing alcohol. That was followed by tears, drunken apologies, and an emotional meltdown from the same girl who just minutes before could've been crowned the queen of the Women's Wrestling Federation.

The rest of the girls were fed up with Bebe as well and had formed a protest group to get her fired. It'd been time for Bebe to go home.

Two days and a plane ticket later, Bebe was ready to go back to Texas.

"Chris, thanks so much for helping me," Bebe had said as she hugged me.

"Nobody really cares about me. All they want is to make money off me or get sex when I get messed up. They all think I'm stupid, but I know what's going on. I just can't control it when I'm fucked up. You're the only one who wants to help me get straight. I'm really sorry I tried to beat the shit outta' ya. I wanna be straight, but I can't do it here. It's too hard."

But like clockwork, two weeks later, my uncle had let her come back. Big surprise.

I looked back at Lynette.

"Ya think he just wants to justify why he believes it was okay to bring Bebe back?" I asked. "The rest of the girls don't want her here, and I agree with them. She'll just go back to breaking all the rules. I told the girls, bottom line is, Jay owns the club, not us."

"Yeah, how'd that go over?" Lynette laughed.

"They told me my uncle is a greedy bastard," I replied.

We looked at each other as if to say "What can we do?"

The door to the office opened.

"Morning," Uncle Jay said.

"Morning," I answered. "Lynette said you wanted to talk to me about something."

He sat next to me at the conference table, looking more serious than expected for a Bebe conversation.

"This isn't about Bebe, is it?" I asked.

He laughed. "Bebe? No. She's temporarily living with me, and today, she's with your grandmother learning how to put rhinestones on G-strings."

"Bebe's with Nana?" I asked, laughing now too.

Wow! There's a picture.

"Who do you think will be left standing at the end of the day?" I asked.

"No telling," he said, shaking his head, then got serious again.

"I want to talk about your wedding."

"My wedding?" I wondered what in the hell he needed to know.

"Yeah, your wedding."

I didn't respond. I sat, waiting for Uncle Jay to make the next move.

"Are you sure you're ready to get married?" he asked.

I replied automatically, "Yep. Why?"

"Because you don't seem like it. Is there something I don't know?"

Suddenly, it was as if we had been talking about the wedding and my issues all along. It was as if he knew and understood how I felt.

"I feel like I'm making a big mistake. I look forward to coming to work more than I look forward to seeing my future husband. Just the word 'husband' makes me nauseous. I don't think this is the way I'm supposed to feel two weeks before my wedding."

We sat in silence for what seemed like an eternity. I could see my uncle thinking, but words weren't coming out.

"Okay, I'm gonna share some info. I'm not gonna tell you what to do, I'm just gonna tell you what I see, okay?" Uncle Jay said.

Having no idea where he was going, I said, "Okay."

"When I watch you and Carson, I see two people I like, but two very different people. I look at you now, and I see you both as you are. Then I look into the future. I see Carson exactly in the same place as now, happy and content. But when I look at you in the future, I see you in a different world. If Carson left this place and went to work somewhere else, he'd find another solid, steady, ordinary job that would keep him in a secure, upper-middle-class world. You, on the other hand, I see taking major steps in life."

He stopped long enough to make a gesture with his hands like moving up stairs.

"I can't visualize you working for another person. I see you as someone who will make your own position in life and probably own your own business. You have so much drive and energy." Uncle Jay paused and looked at me seriously, as if the sentence should have ended with "but."

I silently and intently looked back, waiting for him to say the word.

He didn't say anything. So instead, I said it, hoping he would contradict.

"But . . . ?"

He looked at me and smiled.

"But *you* have to ask yourself: What is the most important thing in your life and *your* future? I'm not telling you what to do. I'm asking you to take a good look at yourself. Do you want to be married to what you know Carson will be for the rest of his life? If so, that's great, and there's nothing wrong with that. Or . . . do you want to take risks and explore the unknown? The only thing I'm saying is that I don't think you'll be able to do both with Carson. So, what you do two weeks from now could be a large factor in what your future holds. But I will warn you against one thing. Whatever you do, do not lose yourself in work. It's just not healthy. Don't end up like me. I've spent the last seven years of my life lonely." Again, he stopped.

And smiled. "Rich, but lonely. I have fun, but it's not healthy, and I've forgotten how to live with another person. You're young enough now to really explore what you want out of life. We're not all smart enough to see where we're going and where we might end up. Ironically, we're all kind of like them," Uncle Jay said, pointing to the dressing room, referring to the dancers.

"We joke about them living fifteen minutes at a time because that's how long each entertainer's stage set lasts, but most of us live a lot like they do. We use the crazy energy for work, we take chances, throw caution to the wind. But somewhere along the way, we get so caught up in striving to get better and go further that we forget to stop and enjoy life once in a while. You know what I mean?"

Great. Come to find out, I'm related to Yoda!

"Yeah, I know. The sad part is that this wedding doesn't seem like it's about what I want at all. It feels more like it's about what will make everyone else happy. I'd feel horrible if I hurt Carson and wrong for not wanting to marry him," I said, knowing damn well I was lying to myself.

Again, my uncle sat there in silence.

"But it's not only that, it's my mother. You remember her, right?" I said, trying to joke. "She'd have a bird! I tried talking to her about it, but she told me it was normal premarital jitters. She doesn't want to hear it. She believes if anything goes wrong, it would be an embarrassment for her, and she'd have no issues telling me that. This is about her."

He laughed, hoping to lighten the mood. "Hey, I never mentioned your mother. You're on your own with that one."

Uncle Jay had no idea how truthful that statement was.

I laughed back. "Thanks."

"Like I said, I can't tell you what to do; all I ask is that you think it through. And whatever you decide, I'll support you, okay?"

Uncle Jay got up, walked over to me, and kissed me on the top of the head.

"Now get the hell back to work," he said, smiling.

On instinct, I got up, shoved the entire conversation into the emotional vault in my head, and happily returned to what I did best.

1990 – twenty-five years old

Chapter 35

Something weird was happening within the club. I couldn't put my finger on it, but it felt unsettling.

Chuckie, a sleazy agent that my uncle had recently hooked up with, recruited girls for the new Monday Amateur Night promotion. On Amateur Night, any girl could come in and audition live on stage, and the guys in the crowd got to pick a winner. And ultimately, we would end up with new girls on our regular roster.

My gut told me Chuckie was involved in something illegal, and whatever that something was, my uncle was also involved. One night he dropped by with six Brazilian girls and informed me, per my uncle, to added them to our regular dancer schedule. He promptly left, leaving me with six non-English-speaking foreign girls.

I'd quickly learned that all but one understood English when convenient, such as dancing on stage and conversing with the guys, but off stage, they'd clam back up.

Gisele, by far the prettiest of the bunch, kept apart from the rest. She knew only a few English words, rarely spoke at all, and, for whatever reason, had grown attached to me like a puppy. She stood about five foot, with long, naturally bouncy, curly blonde hair and a petite, cute, curvy body. The guys loved her.

I'd heard guys say things to her that would—and should— piss-off the other girls, but not Gisele. She'd smile, nod, let the guys place dollars into her G-string, and keep on dancing, because she literally had no idea what was actually being said. Gisele was making a bundle.

I walked into the dressing room and heard laughter.

Everyone was laughing except Gisele, who stood silently in the middle of the room, one hand on her hip and her tip bucket in the other.

"Okay, what's going on?" I asked.

"Saphire, you tell her," Cherry said.

"Chris, Gisele has a question, and we think you should answer it," Saphire said.

Again, the room burst into laughter.

Gisele stood looking as innocent as a baby deer.

She shook her head as if to say she had no idea what could be so funny.

That only made the laughter get louder.

"Gisele, do you have a question?"

Not really understanding what I had said, she looked back at Saphire for help. Saphire motioned her hand toward me, and Gisele seemed to catch on.

"Quiss?" Gisele asked, using her own version of my name.

"Yes?" I answered.

"What-a is-a . . ." She stopped to think about how to say the next word.

"Yes?" I asked again.

"What-a is-a . . . blow-a job-a?" As she finished, the room roared, and I went speechless.

I looked over at Saphire.

"So much for our innocent little puppy." I smiled.

Before I could answer, we were interrupted, sort of like being saved by the bell.

"Chris, there are two guys out there looking for Gisele. They look important, not like customers, if you know what I mean," Matt said, looking directly at me as if more needed to be said but this wasn't the place for it.

"Um, okay. I'll be right out. I'll be right back," I said to the girls.

As I left, the room returned to chatter as Saphire attempted to explain a blow job to Gisele. God help her.

I left the dressing room and came eye-to-chest with two very important-looking men.

They reminded me of the guys from *Dragnet*. Zero personality.

"Are you Christina French?" one asked.

"Yes."

"May we speak to you in private?" he asked, flashing some kind of badge in my face. At that second, I imagined hearing the *Dragnet* sound when someone got arrested.

The club was dark, and the music was blaring. Instinct told me to obey this man. I nodded and motioned toward the front door. The two men followed.

I led them through the front door and down the stairs toward the office and stopped in the vacant bachelor-party room.

"It's hard to hear upstairs. Is this better?" I asked, scared to death.

"Yes, ma'am," the Joe Friday-looking guy answered.

As both men flashed badges in my face, I wanted to reach out and touch one of them just to see if they were real. These guys were no-nonsense.

One spoke after the other.

"Christina, I'm Agent Packard, FBI," one said.

Then the other. "Agent Greene, ma'am."

FBI? Holy fuck!

I felt my knees begin to shake.

"FBI?"

"Yes, ma'am. Is Fanny working tonight?"

"Fanny? No, sir."

Agent Greene pulled a folded sheet of paper from his breast pocket and opened it.

"Is this girl working tonight?"

I looked at the photo and thought they were trying to pull some kind of joke on me.

"That's Fanny, sir, the girl you just asked about. She's not here tonight."

Agent Greene got mad. "This isn't Fanny, it's Gisele."

"No, that's Fanny," I explained.

"Ma'am, I would not advise lying to the FBI." Agent Packard was now in my face.

"I'm not lying. I have their IDs, and as far as I know, that *is* Fanny," I answered, praying to God my knees wouldn't cave in.

They both stepped back a little and seemed to relax.

"Ma'am, is this person whom you refer to as Gisele working tonight?" Agent Packard asked.

I decided I liked him best for no other reason than his hands were smaller and softer than the other agent's, whose hands could probably slap me into next week.

"Yes, sir," I answered.

"We would like to speak to her."

"Okay, she's in the dressing room. Would you like me to get her?" I asked.

"Yes, ma'am, but we'll come with you," Agent Packard answered.

I turned to head upstairs and caught a glimpse of Matt peeking through the office door down the hall.

Thank God. I hoped he was calling my uncle to help me, because I needed rescuing.

How I managed to climb back up those stairs, I'd never know. As I opened the door leading into the main club area, I passed our ticket-booth guy, Kenny, and the look on his face was priceless.

We walked through the door, passed at least one bouncer, oddly still, acting like a queen's guard, and headed for the dressing room. I didn't expect the Wonder Twins to follow me into the dressing room, but they were right on my heels.

We walked in, and the room went silent. Every set of eyes looked terrified.

"Gisele, can you come outside for a minute?" I asked.

As the last word exited my mouth, you could hear the sound of relief flow through the rest of the room.

I looked back at the two suits. They were impressive. A room full of naked women, and they had two of the best poker faces I'd ever seen. FBI or not, there had to be some weird thoughts going through their heads.

Gisele looked up, not understanding quite what I meant.

I motioned for her to come with me. She looked beyond me to the two suits, instantly frightened. Again, I motioned reassuringly. She hesitantly moved toward me.

The four of us left the dressing room to return downstairs, passing the Italian-looking queen's guards and shocked-looking ticket man.

Agent Packard pulled two chairs out from under the bachelor-party stage and motioned for us to sit.

We sat.

"Ma'am, you say your name is Gisele?" Agent Green asked.

Gisele looked at me, obviously scared. Gisele was afraid of big men—possibly a victim of prior physical abuse? I understood her fear and instinctively feared for her too.

I nodded for her to answer, hoping she understood what the FBI agent had asked.

"Your name?" I repeated to her and pointed to the agent.

She shook her head violently, motioning no.

"It's okay."

She shook her head again.

"Please, Gisele. It's okay."

She stopped, looked at me, eyes saddened, and gave in.

"Yes, Gisss-ele." And clammed up again.

The two agents pulled up chairs and sat next to us.

"Gisele, we are not here to hurt you. We just want to ask a few questions," Agent Green said.

Gisele's head shook back and forth. No.

What the hell is going on? What the hell has my uncle kept from me? Why hadn't Matt come out to let me know my uncle is going to take care of this?

Gisele looked back at me, hoping for the okay to leave and go back to work, but I couldn't give her what she wanted.

I turned to her, pointed to the two agents, and nodded my head. She got mad.

I made the prayer symbol with my hands.

She exhaled and calmed down . . . stubbornly.

"Gisele, you came here from Brazil, right?" Agent Packard asked.

She glanced over to me, and I nodded that she should answer.

Reluctantly she answered.

"Brazilllle. Yesss," she said.

Christ! This was going to take all night. I wondered how the club was running. It was Monday night, Amateur Night. I hoped the DJ was running things for me.

"When did you get here?" Agent Green asked.

She didn't understand the question.

"She speaks very little English. When she first arrived, she spoke only two words: 'yes' and 'thank you.' "

The two agents contemplated, wondering if I had told the truth.

"I'm pretty sure I'm right. There were a few other girls who started at the same time who supposedly didn't speak English. But once they began working with the other dancers and listening to vulgar remarks from customers, the truth came out and the English revealed itself," I explained.

"But I watch Gisele's face onstage, and she honestly has no clue what guys are saying to her. No woman could handle some of the words that come out of some of these guys' mouths, but this one just smiles at everything, so either she doesn't speak English, or she's deaf," I said.

"Ma'am, we're the FBI, not the local police. So, I assume you know this is a serious situation. We are not interested in her, we're interested in how she got into the country. She needs to answer a few questions. Can you get her to help us?"

"I honestly don't know. I really don't know Gisele that well," I answered.

"Well, it seems she trusts you, so we're asking you to work with us. We'd like to come back tomorrow and try this again. We'll meet you here at 10:00 a.m., okay?" Agent Packard asked.

Okay? As if answering no was an option.

What the hell did I know? I didn't have experience dealing with the FBI!

"Okay."

"Ma'am, if I were you, I'd make sure she stayed with you tonight," the agent said.

"Okay."

He then held out his hand for me to shake. I did, and he pulled out one of his cards.

"Ma'am, if for some reason she is not here in the morning, please give us a call. Okay?" he asked.

I took the card. "Okay."

The *Dragnet* twins turned in unison and headed up the stairs in silence.

Gisele looked at me and smiled, thinking it was all over. I smiled back, knowing that was as far from the truth as possible.

She got up and ran up the stairs, happy to go back to work. I continued to sit for fear that if I stood up, I'd faint. And I'd thought the worst part of my night was going to be explaining a blow job to a Brazilian.

The door at the end of the hall opened, and Matt popped his head out.

"Are they gone?"

"Yeah, they're gone."

Matt, now feeling safe, walked toward me.

"I heard one say they were FBI. Is that true? What the fuck is going on?" he asked.

I looked up at him to see if maybe he was bluffing and knew something I did not, but by his facial expression, he, too, was dumbfounded.

"I have no idea what's going on, but it's definitely something big, and it's definitely important, because that really was the FBI," I answered, staring into space. "Matt, you've been here forever, right?"

He nodded.

"Have you ever had to deal with the FBI?"

"Nooooo. But this club isn't anything like it used to be. You and Jay made it huge, and some crazy shit is definitely going on right now," Matt replied.

"No shit," I answered, dumbfounded. "Did you get in touch with my uncle? What did he say? Is he flying back now?"

"Yeah, I talked to him, but you don't want to know what he said," Matt answered, almost whispering.

"Why?" I asked.

"He told me to have you deal with it. He said not to even mention his name and say you hire all the girls and that he's never met Chuckie. He said you won't get in trouble because you don't really know anything, and it's better if you don't talk to him till after you get done with these guys," Matt explained, sounding sad.

"What!" I thought maybe I had heard that all wrong.

Matt whispered again, "That's what he said, Chris."

"Does he know that was the FBI?" I asked.

"Yeah, he knows . . . . You okay?"

"I just got a visit from the FBI, who knew me by name. I gotta let Carson know a dancer is spending the night at our home because that dancer and I are having breakfast with the friggin' FBI. So, sure, I'm just fine, Matt." I laughed sarcastically.

At 9:45 a.m., Gisele and I sat in silence on the steps outside The Diamond Mine, waiting for the FBI to pick us up for breakfast and "harmless" questioning. I had no idea what we were in for. We were both terrified.

At 10:30 a.m., still no FBI. Gisele stood up from the step, turned to me, smiled, and said, "All good? Work now?"

I literally had no idea what to do, so I answered, "Yes."

She smiled and continued on, seemingly unaffected.

I was terrified. I sat on the step till 11:15 a.m., then I, too, went inside.

I never heard back from the blue-suited twins, and it was never mentioned within the club.

It was as if it'd never happened. But it had.

1990 – twenty-five years old

Chapter 36

Someone was cussing while forcefully pulling and intertwining baby's breath flowers into my gelled-up hair as another person smeared layers of makeup on my face. Everyone was talking over each other.

"Chris, do you have something new, something borrowed, and something blue?"

"Chris, where's your garter belt?"

"Are you wearing a push-up bra?"

"I can't believe it's snowing!"

Snowing? I leaned over and looked out the window. Yep. It was snowing—in April—on my wedding day. I sighed.

Black-and-white satin-gowned, overly made-up, stiffly hair-sprayed bridesmaids were scattered about, with my mother and grandmother supervising the chaos like a couple of wedding nazis.

Even though they hadn't approved of the idea, Mom and Nana now admitted the girls looked quite sophisticated in their black-and-white gowns, a bold statement considering four of the five bridesmaids worked at the club.

I looked like Little Bo Peep accompanied by three beautiful—as my mother called them—floozies and one out-of-place college grad. Anyone could see this wedding was just wrong.

"Christina, sit down. Can one of you fix her makeup?" my mother demanded, assuming one of the floozies would hop to immediate attention.

"Paige, does my dress make me look fat?" my grandmother asked, paying attention to no one.

"Mother, please wait, Christina needs to look just right!"

What the hell was "just right?" Was Carson going to reject me if I didn't look dolled up enough? Weddings were the dumbest things ever!

"Christina, sit down please," a voice instructed.

"If I sit, all the puffy shit at the bottom of this dress will pop up and smack me right in my sticky face," I answered.

"Awww, come on. Lighten up. This is supposed to be the happiest day of your life. Smile! It's all going to go just fine," one of the girls remarked.

"Here, have some wine," someone said, shoving a glass in my face.

"Wine! Dear God, no! If I have any alcohol, I won't be able to function. I'm barely seeing straight now!"

There was a synchronized sigh from all.

"How cute. She's nervous."

"It's going to be perfect, Chris. You look beautiful. Carson's going to be in awe."

They had no clue.

At some point, I went from my parents' kitchen to walking down the aisle, escorted by every *other* girl's dream: her father. But it wasn't my dream, it was my nightmare. I, on the supposed happiest day of my life, walked down the aisle of the Cathedral of Saint Paul arm in arm with a monster. With our arms intertwined, the evil, self-proclaimed dad of the year, hypocritically proud, led me to the presumed love of my life. My body stood upright, but my vision and comprehension drifted in and out. Clarity returned in the middle as the priest recited what I thought were our vows.

Then someone pulled my dress from behind.

I turned to see my little niece, our flower girl.

"Auntie—blah, blah, blah?" she spoke, but my head only heard sounds, snagging my attention long enough to gather my bearings.

I nodded, hoping that was the correct response to whatever she'd asked, and turned back to face the priest and Carson.

We left the church alongside congratulatory guests and cars full of bridesmaids and ushers spilling raised champagne bottles as they toasted to anything and everything.

When we arrived at Roger Williams Park Casino for the reception, the sun was shining, and spring was in the air as if the morning snow had been imagined. The casino, a beautiful, historic Victorian mansion, was exquisitely decorated in black and white, with each table setting in alternating black and white china. It looked amazing.

The day pressed on in odd sequences of blurriness and barely cohesive vignettes mixed with endless thank-yous and kissing and hugging hundreds of people I either didn't know or hadn't seen in years. I hated strangers touching me. We had photos taken in every variation possible. I was offered a drink about a thousand times but declined for fear that one might just push me over the edge.

Carson had a drink in his hand from the time we'd entered the venue and appeared to be having the time of his life.

The DJ banged a spoon against a wine glass for what seemed like the billionth time, and because it was an unwritten law, we kissed—for the billionth time.

"Good afternoon, folks. I hope everyone enjoyed the dinner," the DJ announced.

Dinner? Wow! I hadn't even realized we were sitting down. It was a scary feeling not being in control of your senses. Dear God, I hoped I didn't pee myself.

"It is now time for the father-daughter, mother-son dance," the DJ continued.

Christ! I'd dreaded this even more than the walk down the aisle. Dancing face-to-face with *him* in front of hundreds of people, acting as if it was a priceless, memorable moment. It was going to be excruciating . . . and he knew it. No one else knew how much I despised this man, not even Carson, my new partner in life.

I flashed back to my mother pushing her teasing a bit too far by suggesting that I dance with him to "Daddy's Little Girl."

"Will you stop singing that song every time I enter your house? I hate that song! If I have to do that stupid dance, I'll pick a song that I like," I'd snapped.

How f'ing delusional was she?

Carson and I had decided that instead of each of us looking like dorks dancing alone with our parents, we would both dance to both songs—kind of like a misery-loves-company deal. Therefore, the two songs would be generic.

The world faded back in, and Carson turned toward me and held out his hand for me to take, then escorted me to the dance floor, where he joined his mom and I joined *him*.

Things went blurry again as happy Disney music, apparently chosen my me, faded into the background.

I gritted my teeth, touched the tops of his shoulders, and focused intently on the walls slowly spinning by. I knew the dance was over when the people started clapping. And reality hit me like a slap in the face when my father forcefully grabbed me and kissed me right on the lips before I had a chance to break away. I turned, wiped my hand on my face, and walked directly to the ladies' room, where I sat in a stall in complete silence for who knew how long.

So far, this was going to go down as the worst day of my life.

I didn't know when the reception ended or even how we arrived at the Plaza Hotel. All I did know was we were alone, and I was sitting on a big, puffy, three-million-count linen-covered bed surrounded by thousands of dollars.

"This day just continues to get weirder and weirder," I said unknowingly aloud.

"What, honey?" Carson asked, intently focused on counting money.

He was in awe of all the cash.

"Oh, nothing," I answered.

Carson laughed uncontrollably. "I can't believe all this friggin' cash! I gotta hand it to you, calling your uncle for a job was the best move you ever made!"

"Believe me, I had no idea it would be like this," I said truthfully.

Looking at all the money, knowing that it was well over $10,000, was actually kind of creepy. I felt like a Gambino daughter. Many cards were filled with large checks and cash from club-owner-related "friends" that we'd never met. I didn't think they were just thoughtful gifts. Something inside felt weird, but that could have been anything at this point.

Carson, still counting money, seemed unaffected by the absurdity.

I looked at the man I had just married. Everything felt completely foreign, and I wondered how the hell I was to pull off happily ever after.

Carson turned to me, as if he knew what I'd been thinking, and said, "I love you too."

1990 – twenty-five years old

Chapter 37

I'd been married almost three months, but this morning I woke up on a mission. I just couldn't live like this anymore. I had tried to make myself love Carson, but I couldn't, and now I was angry at myself for being such a wimp about everything. Though I hadn't expressed it verbally, Carson must have sensed something, because he'd become so sweet and overly happy it was literally sickening! Every day, he'd do one more thing that would inadvertently annoy me, and each time, I'd thought to myself, *If I was "in love," this would have the exact opposite effect.* All this, and we'd still never had one, single real fight! I guess I just didn't care enough to fight for anything. Carson deserved a wife that loved him back. All I wanted to do was work, and the longer this went on, the worse it would get.

I turned on my side and looked at his sleeping body, innocently happy in wedded bliss, and I sighed.

Our home was a lovely, rented townhouse with zero personality. We didn't have pictures of us or other relatives on any of our walls, and our wedding photos sat in a box somewhere in the house.

Carson would have loved it if we were surrounded by photos of us and various relatives. But that was just it: it didn't matter to me what Carson might have wanted. It should have mattered—a lot—but I couldn't get my heart to feel or even act as it should. I wished there was an internal switch you could turn on to make you love someone, but I simply was not in love with him, and I had been too weak to tell him.

Today I was going to become a new me! Today I would have the courage to fix this.

"No chickening out, Christina. Today's the day we will talk, and we will break up!" I said aloud.

Carson had woken up and was enjoying a cup of coffee. "You wanna go out for lunch?" he asked.

"I'm not very hungry, but I'd like to talk," I replied, trying to keep my nerve up.

"Talk? Talk about what?" he asked.

"Us," I answered sternly.

"Us? What about us?"

"Well, I don't know if you've noticed, but there really isn't an us. There are just two people who live here in the same home," I courageously began.

"Wow, honey, I didn't know anything was bothering you. What can I do to make it better?" Carson asked, thinking our problem was a tiny divot in the day.

It was time to just come straight out with it.

"I don't want to be married," I said.

"What? Are you fucking serious?" Carson asked, totally shocked.

"Don't you think our relationship is odd? Don't you want more from a wife? Don't you want someone who is home more? Someone to spend more time with?" I asked, trying to calm him down.

"Odd? I think it is odd that I married someone ninety days ago who's now telling me she doesn't want to be a wife. THAT'S odd! And let me tell you, when I got married, I got married for good. We WILL make this work. This is your uncle's fault. He thinks he owns you, and you allow it!" Carson had lost control and was angry.

Carson never yelled, and I felt my courageous self begin to weaken. I hated yelling. I sat quietly, hoping to see my next sentence floating in midair, when the phone rang.

Ahhh, saved by the bell.

"Hello?"

"Is this Christina?" an unfamiliar voice asked.

Oh, great. A telemarketer.

"Yes," I answered.

"This is Gertie, your father's wife," the voice said.

"Yeah?" I responded without even hesitating.

Wait a minute . . . . What did this woman just say?

"Wait, who?" I asked.

Carson, initially annoyed that I'd answered the phone, was now looking at me curiously.

"Gertie. I have your father here. Would you like to speak to him?" she asked, as if she called every day.

"Are you sure you have the correct number?" I asked, agitated.

"You are Christina, right? The same Christina that recently married a Carson Stone?" she asked.

I waved my hand at Carson to listen with me, as I needed someone else to hear this too.

"Yes, I am the same Christina that just married a Carson Stone. Who are you again?" I nervously asked.

"My name is Gertie. I'm married to your real father, Lorenzo DiMaggio. He'd like to speak to you if that's okay?" she asked, again as if it was no big deal.

I looked at Carson like he'd have the answer. With the ring of a phone, the most important conversation of my life had become trivial. And by the look on Carson's face, he was in agreement.

I was about to have a conversation with my father . . . my real father . . . the guy I'd wondered about all my life.

How in God's name could two substantially life-altering things be happening simultaneously? Somebody up there was seriously messing with me!

"Okay," I answered, for lack of anything else to say.

I heard this woman who'd called herself Gertie hand the receiver to someone she'd called Lorenzo. My father.

"Hello, Christina," a voice said.

"Hello," I replied back.

"This is Lorenzo, your father," he said, nervousness evident.

"Okay." Again, I answered with one word because I was nearly speechless.

"I've been trying to find you for years. My father, your grandfather, saw your wedding photo in the *Rhode Island Gazette* and mailed it to me in Las Vegas. I knew it was you as soon as I saw the photo. Gertie called information to get your number, and here we are," he said, as if that explained the last twenty-five years of his absence.

"How long have you lived in Las Vegas?" I asked, still in shock.

"About twenty years. I'm a maître d' at the Desert Inn restaurant at the casino. I've met all kinds of famous people," Lorenzo said, trying to make conversation.

"Oh, that sounds like a nice job," I replied, still in shock and emotionless.

"Look, Gertie and I are coming out to Rhode Island to visit my father, and I'd like to see you too if that's okay."

I looked at Carson, who had his ear next to the phone, listening along with me. He nodded as if to say "Go for it."

"Sure. When are you coming?"

"Next week. Can I call you with more details when we get our flight information?" Lorenzo asked.

"Yes. Thank you," I answered politely.

I hung up the phone and sat in silence. If Carson hadn't spoken, I probably would have sat there all day.

"What the hell?" Carson asked.

"I guess I'm going to meet my real father next week," I mumbled.

"After twenty-five years, the guy has his wife call and ask for you? And all he has to say is let's meet next week?" Carson asked.

"Yep," I answered, again without feeling or emotion.

"That's fuckin' weird," Carson said.

"Yep."

"You okay?" Carson asked.

"Nope," I answered.

"I don't know what to say next," he said.

We just looked at each other and laughed. It was the only thing that made sense.

My head was spinning, but I had started the day on a mission, and I had to stick to my guns and make it happen.

"That was the weirdest phone call I've ever received, but we still need to deal with us."

"I don't get it, Chris. Why this all of a sudden? Are you scared? Is it something I did wrong?" Carson asked.

The mood had gone from hostile to solemn and sincere.

"No, you didn't do anything wrong. I've thought about it for a long time. I even tried to talk to you before we got married, but you didn't want to think about it, and I guess I took what I thought was the easy way out," I explained.

"Easy way? You call marrying me and then breaking up ninety days later easier?" His voice was growing angry again.

I reminded myself of a choice I'd referred to a few months back as the lesser of two evils was still an evil and noted that it was about to dish out its consequences.

"No, 'easy' is obviously not the right word. Before our wedding, both you and my mother gave me the same 'it's just premarital jitters' speech when I tried to broach the subject, so I thought maybe you were right. But now, I know you weren't, and it's not fair to make you live like this."

"Don't give me that bullshit. This *can't* be what it's all about! It's that damn uncle of yours, that's what I think. He has you believing he's more important than me!"

My head hurt. Everything inside my brain knew this marriage was wrong, but I couldn't get it out into words that made sense. I was so tired of keeping everything inside, bottling up all of the wrong while choosing what was expected instead. My inner self was well aware that I should be able to share everything with my husband. Everything. But I couldn't bring myself to do that with Carson, and that might be the real reason this marriage would never work. But since I wouldn't share *that*, I had to convince him it was something else.

"I know I made a mistake getting married. I'm a horrible person. If I had to choose between work or home right now, unfortunately, I'd choose work. That's not the way it's supposed to be. And the sad part is I like it that way. Do you understand why you shouldn't be married to a person like that?"

"I don't understand any of this! It's insane! And I will not let you decide whether or not this marriage will work! Besides, what would we do with all of these gifts?"

Gifts? Okay, that wasn't rational thinking.

"I don't care what we do with the gifts. That's the least of our concerns," I said quietly, hoping to calm him down with my voice.

He stopped as if in distant thought for a moment and said, "I'll be right back."

He got up from the sofa and ran upstairs. I sat alone in silence, wondering what had become so pressing to Carson. I heard the shuffling of feet minutes later.

"Okay, here's what I'm going to do. I just called my aunt, and I'm going to visit with her family in Vermont for two weeks. I hope this whole thing will have blown over by then, and it'll give you time to meet your dad and come to grips with that, okay?" Carson stated.

I thought about it, knew I would still feel the same in two weeks, and answered, "Okay."

So much for courage. The double whammy thing with my dad was just too much.

We coexisted in silence for the next few hours while Carson packed.

"Okay, I'm ready to go," Carson said as he came down from the bedroom and stopped in front of me in the kitchen.

He squeezed the top of my shoulder, pulled me toward him, and kissed me.

"Everything will be okay when I get back. We'll have no communication for two weeks. It'll be good for both of us; we'll learn from it and move on," Carson said, as if we were each taking an adult-education night class.

"I don't think it's that simple, Carson," I said.

He quickly replied, "I do. You'll see," and turned toward the door.

I listened to the doorknob click, the buzzing of the garage door opening, his car engine start, the garage door closing, and then the humming of Carson's car fading away as it left the driveway. Then I massively exhaled.

There I was, alone in complete silence. This was where I'd thought I be when I left Harry. This is where I should have been. This whole mess was my fault.

I'd convinced myself I was making the right choice, but I was broken, and Carson was a ray of sunshine sitting at the apex of an emotionally distraught fork in the road. What seemed so right back then was so obviously wrong and crystal clear today. I had chosen the path of least resistance, the secure one.

I'd let so much get out of hand, taken too many easy roads instead of the right ones.

Two weeks, he says, huh?

"Well," I said aloud, "I don't think he's right, but I'll see what happens."

I walked upstairs to shower, unsure whether I hoped to wash away the guilt or thoroughly enjoy a long-awaited rejuvenation.

1990 – twenty-five years old

Chapter 38

I sat in an oversized dark-purple plush chair in the Providence Marriott lobby, waiting for the man who claimed to be my father. At ten in the morning on a Saturday, the entire lobby, adjacent to the hotel restaurant, smelled of French toast and maple syrup. I had a magazine in my lap, completely oblivious to title or story content of the page I was supposedly reading. There was just enough activity in the hotel lobby to convince myself I didn't stand out as the weirdo in the lobby, looking for her long-lost dad. The overhead speaker system was playing a generic Muzak rendition of Alannah Myles's "Black Velvet." As nervous as I was, all I could envision at this very moment was one of the dancers on stage, as that was her over-requested favorite song.

I heard a ding from the elevators down the hall and looked up as if I was meeting someone I saw daily. Instead, at twenty-five years old, I was meeting my father and some woman named Gertie for the first time. Six people exited the elevators. There was an elderly couple. Nope, too old. A single woman I assumed was a Mary Kay cosmetics representative, dressed head to toe in pink, otherwise an unfortunate outfit choice. The pink lady was followed by a room service waiter and another couple. Possibly my father and his wife?

I sat still while they approached the lobby. As the man got closer, I knew it was him. This was my father—a man I'd never met, a man I'd never even seen a photo of—and yet I was sure he was the one, because I recognized myself in him. This was the strangest feeling ever. It wasn't that we looked alike, but we had similar facial features that were easily recognizable as father and daughter. This man, my father, had bright crystal-blue eyes, unlike my dark-brown eyes, but even so, we resembled each other. Our mouths, chins, and cheekbones, definitely from the same genes. It was as if I was looking at myself for the very first time. It was indescribable. He was tall, a little over six feet. I had no idea why I'd expected to see him in a suit, but instead, he wore a paisley-patterned polyester shirt and knit pants. Very 70s. Not quite the cool guy I had imagined. I'd envisioned a healthy, calm, sure-of-himself, Rat Pack-kind of guy. Or at least that was what my imagination had created over the years. Gertie was a short, stocky blonde woman who walked with a lot of energy. I could tell they recognized me, so I waited for them to get closer and then rose from my puffy chair.

Gertie spoke first.

"Christina? That's you, right? Oh, we know it is. Come here."

Gertie spoke loudly and held out her arms, expecting a hug. I silently walked over and engaged even though hugging her was the last thing I wanted to do. I hated being touched by strangers. I released, stepped back, and turned toward the man who was my father.

"Hello," I said.

He smiled and quietly spoke, "Hi, Christina. I'm your father, Lorenzo." And he too held out his arms.

I had the same feeling as when Gertie had done it, but I did what was expected.

"Let's go over to the restaurant and have some breakfast?" Lorenzo asked.

"Okay."

A maître d' greeted us at the entrance and sat us off to the side, away from other diners, as if he knew we needed privacy.

I sat at a fancy, white-linen-covered table in an expensive, thick leather chair, looking at two strangers, wondering what was going to happen next.

She spoke first.

"So, we hear you work for your Uncle Jay?"

"Yes, I have for about a year," I answered, wondering how this woman had learned that.

Then he spoke.

"We talked to your uncle this morning. We used to be quite close."

He stopped to take a breath, just long enough for Gertie to jump in.

"That uncle of yours sure has made a name for himself. He's done quite well. You'd be best sticking with him. He's loaded, you know. He's a smart guy, just like our family. Everyone in my family is a doctor except me. My father and my brothers—all doctors, you know, followed right after him. My daddy was a big shot in Chicago, and we built quite a name for ourselves up there. They're a wealthy bunch—all doctors, you know. And me, I was Daddy's little girl. So, Daddy made sure I was well taken of. Of course, he took care of my brothers too. But they have no problem taking care of themselves. They're all doctors, you know."

A waiter came to the table and interrupted what I assumed would be another round of Gertie's verbal diarrhea. We ordered.

Before Gertie had a chance to begin again, Lorenzo, spoke. "So, you just got married, huh?"

"Yes, in April," I answered.

And she began again.

"Where's your husband? Is he working? What does he do? Carson, right? Oh, wait a minute. Jay said he works at the club too. Right? That's a good move. You stick with your Uncle Jay. He's got money, you know, not like Lorenzo here. Oh, he's had his chances. He's made plenty of money. Says he won't do it again, but we'll see. Right, Lorenzo?" she said, scolding the grown man, her husband.

Lorenzo looked embarrassed but laughed it off as if it was some kind of joke.

"Oh, c'mon, Gertie. Stop teasing. Christina isn't here to listen to all of this."

Jesus Christ! This little round blonde lady is a fucking nut—and a greedy too!

"Lorenzo, I'm gonna go upstairs to our room. I'll be right back," Gertie said.

And just like that, she was gone.

"I've been looking for you for a long time," Lorenzo said. "I tried to contact your mother years ago, but she'd have no part of it."

"Really?" I asked.

Wow! She'd never told me that. God, that made me angry.

"How is your mother?"

"She's fine," I answered, as I was supposed to.

"And your grandmother? Is she still in control of your mother? Can she still do no wrong?" He smiled.

That made me laugh. I guessed things had always been the same.

"That's about it, yep." I answered, nodding.

"You have no idea what it was like living with her. And that grandmother of yours, she's a handful. Made our lives a living hell."

"Oh," I answered, waiting for more information.

"You know, I tried. I tried my best," Lorenzo explained, as if it was some kind of apology.

I sat in silence.

"I just couldn't live like that. And when you came, it got worse. Between your mother's moods and your grandmother's control issues, it was just too much."

"Oh?" I didn't have anything else to say.

"Not that I was an angel. I was bad too. I made bad decisions and got wrapped up in some pretty bad things. This *is* Providence. It was different back then. That was almost thirty years ago." Lorenzo paused, and I could see he was reminiscing about whatever it was that had actually happened.

"I don't think it's changed as much as you think it has." I laughed, trying to lighten the mood.

"Oh? Well, maybe not. But back then, I had to leave. I didn't have a choice. I got mixed up with the wrong guys, and I had a problem with gambling. Leaving was the best choice. But believe me, leaving had nothing to do with you. I tried to get your mother to go with me, but she wanted no part of it.

"The day I left was awful. There was a lot of screaming. Your mother can do some serious screaming."

I had to laugh, because I didn't think he really had any idea how debilitating her yelling could be.

"And that grandmother of yours . . . She said she put a hex on me. She's crazy. I left this city with nothing but the clothes on my back. I had enough money to take a train to Washington, D.C. I ended up spending a few years there, and then I met someone who said they were looking for people like me to work in Vegas, and I've lived in Vegas ever since."

"Is Vegas as fun as it looks? Is that where you met Gertie?" I asked.

"Yes, Vegas is a city like no other. It's an amazing place. You should come and visit. I work at the Desert Inn as head maître d' at the finest restaurant in the hotel. I've met all kinds of stars." He stopped and bent down to pick up a folder I hadn't noticed before.

He placed it on the table, opened it, and began to speak again.

"I have pictures to prove it too."

This was weird. Did this guy think I'd be more impressed with him if I saw photos of him with movie stars?

"See, here I am with Dean Martin, and here's one with Wayne Newton. He's a big shot in Vegas, you know. And here's one with old blue eyes himself, Frank Sinatra. I've waited on Frank Sinatra! He'd even ask for me by name. I've gotten some big tips too. Some in the hundreds!" Lorenzo boasted.

"Cool," I said.

"Gertie and I have been together for almost twenty years. She's another one. Gertie's always on my case about this or that. I could tell you some stories that would make your head spin. I have my hands full with her. I could use your help and advice . . . ," Lorenzo said.

My help and advice? Oh, man! Wasn't he supposed to be the parent? He was supposed to be my father, the one I should be able to go to for support, guidance, and love. Christ! Was he just like my mother? No wonder those two had hooked up.

He hadn't asked about my life at all. So far, I'd heard about how cool he thought he was and why I should feel sorry for him. Maybe he was just nervous.

"I've tried to leave her before, but she has a hold on me. She's got the money, and it stays in her wallet. She even gets my paycheck. Says she's trying to keep me straight," Lorenzo explained.

"Straight?" I asked.

"Well, I used to have a problem with gambling. Blackjack, but it's under control now. I'll be retired soon, and I have a big pension coming, so then I'll be able to do what I want. I won't gamble it away, you know," he said, as if I doubted him.

Great. My real father was a guy with a gambling problem living in Las Vegas.

Gertie came back to the table just as the food arrived.

"Well, from what I hear, you're doing well. Is Carson treating you okay?" Lorenzo asked.

Since he really hadn't asked me anything about myself or my life, I found it was best to keep the responses as short as possible.

"Yes, Carson treats me fine," I answered.

"Good. That's how it should be. If Carson doesn't, then you just go and tell that uncle of yours, and I'm sure he'll fix everything," Gertie said.

What did she think? Just because my uncle was rich, he was a superhero? The guy she saw as a superhero was the same guy who'd thrown me under the bus with the FBI. Didn't take a genius to see how she rated people.

I looked down at my plate and pushed the eggs around some more to make it look as though I was actually eating something. I had so many questions that now seemed inappropriate because this was so far from the experience I'd expected.

"Did you two ever have children?" I asked, wondering if I had any brothers or sisters on the other side of the country.

"No. You're my only child," Lorenzo said.

The waiter had come and gone with the check, and we sat in silence for a moment.

"We're gonna come visit you at work tonight after Lorenzo visits his father. Jay invited us!" Gertie boasted, as if it was some kind of royal honor.

"You're coming to The Diamond Mine? You know it's a topless dance club, right?" I asked.

"Honey, we live in Vegas. Remember? We've seen it all. Besides, there's a lot of money in that business. Not that I'd do that, because I don't have to. My daddy was a doctor, and all my brothers are too, you know. You stick with your uncle, and you'll be just fine. Tell that husband of yours too. Is he working tonight?"

I swear, if I had to sit here one more minute, I was going to punch this woman.

"No, Carson's off tonight," I answered.

"Too bad. It would've been nice to meet your husband," Gertie said.

They both rose from the table, and I followed. When we got to the exit of the restaurant, they stopped.

"Well, we'll see you later tonight, okay?" Lorenzo asked.

"Okay. But I'm usually pretty busy keeping track of everything, so I might not get a chance to talk to you too much," I answered, hoping he would follow with something that would make me feel like he had an interest in my life at all.

"I understand. It was nice to see you today. I'll make sure Gertie gives you our address and phone number tonight so you can call anytime you want to, because, after all, I am your father," Lorenzo said, and held out his arms for a hug.

Emotionless, I hugged him while Gertie babbled something I wasn't listening to.

I walked out of that hotel feeling emptier than I had during my years of growing up without him. After all these years, the man I'd thought would rescue me was not only a complete stranger but also would probably never become my friend. Never once had he asked: "How was your life? Were you treated okay? Did you get everything you needed? Is there anything I can do for you?" or "How do we grow from here?" Nothing! Not even once.

By the time Lorenzo and Gertie arrived at the club, it was in full swing, and I was far too busy to chat, but it seemed not to matter much at all, as they spent all of their time in the VIP section with my uncle. I didn't even see them leave the club.

I drove home that night, took a shower, and crawled into bed hoping I'd wake up the following day to learn I'd imagined the entire event.

I got up the next morning, laughed at the harsh reality of the prior day's event, and reminded myself that Carson was arriving home today . . . to resume our lives together. Carson wanted to believe that two weeks away would fix everything. I made myself a cup of coffee, sat at the kitchen table, and wrote Carson a note:

Hi,

I am very sorry that I still feel the same way as when we last spoke. You really do deserve someone so much better for you than me. I wish it didn't have to end this way, but it truly does need to end.

I do not want any of the wedding gifts, and you can have the stereo system and whatever furniture you'd like, but if I could keep the bed, that would be great. If you'd like to talk about our next steps, I will be home after work tonight.

Chris

When I got home that night, Carson and some of our furniture was gone. I was not surprised and figured he'd call soon so we could be adults and make plans.

I got to work the next morning and learned Carson had quit his job at the club. Later that day, I took a break to go to the bank and then learned that he'd taken our entire savings account with him too.

I told myself that was fair play, and it took a small dent out of the enormous crater of guilt I'd deservedly laid upon myself.

I felt like Alice coming out of the rabbit hole as I exited that bank. Between the wedding, meeting my real father, and being solely responsible for the dissolvement of a ninety-day marriage, I'd been balancing a lot!

I got in my truck, slowly inhaled a deep breath, exhaled, and told myself, *TODAY is the first day of the rest of my life.*

1990 – twenty-six years old

Chapter 39

I walked into the club feeling a sense of accomplishment.

The Diamond Mine had become the top adult entertainment complex in New England, resulting in facsimiles popping up in New York City and surrounding areas.

Strangely, it felt good to have played a significant role in making a mark admired by many businessmen. In fact, it felt great, but what was next? Sure, being part of its success was fantastic, but it was now leading the owners down a questionable, greedy, ego-driven path, which was a bit unsettling.

My uncle had gotten friendly with a successful—though not so reputable—adult-club owner in Texas. And because that man was ahead of my uncle in adult-club accomplishments, my uncle hung on his every word. It was sickening to watch, because my uncle was more than capable of accomplishing everything that man had and more. But his greed and ego and insecurity were driving him to *be* that man in Texas, whom I didn't think was admirable at all.

Over the last month, Jay had deepened his relationship with the shady agent delivering girls from Brazil and was working with the Texas club owner as his personal advisor of sorts.

Shady guys had been shipped to us from Texas and put on the payroll as departmental managers of things we didn't even have departments for. Drugs were everywhere. Some girls used the new guys to their advantage, and some girls were scared, but no one seemed to care that this was headed down a very dangerous road.

I sat in my office, wondering if my uncle had forgotten the club wouldn't exist without the 150 dancing girls on his weekly roster.

A dancer knocked on the office door.

"Chris?" Elise asked.

"Yeah."

"We have a T-shirt promotion in ten minutes. Are you coming in to give out T-shirts?"

"Yeah, I'll be right in," I answered, though my head was still swimming in other thoughts.

"You okay?" she asked.

"Oh, yeah. Just daydreaming." I smiled.

That satisfied her, and she pranced back to the dressing room.

If she only knew what I had been ordered to do next.

I felt my life changing again. And . . . I was scared to death.

The dressing room was buzzing with energy as the girls ranted and raved about a club full of military men in fatigues. I grabbed an empty chair, pulled it to the front of the dressing room, and stood upon it to get everyone's attention.

I cupped my hands around my mouth and yelled, "Hello, exotic dancers!"

The room became silent.

"What the hell are you doing?" Saphire asked.

Cherry yelled from the back of the room, "Hello, crazy woman standing on a chair!"

"I need your attention for a minute. It's important," I said. "I know things are changing rapidly around here, and I want to discuss something before it happens . . . ."

"Changing? That's a fuckin' understatement!" Saphire yelled.

"Yeah, what the fuck is going on in this place?" Brandy yelled.

"Those greedy bastards don't give a shit about us anymore! And now they got some slimy-ass Texas manager trying to push cocaine on us. It took so long to make this place what it is, and now Jay's letting it go right back there cuz he wants to be some fuckin' big shot. It ain't fair!" Saphire was again speaking for everyone. I saw heads nod in unison.

I had to laugh. Jay and the other owners didn't give the girls enough credit. They didn't miss a beat. They had seen what was happening and didn't like it one bit.

"I know. That's what I want to talk to you about. I know things are changing, and believe it or not, Jay thinks it's for the best."

The room got quiet. I tossed the pile of T-shirts to the dancer closest to me. She took one shirt and passed the rest around, assuming I was going to continue to explain.

"Okay. Everyone knows our slowest night is Tuesday, right?"

Heads again nodded.

"Well . . ." I paused and took a deep breath. "Jay and the new, Kenny Rogers-looking Texas guy have come up with a promotion."

"Cool. Let's hear it," someone in the back said.

I paused.

"Well, every Tuesday night, we are going to auction off a date with a dancer. The ad is going to read 'Win a Date with a 24-Karat Dancer!' Every Tuesday, at some point during the night, we are going to introduce each girl with a cute little bio, like *Playboy* does for their centerfolds. And later in the night, we are going to sell a date to the highest bidder. Then we will send that guy and the girl of his choice out in a limo for a night on the town. The dancer of his choice gets to keep half of whatever the highest bid is." I stopped for a breather, and the room went wild.

"Chris, are you fuckin' insane?"

"What the fuck. That's prostitution!"

"There is no way I'm going anywhere outside this joint with some drooling loser!"

"Hey! Ain't that illegal?"

"Fuck that! I ain't never working another Tuesday night!"

And the room went silent again. I could see each dancer's reasoning turn as if a light above had just lit up.

And the responses went wild.

"Me neither!"

"You ain't never gonna see *my* ass on a Tuesday!"

I stood on the chair in silence. I was not surprised by the reaction at all.

"Chris, what are you going to do?" Mercedes asked.

"Yeah?" another asked.

"Well, the best I can tell you is that I will talk to him. Maybe we can come up with some kind of compromise," I answered.

"Good luck! That ain't no compromising man down there!" Bobbi said.

"You got that right," Saphire added.

"Yeah. But Chris won't let us down. Right?"

I sighed and got down from the chair. "I'll just promise to do my best."

There was always at least one in the bunch who was greedier than everyone put together.

"I don't know what y'all are so uptight about. I'm fine with all this new shit. I get all the drugs I want for free, and I ain't got no one on my back. I'll go out with some loser who wants to pay for it anytime. Besides, I'll get a free meal, and you bet I'll get my money's worth and ride home in a limo to boot!" Paris said, as if all of the others were looking at it wrong.

"Fuck you, you money-grubbing, two-bit hooker!" Brandy yelled.

I walked out slowly, because I had physically and emotionally run out of energy.

Gabriella was standing at my office door.

"You look wiped," she said.

We'd become friends since she had started working at the club.

"Thanks for the compliment," I said.

"That's what you get for uninviting me to your wedding," she teased back.

That had become her response to everything she didn't agree with. I knew she felt bad about it, but when her and Mikey had broken up, my mother uninvited her. But hey, what did it matter now anyway?

"Wedding? What wedding? I'm not married. What the hell are you talking about?"

"Aaaah, shut up. What the hell's wrong in there, anyway?" she asked, pointing to the dressing room door.

"You don't even want to know," I answered, rolling my eyes.

She laughed and shook her finger at me.

"I keep telling you, we oughta write a book!" Gabriella said, snapping gum and walking away.

1991 – twenty-six years old

Chapter 40

I spent most of the night wide awake, thinking about how to get through to my uncle, and wondering why it I felt it necessary to continue to fight this insane battle.

Did I feel a responsibility to a group of girls I had spent all of my life trying *not* to be like?

Ironically, when it came right down to it, caring about these girls' well-being was primarily the reason I continued to stay. I felt like I had accomplished things with them that no one else had. We'd learned to work together in a relationship built on shared experiences of right and wrong and mutual respect and trust. Somehow, I had formed, in a completely unconventional way, a more intimate bond with 150 topless dancers than I had with anyone else.

I thought about how much of my life was spent working. I thought about the late nights spent bailing dancers out of jail or consoling phone hours due to cheating boyfriends. Or the temporary roommates I'd inherit while a dancer's new boob job healed. The countless times I'd lent money because they'd foolishly spent the thousands of dollars they'd made on a fur coat and didn't have anything left for rent.

Okay, my life was really fucked up.

I walked into the club a bit earlier than usual. As I was walking in, Terry, the funny but crazy owner, was walking out.

"Hey, kid. How's it going?" Terry asked.

Terry started every sentence he'd ever spoken to me with that same opening.

Out of politeness, I lied.

"Okay. How are you?"

He stopped walking and leaned against the lobby window.

The newly constructed lobby was architecturally beautiful. My uncle replicated a design from a local contemporary office building. The club had an ultramodern look from the outside, allowing a great view of the city from any of the artistically angled lobby windows. The lobby was, of course, the only room with windows. The rest of the club was like walking into an X-rated black hole.

I stopped and leaned too. The view was certainly beautiful.

"Nice, huh?" Terry said, reading my mind.

"Hmmm."

"Not a bad view for a place that's gonna be yours someday," Terry said.

"Mine? I don't think so." I laughed.

"Why the fuck not? You and your uncle made this place what it is today. That's all there is to it. You've earned his part of this when he retires. Hell, you've probably earned mine."

"Terry, I don't think my uncle sees it that way. And besides, I honestly don't know if I want *all this*," I said.

"Who cares if you want it? Just fuckin' take it! You'd have to be crazy not to!"

"I want to do more with my life than this." I waved my hands out to the club entrance.

"My uncle only sees *this*, and right now, he only sees it with the guy from Texas. I don't think we see eye to eye anymore. I tried talking to him about a month back. I even tried to sit with him to explain that I'd like to own my own business, a little restaurant. But he went nuts when I mentioned it! Instead of being supportive, he went on an insane yelling spree about how I was spending too much time thinking about things other than this club! Then there's the FBI thing, and I haven't forgotten about the Ricco incident either."

"Christ . . . don't even mention those feds," Terry whispered, as if they could actually hear us.

"As for the Ricco incident, you have to understand thugs. Your uncle had to let them do that to your brother. It's a respect thing. It's the Italian way."

"Terry, I don't care if it's an Italian thing or a respect thing. When it came right down to it, he should have stood up for my brother just as he should have stood behind me when the feds came in. My brother had only been floor manager for one night! As far as Mikey knew, closing the club at 1:00 a.m. was his job. Leaving it open for a bunch of bottom-feeding mobsters was not, and he did what he thought was right."

"Well, unfortunately, once it was done, it had to be seen out. Providence has its own way of doing things sometimes. You know that. Your brother is okay now. That's all that matters."

"The fact that he is okay has nothing to do with it! My uncle sat in his own office while some fat mobster bashed my brother's face in with a telephone receiver. That's just sick, and it makes my uncle look like a coward. I don't understand what's happened to the guy I once looked up to. No—I take that back. I know what's happened to him. It's greed. He got too rich too quick. And he doesn't wear it well."

I saw Terry getting nervous because the conversation was becoming too much for him.

"Ahh, don't worry. It'll all work out. Just take it easy. Jay will come around," Terry said.

"Yeah. You're probably right," I lied.

"Hey, kid, have a good day, okay?" Terry said as he walked out.

"I'll try, Terry. Thanks," I answered, and began my descent downstairs to the owner's office.

"You're late," Jay growled.

These days he was always in a bad mood.

"You'd think as a manager you'd give a fuck what happens here."

"What do you mean? I wasn't late at all. I've been upstairs talking to Terry."

"We've got a lot of work to do. You've got ads due this morning. You'd think that'd matter more than wasting your time thinking about stupid ideas like opening a restaurant. There's no Goddamn money in food, anyway. Besides, I lost almost sixty grand last month. You should work extra hours for free."

Extra hours? I worked almost every day and night.

I wanted to scream at him. God only knew how they lost sixty grand! Thank God I never touched any of the money nor did I know how to crack a safe. I wondered how a place like this could get robbed of that kind of money yet choose not to call the police.

"Do you have the ad ready for the Tuesday night promotion?" Jay asked.

I took a deep breath and prayed.

"I do have an ad ready, but I think it might be a good idea if we talk about the promotion first," I said politely.

"What's there to talk about? Is the ad done or not?"

"I think this might be illegal. I mean, well, isn't selling a dancer to a stranger kind of like prostitution?" I asked, hoping he might see the light.

"I don't care what it looks like. I can do anything I want here. You hear me?" he screamed.

Oh, boy. This wasn't getting any better.

"Well, I don't think you're going to be able to get enough girls to work on a Tuesday night, so it will actually hurt the night instead of helping it."

"How the hell do you know that?"

"I went over the promotion with the dancers, as you asked. Most of them are *really* against this one."

"Fuck those pigs! They'll do whatever I tell them to do. I made this club, and if they want to work here, they'll do as I say. They have no idea how fuckin' lucky they are!"

Huh. I guessed the club's success hadn't been a team effort. And my devotion to him had meant nothing? So, this was him, only him. Right.

"You better fix this now! Tell them they have no choice. In fact, go get me the list of all the girls that work here. I'll give you a mandatory rotating schedule, and they'll all have to work the schedule posted. Who the hell do they think they are? I can get fifty girls here with just one phone call. Fuck them. I'll call Texas and have girls shipped like UPS boxes. You tell them that."

"Jay, I can't do that," I answered quietly.

He sat in silence for a moment.

"Well, I don't know if you're just too fucking lazy or too damn stupid, but you better straighten up immediately. Do you hear me?"

Lazy or stupid? Did he really say that? That was the meanest thing he had ever said to me. Wow, that hurt, but now I was mad.

There was a rage in my voice when I answered.

"I fucking hear you all right. And I am pretty fucking far from lazy or stupid. In fact, I am smart enough to know it's time to quit! Do you hear me? I quit!" I ended screaming.

I turned to walk out the door, and Jay started again.

"Fuck you. You can't quit! I made you!"

Oh, God. Now he sounded like my mother.

"You aren't quitting. I'm firing you. You're worthless! And don't even think about getting another job in this city, because you'll never work in this fuckin' city again! You'll come crawling back here, begging me for your job back. Everyone comes crawling back to me. Just wait!"

He was still yelling hurtful things as I climbed the stairs and exited that building for the last time.

Tears ran down my face as I drove out of the parking lot of The Diamond Mine. My uncle had just hurt me more than anyone. I promised myself never to go back to him. I'd be homeless before I'd beg for my job back. I'd never forgive the man I'd used to look up to as the dad I never had. I would never allow myself to be that close to anyone ever again.

***

"Christina, I shouldn't be telling you this, but it's about time someone stepped up here. Jay knows you have an interview with our company today," the man on the phone said.

"And . . . ?" I asked.

"And . . . we can't hire you. If we do, Jay threatened to cancel the club's advertising campaign. We can't afford to lose them as a client. But you should know he's telling everyone in the area, including my boss, that you stole $20,000 from the club before you left. You should think about calling a lawyer. You're being blackballed throughout the city," he said.

I politely thanked him, hung up the phone, and sat on the sofa, dumbfounded and mentally exhausted.

Hours later, I sat in my two-room apartment, wondering how my life had come to this. It was time to admit to myself that leaving the club had taken a significant toll on my mind and body.

Morally, I had made the correct decision to leave the club. I could have given in to my uncle's ways, I could've turned a blind eye on his wrongdoings, but I had not. Yet here I was, left with nothing in the world that didn't make sense to me.

I'd left The Diamond Mine, choosing to be a better person because I had faith in an unknown power above and believed that in the long run, everything would be okay. I had since learned things were not always as they appeared, and the so-called power above, if it existed at all, didn't always seem to care. The reality was there were people here on earth more powerful and evil than I could've ever imagined.

Whatever savings I'd built up after Carson left had quickly run out, leaving me practically penniless, landing my ass back at home, right back where I'd been when I'd left Harry. Though instead of living *with* my parents, I rented a tiny, converted half basement with a street-level walk-out from them.

Total ceiling height throughout the space was six feet. I stood five-foot-seven, so it worked. I was sure the space wasn't legally rentable, but it was viable enough for my parents to charge me $300 a month. I had to laugh, because they'd charged the previous renter $275 a month.

Now jobless longer than I'd planned, I found myself collecting unemployment, allowing for just enough to pay rent, my truck loan, and its insurance.

It was a far cry from a year ago when I'd literally forget to cash paychecks, but I was still determined to do it alone, and I'd still never go crawling back to that man.

I had heard all kinds of horrible rumors initiated by my uncle, but being accused of stealing had crossed the line. This had to be illegal.

That nice man on the phone was right. I needed to do something!

I got myself off of the sofa, got dressed, and drove to the club.

I parked my car in the lot, slammed my door shut, and marched right past the parking lot attendant waving his arms, trying to inform me I was not allowed in the club.

I walked in with determination, stormed past the meatball guy sitting inside the entryway, and headed down the stairs.

I knocked on that office door like there was a fire in the building and everyone was about to die. Lynette, the bookkeeper, opened the door.

"Where the hell is my uncle?"

She looked scared.

"He's not here, Chris. Is there something wrong?" she nervously asked.

She knew right damn well what was wrong. She knew everything that went on in that office. Quiet or not, she listened to everything.

"Wrong doesn't even *begin* to cover it! Who's here if he's not?" I yelled.

"Hey, kid, I'm here. C'mon. Sit down, relax. Tell us what's wrong," Earl said.

He was so fake, but he was better than no one.

I explained what had happened over the past few months, including the stealing accusation.

"So, my next move is to call an attorney, but I came here first hoping there'd be an ounce of dignity left in that man."

"Sit right here, kid, I'll be right back," he said, getting up and walking into Lynette's office area. He picked up the phone.

He returned a few minutes later.

"I just spoke to Jay. He'd like to see you at his house in Forestville. I think he's sorry, I really do. Go talk to him, will ya? You're family. Family shouldn't be like this. Whaddya say, kid? Will you go see him?" he asked nervously.

Because I couldn't sit there listening to that man any longer, I agreed.

He got up and smiled, shook my hand, and hugged me.

"Good. Good luck, kid. You're doing the right thing, trust me," he said.

I didn't believe a word he'd said, and I knew he didn't like me, but he liked negative publicity even less.

Less than ninety minutes later, I was on my way back from the secluded country mansion, feeling disappointed.

The visit had lasted a total of fifteen minutes. It wasn't a total loss. I'd vented and he'd listened, and while he'd agreed to stop blackballing me, he never apologized or even hinted to feeling sorry. Sadly, it wasn't surprising, as along the years I had learned, through experience, to expect nothing from anyone.

1991 – twenty-six years old

Chapter 41

My nightly entertainment consisted of sitting in the claustrophobic, dungeon-like living room of my apartment, looking out the window, and watching dirty toddlers dressed in nothing but diapers run barefoot in the street. Across the street, I saw the druggie mom sitting in the open second-floor window, chain-smoking, using the sill to keep herself propped upright. I prayed she was coherent enough to care for the tiny, doomed future adults playing fearlessly in the street.

I'd finally found a job, making pennies above minimum wage, working customer service for the telephone company. Each day, along with countless other human army ants, I'd file into the multilevel office building, take the elevator to the eleventh floor, and sit at my desk adorned with no more than two personal items in a cubicle maze that could easily double on off hours as a scientific rat experiment. It was a failed attempt of individuality, as from a birds-eye view, we looked like drones, answering monotonous incoming customer issues via a dog-leash-type headset. But, after jobless months of being blackballed within my field, working for Satan's version of customer service was better than being unemployed.

When not reading romance novels borrowed from my mobster neighbor or watching feral toddlers run in the streets, I enjoyed going out to dance clubs with Gabriella. We did silly things that most young adults did, but for me, carefree nights at dance clubs followed by late-night diner breakfasts were completely new experiences. Gabriella taught me how to have plain old girl fun. It felt good. It felt human. Gabriella was a godsend.

I got into bed thinking about the irony of my life. It was a mess, but for the first time in years, I felt relaxed and I was losing weight. I'd cut down on fast foods and added a bit of exercise to my daily routine.

I woke in the middle of the night to the sound of sirens close by. Not so unusual in the city. I sat up and peered through the curtains, and sure enough, there was an ambulance parked on the sidewalk within a few feet from my window. They were probably looking for the mother of the toddler street gang. I didn't care much for that drug-addled woman, but I hoped she was okay and crawled back into bed.

The ringing of the phone woke me up again. I sat up, still groggy but with the eeriest, overwhelming feeling like I'd just had the best sleep ever.

I'd always been a light sleeper, obviously. Maybe I'd just dreamt of sleeping like a rock?

The phone was still ringing. I glanced, squinty-eyed, at the clock; it read 4:20 a.m.

Who would be calling in the middle of the night?

I stumbled out of the bedroom and through the doorway, aimlessly grabbing at the wall in a foggy attempt to stop that incessant ringing, and I grabbed the telephone receiver like I'd just won a marathon.

Before I could say a word, I heard sobbing and yelling.

"Christina? Christina, is that you?"

"Hello?" I answered.

More hysterical sobbing.

"Christina, it's Mom! We're at the hospital. It's your father. He's had heart attack! Can you come now? Please come help me. Please come now!"

"Okay," I responded, by instinct.

I hung up the phone, and that eerie feeling I couldn't place was still there. I couldn't put my finger on it, but it was weird and oddly smooth.

Okay, I must be losing it.

My mother had just called with a major emergency. Maybe I hadn't fully woken up yet? I needed to snap out of it!

What felt like moments later, I found myself walking into the hospital with a pair of glasses in my hand.

"Where can I find a Mr. French? He was admitted this evening," I asked the nurse at the desk.

She pointed down the hall as she began to speak, but my mother, dressed in a nightgown, slacks, and bedroom slippers, came running toward me, crying hysterically.

"Christina, it's awful. He's gone. My husband is gone." Then the sobbing got louder and more uncontrollable.

"Mom, calm down, I can't understand a word you're saying," I said.

"He's gone! My husband is gone! The doctors tried to save him, but he's gone! What am I going to do? Why did this happen to me?" She sobbed, grabbed me, and pulled my body against hers.

I looked up out of desperation for help—any help. I found the nurse staring blankly into my face.

"The rest of the family is down the hall. Maybe it would be best to join them," the nurse said quietly.

I nodded.

"Is everyone else here?" I asked.

"What?" Mom looked up but didn't let go of my shirt.

"The boys? Are they already here?" I asked.

"Oh, yes. The boys are sitting down in the hall, waiting for you." She stopped outwardly crying just long enough to answer.

"Let's go to them, okay?" I said.

She stopped and thought.

"Yes, okay," she answered, and went back to sobbing hysterically while grabbing my body and clothes to keep her upright.

I walked down the hall with her sobbing and hanging on to my side. I didn't utter a word or release a hint of emotion. I was unsure about how I felt. But whatever it was, this was not the time to show it, because she was as needy as she could ever be. She'd lost the love of her life.

When we reached the end of the hallway, I found four grown men also sobbing hysterically.

A doctor came out of a pair of swinging doors off to the side.

"Ma'am? Are all of your children here now?" he asked.

Mom looked up from my sleeve and answered, "Yes, everyone is here now." And buried her head into my tear-soaked sleeve.

"You may come in to say your good-byes," he said, then turned toward the same doorway from which he had come.

To him, this, unfortunately, was a regular occurrence.

The boys, who had all been looking down at the floor, crying, looked up, first at each other, then at me.

I nodded for them to go first because I had my mother attached to my shoulder.

One of them nodded and got up. The rest followed.

As we entered the room one by one, I listened to my brothers speak about our father like a god they worshiped. Each brother left his side, devasted and helpless. This was their father, a man, though unfathomable to me, they looked up to.

When the boys finished their good-byes, my mother let go of my shirt sleeve. And gravity took over as her body fell over his body, howling and crying like a woman who had just lost her soulmate. "What am I going to do? How am I going to survive? Why did this happen to me?"

It was then that it really hit me. When all was said and done, she was going to expect me to be there for her—for everything—because she was incapable of taking care of herself. That was when I, too, began to sob uncontrollably.

Dad's death was followed by blurry days of visiting, food-toting, consoling people and a trip to the funeral home. My mother, although grief-stricken, was embracing the focused attention on her and was really taking this whole needy thing to new level.

Through the years, my parents had never been afraid to borrow money or ask for help from anyone, and my father's death was no exception. My mother didn't have the kind of money it took to bury someone. As if on cue, in her time of need, my uncle appeared like Superman. When needed, my uncle was always there to spread his generosity, using money to swoop in and play the hero. My uncle, a man she had been cursing for the past year, she now welcomed with open arms; a man she blamed, when she wasn't blaming me, for the many changes in her precious youngest son; a man she knew was as corrupt as a day was long. But now he was a man that she needed. And when she needed something, she could act better than anyone I knew.

The boys were sacked out in the living room from a day of morbid chaos. I sat at the kitchen table with my mother, who sat across from me, staring sadly and looking as pathetic as possible.

"Christina, we're going to need you to do something for us," she said.

"We?" I asked.

"Yes. I talked to your brothers, and we all agree you're the strongest one," she explained.

"And . . . ?" I asked, wondering what the hell was coming next.

"Well, we'd each like to speak at the funeral, but we're too upset to think about what to say. So, I figured that since this is your father too and even though he is not your biological father, he is still the only father that you know . . . ." She paused.

What the hell was she getting at?

"And . . . ?" I asked again.

"Well, we'd like you to write a eulogy for each of us to read aloud. You're a better writer than we are, and maybe you can put into words what we feel for your father. Please, it would be such a great help. I would like you to convey how much we all loved and cherished your father and how he was different to each one of us," she said in a sympathetic voice.

I could feel a knife slowly being pushed into my heart and twisted.

"So, you want me to write a speech for each of the boys and for you?" I asked.

"Yes. And I assume you will want to speak too, so obviously one for yourself. Maybe you can note how much Dad did for you and how many times he made you laugh?" she suggested, as if happy thoughts would come to me naturally.

Had she gone completely insane? Why would she make me do this? Was this a way to get back at me for something? I *knew* she knew what he'd done to me. I *knew,* deep down inside, she knew. No one in their right mind would ask such a thing.

But I couldn't bring myself to argue against it. How could I, when everyone else appeared so in need, talk to her about *that*?

So, I did, as usual, what was expected of me.

I spent the next three grueling hours banging out personal eulogies about a monster for the other people who loved that monster. I sat at the kitchen table by a window that offered a stunning view of the paved driveway between the two houses. Fall was in the air, but there wasn't a single leaf in the driveway because there weren't any trees on our street. Just triple-decker houses, packed like Legos, separated by anorexic driveways. The air in the house was still . . . or maybe dead. I was surrounded by dozens of platters and containers of food that had been dropped off as if a cure, like aspirin for a headache, to make pain disappear.

There was no shortage of lasagna. Must be an Italian thing.

I awakened that morning with an excessive amount of energy.

Where had it all come from?

Was it a sense of peace being released as energy?

And I smiled because I knew that feeling was here to stay.

September 10, 1991, one day before his birthday, would go down in history for me, but the night after his death, September 11, 1991, was a personal celebration of something new: an uninterrupted full-night's sleep. It was indescribable.

Blissfully energized and restrengthened, I began writing. I wrote for Zac, Andy, and Mikey and finished a rough draft for Mom for her to adapt and personalize to her liking. I had one to go. One big blank piece of paper.

How in God's name was I going to write one for Daniel? I didn't think I could bring myself to explain the relationship between those two despicable humans. No one should have to hear what those two meant to each other.

I put pen to paper and tried to write something—anything—resulting in a hole in the top of the page from bearing down too hard. This was torture.

Why ask me to do such a thing? She knew exactly how I felt about Danny. She knew he was barely even human. It wasn't my fault Danny was too stupid to write something.

I put that aside, and I started one for myself. I had to write something these people would want to hear. This would be the most hypocritical thing I had ever done.

Maybe, with the right wording, I could stay true to myself?

From as far back as I can remember, my dad was a man liked by everyone. Al, as most people knew him, was different from everyone, especially to me, because when I was four years old, Al became my new dad. My dad taught me to take care of myself, and my dad taught me to be strong mentally. But most of all, my dad taught me how to survive. Al spent so much time with me that went unnoticed yet shouldn't have. But of course, I noticed, as those are memories I'll never forget . . . because Al was my dad.

I would read it aloud to everyone, but this was for me, as I had thought about those words carefully.

He couldn't get away with things now. Al couldn't hurt me anymore because Al was now dead.

1991 – twenty-seven years old

Chapter 42

The tiny living room was jam-packed with Christmas presents and people. I was surrounded by my brothers and their significant others. Zac and Samantha, now married, were accompanied by their two young girls, who would most likely be the stars of the day because, after all, Christmas was more fun with little ones. Andy was busy entertaining the girls by making fart noises. And because some things never changed, Danny was bragging about buying some company and how successful the company would become now that he was in charge. Danny was still an asshole.

Mom walked into the room, singing a high-pitched version of "Merry Christmas."

"Okay, everyone. It's time to open presents."

"Yay!" the young ones hollered.

"I'd like to start the present madness by giving you each a gift from me," Mom said, holding a big box full of wrapped gifts.

As she handed wrapped gifts to each of us, she said, beaming with pride, "I've put a lot of thought into this, and I think you'll cherish this forever. I am so proud of myself. Danny, you open your gift first."

We sat in silence while Danny opened the small gift.

"Aww, Mom. It's great!" Danny said.

"Yes. I know. I gave you Dad's old money clip because I know how much you like money, and it will be special to you because it belonged to your father," Mom said in self-elation.

She gave Zac Dad's gold cross necklace and Mikey one of his gold bracelets, and Andy got Dad's watch.

The boys were emotionally grateful.

Samantha and I were next.

"You can both open yours now. Both gifts are the same." Mom smiled, looking at us as if we were about to uncover the Holy Grail.

I opened the box and found a gold chain bracelet. I picked it up and looked at my mother and then Samantha.

"I had them made for the two of you. The bracelets are made from Dad's gold necklace. Now you have something to wear every day that will make you think of him. Isn't that special? Isn't that a terrific idea?" Mom was on cloud nine.

Samantha cried in gratitude and hugged my mother. Then everyone started talking about what a great man our father had been and all of the great things he'd done for everyone. By the end of the night, I was sure they were all convinced their father had been a god.

I'd never understand why once a person died, we chose to gloss over all of their flaws and wrongdoings and opted to deify an imaginary version of themselves that had never actually existed. Rewriting history didn't make any sense. It made us hypocritical.

I sat in total silence, holding that gold chain like it was a poison. It made me want to vomit.

What the fuck was wrong with her? She *had* to know, and yet she still went on about how great he'd been. Was it because she loved the pity and attention? Had that overshadowed the reality of the past and regard for her own daughter's feelings?

I took a deep breath, sucked up my pride, and got up to hug her.

"Thank you," I lied.

"I knew you'd like it," she said.

The rest of the evening was happily focused on the young ones. My mother was perfectly content.

Finally, the holidays and never-ending food condolences were behind us. And now, looking at myself in the mirror, I was actually impressed. It had been a long time since I was happy with my appearance. I'd gone from a size sixteen to a twelve and was still losing weight. My life wasn't a barrel of bubbles and rainbows, but at least something was going in the right direction.

"Chris, you ready to go?" Mikey yelled down to me from Mom's apartment above.

"Yep. I'll be right up," I said, taking one last look into the mirror and wondering if I'd get a date before I died.

My mother, who'd been as needy as expected, seemed to be sucking up the emotional energy of everyone around her, and tonight's dinner out was no exception.

Mikey and I had been guilted into dinner with her at El Torito's restaurant in Warwick.

"How's your job going?" Mikey asked.

"Good, but boring. I make decent money, but there's no challenge in it."

While working for the telephone company, I'd run into the editor of the *Providence Sphinx*, a local Rhode Island arts and entertainment paper. Per our discussion, my uncle had stopped his blackballing vindictiveness, and when the offer of a position with the *Phoenix* came my way, I'd quickly accepted. Selling ad space was leaps and bounds beyond being a leashed customer service drone.

"I hate being alone," Mom whined, pushed her plate away, and looked to signal the waiter.

No matter what meal she was served, there was always something wrong with it. It wasn't as much about the food as it was the attention.

Mikey and I had been listening to her whine since Christmas.

"The friends your father and I had don't come around anymore. They're tired of listening to me complain about trying to survive alone. I don't know what I'm going to do, I just can't be alone. Do you think it's too soon to start dating again?" Mom asked, attempting to sound innocent.

I knew it! I fucking knew it! He wasn't the love of her life. If that man had been the god she made him out to be, and if she was as devoted as she claimed, then she should be in no condition to think about dating so soon after his death! My mother was about what was best for her and her only. Sometimes, I didn't know who was worse, him or her.

I needed to get up from the table before I exploded.

I walked to the ladies' room and leaned against the sink, faced the mirror for a few minutes, hoping to convince myself that murdering my mother in a Mexican restaurant probably wouldn't fly as an act of self-defense.

What was it about needy people that made strong people feel obligated to be their emotional support system? Dining out with her tonight was the last place on earth I wanted to be, but here I was, and now I was going to go back out there and act compassionately.

I counted to ten, took a deep breath, and opened the bathroom door.

I meandered a bit, trying to savor the time before resuming my hypocritically fake compassion.

I exited the bathroom and walked through the overly colorful waiting area, complete with a variety of sombreros and painted wooden shakers like in Disneyworld at Epcot's Mexico. *I think they're called maracas*, I told myself. I took the long path around the hostess station just to kill time, waited for her to seat a party of four, then headed down the aisle that led to our booth.

I moved to avoid a head-on with two other patrons coming my way, a man and woman, walking several feet apart, with the woman leading the way. As the woman passed, I proceeded toward our booth of misery while trying to avoid hitting the man. Then time stood still for a nanosecond.

I looked at him, and he looked at me.

"Hi," I mumbled . . . I thought.

"Hi," he responded . . . I thought.

Then that nanosecond was over; neither one of us stopped. We just continued in opposite directions as if nothing out of the ordinary had happened.

But it had. *What the hell? Was that Luke? Are you kidding me?*

I hadn't seen Luke since the day he'd predicted my divorce. Since the day Luke had said we'd meet again. Since the day he'd told me that we'd end up together!

I got to the booth and sat down. My mother was still babbling about being lonely, though now I wasn't bothered by it in the least. In fact, I couldn't have cared less as to what she was saying. It was my brother who noticed the change.

"Chris, you okay? You look a little weird," Mikey asked.

"Hmmm? Yeah. Weird," I repeated quietly.

He laughed, which made my mother aware the subject must've changed.

Mikey, sitting on the same side of the booth as me, waved his hands in my face.

"Hellloooo. Earth to Chris. Are you in there?"

I must've looked like an idiot.

"Yes. Yes, of course. I'm fine. But I think—well, actually I know—I just passed Luke. In here . . . in this Mexican restaurant, miles away from where we each live. How weird is that?" I asked.

"Luke?" my mother asked.

"Yeah, it's weird, right?" I answered.

"Well, maybe you can ask him, because he's heading this way right now," Mikey teased.

"Oh, shit!"

Mikey was right. I looked over, trying to act inconspicuous by gazing across the table at my mother. As Luke got closer, my stomach nerves kicked into high gear. When he approached, I froze.

Luke slowed his pace, quickly glanced around the table, and spoke.

"How's it going?" Luke asked.

"Good," I answered, hoping he would ask more . . . or at least stop, for Christ's sake!

But he didn't. Luke didn't stop at all. Instead, he continued to walk away and never came back.

"That was fucking weird," Mikey said.

I could only reply with one word.

"Yep."

I wasn't sure what we talked about through the rest of the meal. All I knew was I had made it through the night without murdering my mother.

The next few days went by without any unusual occurrences. But now on Monday, as I drove up the driveway after a long day at work, I still was thinking about Luke. Gabriella had said only fate would decide what was best. Gabriella also used an entire can of Aqua Net before leaving the house each morning, so it could have been the fumes talking.

Shortly after arriving home, my mother uninvitedly stopped by with a handful of mail as an excuse to visit.

"Can I come in?" Mom rhetorically asked as she walked in.

"Looks like you already have," I said, trying to sound like I was joking.

"Well, I brought your mail."

"Okay. Just put it on the table."

"Do you want some coffee?" Mom said, taking it upon herself to grab the pot from the coffeemaker on the counter. My counter.

Oh, God. She wanted to chat. I'd had a long day, and she wanted to talk.

"Okay," I answered.

I watched her put water in the coffee pot and the grounds in the filter and returned to the table to sit.

I waited patiently for a reason for this visit.

"Christina, I'm concerned about you," Mom said.

"About me? Why?"

She was never really concerned about me. There had to be another reason for her behavior.

"Well, because you never talk about your father. It's not healthy. Or if you do say anything at all, it's always sarcastic. I don't know why you do that. I want to know why. And I want to know why you never wear that bracelet I had made for you. I made that from my heart. Why don't you wear it? Is there something you haven't told me?"

Well, well, well. Here it was. Finally, the day she admitted what she'd known all along. A day I'd waited for all my life. Maybe it would be a turning point? Perhaps she was finally coming around.

"You mean to say you really don't know why I will NEVER wear that bracelet? You really have no idea why?" I asked, baiting her.

"No, I've been wondering for months. Every time one of us talks about him, we remember the good things, and I notice how you only bring up the bad things. Did he do something to hurt you?" Mom said, sounding as innocent as possible.

"You mean to tell me you have no idea?" I asked in total disbelief.

"No. No, I don't."

"Well, I'll make it as brief as possible. Let's say that from the time I was adopted to about the age of seventeen when I moved out, Al, that loving husband of yours, abused me almost every fucking night of my life! And his fucking pig of a son, the oldest one, occasionally joined him! How's that for an answer!"

Wow! What an incredible relief. Oh my God, that felt good. Finally, to say aloud what I'd wanted to say for years. With him gone, maybe now my mother would be the caring mom I'd always wanted.

I watched as her facial expression went from innocence and questioning to sorrow and tears of sadness, then anger. I expected questions, maybe a comforting embrace, but what happened next was far from what I could have imagined.

"Oh, my God! Do you think he abused Mikey too?" Mom asked.

Then the tears became a woe-is-me self-pity party.

"I can't believe it! I truly can't believe it! I can't believe my own husband could hurt me like this! My own husband! How could this have happened? How?" She looked up to me as if I was actually supposed to answer that.

I wanted to slap her in the face, and I wanted to scream at the top of my lungs.

I was in shock. Had I heard all of that correctly? After years of being abused by a man she put on a pedestal, after years of keeping my mouth shut for her, after years of acting like everything was normal and biting my tongue, her only response was "What about my son?" and "Why did this happen to me?"

If not for the numbness, I think I'd have instantaneously died from a broken heart.

What the fuck!

A real mother was supposed to love a child from birth unconditionally. A real mother instinctively put their child's welfare first. A real mother was supposed to protect their child in need. A real mother was someone you could always count on, no matter what.

At this moment, I realized that I had been fooled by something so crystal clear it had been invisible to me. This person sitting across from me, biological or not, was by no means worthy of being my mother.

There would never be any kind of a bonding relationship between this person and myself. Never. And it wasn't because I wished that upon us. It was because she had chosen it to be that way.

With new clarity, I looked back at her and saw a woman expecting attention and coddling from the horribleness that had so obviously been cast upon her.

"Are you okay?" Mom asked.

I couldn't tell if she was attempting false sincerity or wondering if I'd forgotten to be concerned for her well-being.

"I'm fine," I answered.

"Oh, that's good."

"Yeah," I said.

"Let's keep this between us for now, okay?" Mom asked.

"I've kept it to myself for this long. Why change now?" I answered.

"This has been a lot for one day. I've got to go lie down," she said, getting up from the table.

"Okay."

On the way out, she stopped, as though remembering something as an afterthought.

"I love you. I just want everything to be okay," Mom said.

"It is okay," I said, and closed the door.

1992 – twenty-seven years old

Chapter 43

The mail usually consisted of bills and other random junk mail, but today's delivery included a big red hand-addressed envelope. The return address was in Forestville, Rhode Island. I immediately knew it was from Luke. I smiled, opened the red envelope, and pulled out the card.

The face of the card read:

I had the most unbelievable dream about you last night! I dreamt you wrote me a letter.

Inside, Luke had written:

Or better yet, call and say hi. My number is still 555-3223. Luke.

Huh. This was an invitation to call, but what about the woman he'd been with at the restaurant? Well, he was the one who'd sent the card. Perhaps I could call and just say hi as he'd suggested.

I sat at the table, looking at the card, waiting for the card to tell me what to do, but no such luck, so I consulted with my personal psychic, Gabriella, who promptly told me to hang up the phone immediately and call Luke.

I picked up the phone and dialed the number.

It rang. *Damn.*

"Hello?"

It was Luke; I knew his voice.

"Hello. May I speak to Luke, please?" I asked.

"This is Luke, smart-ass. You know it's me. I know your voice too. I assume you got the card." His teasing lightened the mood.

"Yes, I got the card. Thanks. How did you know where I live?" I asked.

"My mom is a nurse, remember? When your mom went in for an operation a year or so ago, my mom was working at the hospital. She's been bugging me to send you a card ever since. When I saw you the other night, Ma said it was fate. So, here we are."

"But what about your girlfriend?" I asked.

"What girlfriend?"

"The one you were walking with in the restaurant the other night."

"I wasn't walking with anyone. If someone was walking in front or behind, that person wasn't with me." He laughed.

"I'm not attached to anyone right now. I haven't been for quite a while. But you were with someone . . . ?" Luke asked.

"I wasn't with anyone," I snapped.

"Um, you were sitting right next to him. That was why I kept walking after I said hi. Who is he?" Luke asked.

"His name is Mikey. And you know him because he's my brother, you twit!" I laughed.

"That was Mikey? God, I haven't seen him since he was a chubby little kid." Luke laughed. "Wow, he's grown."

"Yeah. I know what you mean. So, does this mean we're both unattached right now?" I asked.

"It sure looks like it. Must be fate," Luke answered sincerely.

"Hmmm. Must be," I agreed.

***

Luke and I enjoyed every spare minute together. Now months into our adult relationship, it seemed inconceivable that was the same guy that could barely bring himself to kiss me when we'd been kids.

There I was, naked in bed next to that previously shy guy with our bodies contently intertwined and sweaty from sex as we listened to each other's heartbeat slowly return to normal.

Was there a powerful, all-knowing being above that had preemptively planned a life path for each of us?

I lifted my head from resting on his chest and looked into his eyes.

"Remember when we first started dating and it took you months to hold my hand?"

"Yeah." Luke softly giggled.

"Did you ever think we'd actually be here? Doing this?" I asked.

"Of course I did. I even told you we would, remember?" he answered.

I flashed back to that day in the parking lot.

"Yeah, but I never thought it would actually happen," I replied.

"I never doubted it," he answered.

"We're not kids anymore," I said.

"Uh, I think we just proved that," he teased.

"Yeah, we've definitely grown up and become real adults." I laughed, then sighed.

"You never ask me about my dad. Hell, my mother has shared it with everyone. It's okay to ask, ya know," I said.

Shortly after my mother asked that we keep my info private, she, without my consent, had shared that incredibly personal and private information with every family member that would listen. Yet she'd only mentioned the part about my dad, I assumed because that was what would bring more sympathy and attention to her. Mentioning Danny would only open doors she had no use for.

During that horrible experience, I'd learned that my brothers, who had idolized their father, saw the situation differently.

Zac couldn't comprehend how the man he'd idolized could do such a thing. Andy didn't believe a word of it. Andy said I'd probably made it all up, and the subject just made Mikey sad. Mikey looked as though he'd have a tough time handling any of it. Luckily, I hadn't seen Danny over the last year, as he had moved from state to state, continuing to burn bridges as he went.

But once the initial conversation about the issue was over, it had never been spoken of again. So, I'd chosen to push the whole thing aside. My mother was the only one who ever mentioned it, and that was only when it was to her advantage. Needless to say, I was now as uncomfortable as humanly possible around my relatives, and I'd never broached the subject with Luke until now.

"Nope. I'm happy. No need to ever talk about the past. This is now. We're in control, no one else. It's taken a long time and a lot of patience to get to this point. Finally, we can plan our lives together. That's all that matters. I can't wait till we're married and build a home of our own in Forestville that I can share with the woman I love, and someday, you'll give birth to little versions of us. This was all totally worth waiting for," he answered, completely content.

Never talk about the past? Married? Home in Forestville? Give birth? Children?

Did he feel my heart beating out of control? It felt like I had a swarm of bees in my brain.

He wrapped his arms around me tighter, kissed the top of my head, and quietly said, "I love you."

"I love you too," I replied.

The next few months seemed to fly by. Sunday afternoons were spent at Luke's mom's along with his entire family. It felt great to be welcomed into a weekly family ritual of spaghetti and meatballs. Luke's life had barely changed over the past twelve years, and my life had changed direction so often that I'd lost track, but we seemed to fit together just fine. He hadn't pushed the children-and-house idea since our bedroom chat, and I was enjoying the companionship that only a couple could share. *This time*, I thought, *I can make it work*. After all, it was fate.

My last stop of the day was to pick up an ad layout from the Pavilion, a prominent new club-and-restaurant complex in Providence. The Pavilion was the venue with a bigger capacity than The Diamond Mine, but the Pavilion wasn't a strip joint. The Pavilion was a chic, three-level complex with five bars, a marina, a restaurant, and the city's hottest new dance club. Anyone who wanted to be seen went to the Pavilion.

"Hello. I'm here to see the manager," I said to the cute little hostess standing by the restaurant check-in podium.

"Are you Chris from the *Phoenix*?" she asked.

"Yes."

"The manager will meet you in that room," she said, pointing to an area in the restaurant referred to as the pub.

I walked into the pub and saw one guy sitting at a table covered with notebook binders.

"Chris, I assume? I'm Paul, the new general manager. Have a seat." The guy smiled.

"Hi, yes, I am from the *Phoenix*."

I sat silently and waited for the ad layout I had come in for.

"So, are you as good as they say you are?" Paul asked with what came off as a hint of sexual innuendo in his voice.

I was a little taken aback by it. He was awfully bold for someone I didn't know.

"Excuse me?" I asked.

"I've been asking people if they know of anyone that could handle the advertising, marketing, and promotions for this place, and everyone I've asked responded with your name."

I tried to relax, but this guy made me very uncomfortable.

"Well, you're probably hearing things based on what I did at The Diamond Mine."

"Whatever the reason, you seem to be the right person for the job, and this is a great opportunity," he answered.

I hadn't been looking for a different job, but a new challenge was tempting. My favorite part of working at The

Diamond Mine was taking something with a lot of potential and using creativity and energy to make it successful.

I reminded myself that I was enjoying a second chance with a man I loved.

But I had to admit a chance to succeed at a venue besides The Diamond Mine was tempting, and it'd give me a sense of self-earned value. But I couldn't and didn't want to go back to long work hours every day and night. I had a personal life now, and it was important to me. But maybe I could get the job on my terms?

"What exactly are you looking for?" I asked.

And the smart-mouthed man replied with another sarcastic remark.

"What are you willing to offer?" Paul asked.

"I miss the marketing, advertising, and promotional aspects of my old job, but I don't miss the hours and other managerial obligations. I'd be willing to work four days a week, handling the advertising and marketing. Like, part time. And in return, I would only be looking for part-time pay. Who exactly would I be working for?"

"Why do you ask? Does it matter?" Paul asked in a teasing tone.

"I guess it doesn't. I just don't know much about the owners here."

As usual, with any of the successful clubs in the Providence area, the word was that this place was owned by mob-related people. And from my experience, that wasn't hard to comprehend.

"Well, let's just put it this way: if you survived working for the guys at The Diamond Mine, you'll have no problem working here. They're nothing alike, if you know what I mean. One owner is a podiatrist, and the other owns a large metal-recycling business. This is their side project. Besides, you'll be working directly for me. In fact, one of them is here now and would like to meet you, okay?" Paul said.

"Okay," I replied.

Paul led me into a small office where a woman who appeared to be a bookkeeper was working alongside a young, Italian-looking man.

"Nicky, this is Chris. I think she's interested in joining our crew," Paul said, motioning toward me.

The small, Italian-looking man who'd been leaning over the desk, overseeing the bookkeeper, turned to me and offered his hand and spoke.

"Hello."

I instinctively shook it.

"Hello, nice to meet you," I said.

Nicky was nothing like I had imagined. I had imagined a tough-looking, big, rough, old-style Italian man. Instead, this was a well-dressed, clean-cut, small-built, nice-looking man with manners.

I expected Nicky to escort us to another private room for a formal interview of some sort, but instead, he stayed where he was standing.

I remained leaning against a copy machine on the opposite wall, only feet away from where he stood.

"You're the same Chris that worked at The Diamond Mine? The same one who came up with the Monday-night promotion and Legs 'n' Eggs? The same one whose name was in every ad I used to see. And you created those ads too, yes?" Nicky asked rapidly.

"Yes. That's me," I answered.

"Good. You're the one I want. You're hired." He shook my hand again and turned to Paul.

"Paul, you talk to her about money and let me know when she can start," Nicky said, and turned back to me.

"We're gonna do some cool things here. I wanna make this the best place in the city! Take care," Nicky said, then bolted out of the office like Speedy Gonzales.

I wasn't sure what it was about Nicky, but I immediately liked him. I looked around to see if anyone else in the room thought that was the weirdest and quickest interview ever, but no one other than me seemed affected.

I got in my car, wondering what the hell had just happened. I was pretty sure—no, I was sure—I'd just been hired to work at the Pavilion—and on my own terms! I hadn't asked for much because I honestly wasn't sure I was capable of doing the job. In reality, my accomplishments at The Diamond Mine had occurred with my uncle by my side. Now it was time to show someone else what I could do. Actually, now it was time to go back to the *Phoenix* and give my notice. I wondered if I should have talked to Luke about it before I accepted.

I paged Luke and waited for his call.

While waiting, I called Gabriella and filled her in on the news. She was thrilled, and as far as she was concerned, the Pavilion was the hippest place to work, and now she'd be able to get in without standing in line for hours on a Friday night.

Luke was already home when I arrived. We hadn't officially moved in together, but he had a key and spent most nights with me.

"Hi. No wonder you didn't call back after I paged you. You don't normally beat me here." I smiled, happy to see him.

"I've been here for almost an hour. I've already showered and changed. How about a nice romantic dinner?" Luke asked.

What was with him? Had everyone gone wacky today?

"How about I tell you what kind of day I had, and then you tell me what you're up to, because you're looking extra hot tonight," I said.

He'd come a long way from the young teenager I knew. His shoulders were broader, and his hair had a hint of gray speckled through the deep, thick black that made his blues eyes stand out. There was just something about a man who could walk into a house looking like Pig Pen from the Peanuts gang, take a quick shower, shave, dab on awesome-smelling cologne, and come out looking like a country version of a *GQ* magazine model.

I filled Luke in on my day.

"Damn, you've had quite the day!" Luke laughed. "Well, I made us dinner reservations, so how about we chat about it then?"

"Sounds good to me."

***

"May I take your coats?" the hostess asked as she escorted us to our table.

"Coat? No, no, thanks. I'll keep my coat with me," Luke said oddly.

"What was with that?" I asked.

"Oh, nothing. I have my wallet in my coat tonight, and I didn't feel like switching in the middle of the restaurant."

"Oh."

He ordered a gin and tonic, and I ordered a glass of wine while looking over the menu.

The restaurant was just about full, but quiet, with soft, almost inaudible music in the background. The hostess had seated us off to the side, away from other diners, in a quiet booth with high-backed seats for privacy.

"So, are you going to take the job at the Pavilion?" Luke asked.

"I'm not sure. I want to take the job, and I think I sort of already accepted it by not saying anything after Nicky hired me, but I'm not sure I can do it. This is the kind of job my uncle tried to keep me from getting when I left."

The waiter placed our food on the table.

"May I get you anything else this evening?" the waiter asked.

"No. No. We're fine. You can leave now," Luke said, sounding almost angry.

The waiter left as if it wasn't any big deal to him.

"Are you okay?" I asked. "Is there something bothering you?"

"I'm fine. Nothing is bothering me at all. Nope. Nothing at all." Luke smiled.

We talked about the good and bad points of each company. We talked about how I could laugh at my uncle because his evil plan to keep me out of a field I enjoyed would be a failed attempt if I chose to work at the Pavilion.

Everything seemed typical as ever, but Luke fidgeted through the entire dinner, and Luke wasn't a fidgety person.

After the waiter cleared the table, he asked if we would like dessert.

"Yes. Dessert sounds great!" Luke answered, as if someone had just offered him a million dollars.

I glanced up at the waiter, who seemed just as puzzled as me, and shrugged my shoulders.

"Are you sure you're feeling okay?" I asked again.

"Yep. Fine. Just gotta go to the bathroom," Luke said.

Before I could respond, Luke got up from his seat, his coat in hand, and almost ran toward what I hoped was the restroom instead of the exit.

I didn't know what to do next, so I sat and waited as if all was normal and Luke would return shortly . . . I hoped. A waiter came by and placed two cups of coffee on the table. Though I never turned down coffee, I thought it was odd, because we hadn't ordered any.

As the server left, Luke returned.

He put his coat back on the seat next to him and added cream to his coffee as if everything was normal.

"You're not going to run away again, are you?" I asked, trying to joke a little.

"Nope," Luke answered.

I noticed his lunaticish demeanor had become more like a cat's who had just eaten a canary.

Before I could utter another word, two pieces of chocolate cake arrived at the table. We hadn't ordered chocolate cake. As the plate hit the table, everything became perfectly clear.

There, on top of the cake in the center of the frosting, was a diamond ring.

And then everything went blurry.

"Will you marry me?" Luke asked, now smiling.

Why? Why did my serious life-altering moments consistently coincide with one another? Was one life-altering change at a time too much to ask for? Someone up there was totally messing with me!

Wedding proposals should only be allowed to come in through the mail so there wasn't the instant pressure of an obligation to say yes. I'd bet the divorce rate would go way down if someone passed a law that required all proposals to go through the mail. Christ! This had been a rough day.

I was scared to death when I looked back up at him. I was scared to death to answer that question again. I was scared to death to be married again. I was scared to death that I still might not be ready for this. I was scared to death of marriage in general, because what I feared most was another failure.

This offer from the Pavilion had opened a little door inside me that I'd closed the day I walked out of The Diamond Mine. If I said I didn't miss it, I'd be lying.

But I looked into Luke's eyes, and I did what I'd done my entire life. I put my feelings and uncertainties aside and based my decision on what he wanted to hear.

"Yes," I answered.

Fall 1992 – twenty-eight years old

Chapter 44

It had taken me a while to get the hang of balancing a job I loved with the man I loved, but so far, I was making it work. We hadn't set a date for the wedding, and while Luke wasn't pressuring me to do so, he consistently tossed subtle hints of quitting my job and planning a family. The pressure was there. Loud and clear.

"You want me to do what?" I asked.

"I want you to manage the club," Nicky answered.

I had known it was coming. Nicky, who I'd learned was very observant and smart, had been hinting about it for weeks.

"I can't do that," I replied. "That would mean working nights. Advertising and campaign planning require day shifts. I don't want to give up the marketing. I like it."

"So, combine the two. Come in later in the day, make your appointments later. People work till 5:00 p.m., ya know. Look, you're the only one who knows how to handle these club people, and you know a lot of them from The Diamond Mine anyway. I need someone that knows this crowd and can control who comes in and who doesn't."

Nicky was right, and I knew it. But managing a dance club? I'd been in this situation before, and I knew the results. Besides, this schedule would not go over well with Luke. He was already complaining that all I talked about was work. Luke wanted me to quit my current job, never mind add additional responsibility and hours. A woman managing a dance club shouldn't be engaged to a good-natured country guy who worked days and was in bed by 9:00 p.m.

Like Carson, Luke was a great guy. Most women would be thrilled with a guy like that. The problem was me, not Luke. But that little closed door inside my head had just been pried open, and opportunity was knocking. Right or wrong, I walked through.

"Okay," I answered.

***

I quickly fell into working six nights a week. Now, after two straight months of Luke and me working completely opposite hours, it had taken a toll on our relationship. I'd promised Luke tonight would be the night I came home early.

I sat in my truck for a few minutes and took several deep breaths before heading home. We had planned to meet at home at six o'clock, and it was now well after eight. The night was going to get ugly. I could feel it in my bones.

I walked into our apartment, knowing a verbal war was imminent. I opened the door, walked into the kitchen, and listened. Nothing. Complete silence.

Maybe he wasn't here. Maybe he'd gotten fed up and left.

I took a glass from the cabinet and poured myself some ice water. I stood, eyes closed, leaning against the kitchen counter, relieved, and exhaled and turned around.

I opened my eyes to find myself inches from Luke. My back was pressed against the kitchen counter, with his arms and hands locked on the countertop, positioned around my waist. Luke was definitely mad. With only one direction to look, my eyes skittishly settled, looking directly into his. It was killing me.

"Hello," he said.

"Hi," I answered softly.

I didn't think I could possibly feel any worse than I did at this moment. It was time to do one of the most emotionally painful things I'd ever do: deeply hurt the man I had previously hurt so many years ago. I was going to once again lie to that very same man because again, I couldn't bring myself to be honest with someone I was supposed to emotionally trust. But this time, it was me making the choice. And this time, as hard as it was going to be, it was right. It wasn't as if it was a spur-of-the-moment decision; it was something I had been asking myself since accepting his ring months ago.

I'd asked myself these same questions daily: Why hadn't I been overjoyed when this man asked me to marry him? Why hadn't we set a date yet? But I knew the answer. I just hated admitting it.

But why did I always choose work? That was not the way life—or love—was supposed to be. This wonderful man, for whatever reason, was happy with who he wanted to think I was. It wasn't fair to either one of us.

By choice, I'd held myself back when I was with Luke. Luke was great, but he was content with life as it was. And there was nothing wrong with that, but my brain was continuously running wild about things I wanted to do and places I wanted to see, and I'd kept most of that from Luke. If he had been the right man for me, I wouldn't have wanted to be anywhere except in his arms.

I knew Luke knew about my dad, and I knew he wondered, but he'd never inquired because Luke was happy having whatever percentage of me he could get, and whether he knew it or not, that wasn't good enough for him. And that wasn't good enough for me either.

The bond we had, or the bond that I thought we had, was based on mythology. It was a fantasy we'd both clung on to and built up for years, born from two tenth-grade hearts in love based on a relationship that had been taken away by forces beyond our control, leaving us wondering what could have been. Luke wanted that very same relationship back. But the fact was, we weren't those kids anymore. Good, bad, or otherwise, we'd grown and developed into the people we were now.

Unanswered questions, unfulfilled desires, and mixed-up frustrations had been in our hearts, stirring in emotional limbo for over a decade due to a decision made by my fucked-up parents. Once reunited, neither of us had been willing to consider failure in the relationship. Luke was still living our high school relationship, the one taken from us, not this one. And accepting this new me, the grown-up me, or even things about the old me that didn't fit his pretty picture, such as child abuse, wasn't an option. Luke had quickly brushed off with noticeable discomfort all attempts I'd made to open up with him about my years of abuse. That was a place Luke did not want to visit.

A real relationship should be with a man who wanted to know all of me and love me as a complete package. And as much as I loved Luke, I knew it was time to move on—separately. I would miss Luke, but this was the right choice.

I looked into Luke's eyes, knowing they were eyes that would love, take care of, and support me forever. But it was time to walk away from those eyes.

"This isn't working anymore," I said.

"This isn't working anymore because you don't want it to work," Luke said, staying right where he was.

I think he expected a fight, but I didn't have it in me.

"I know," I said, trying to look down, away from those eyes.

"You know? Why do you want this to end?" Luke asked as his voice grew louder, pulling away. "Do you want to date other people? Is that it? Are there guys in the club you want to go out with?" Luke was angry.

My mind raced.

"No, there is no one, but . . . I'm not sure I don't want to date other people. And I know a relationship shouldn't be this way." Tears now streamed down my cheeks.

"What's wrong with us? Why don't you give me a chance to take care of you? You don't have to work the way you do," Luke said calmly.

"I know. That's just it. I know you'd always be there for me, but I want to work. I think it's some kind of dumb sickness, but I'm not ready to change it. It's not healthy for us to stay together. I've had this issue with past relationships too. That's why I try to avoid them, but when you came along again after years of wondering what we might have been like together, I couldn't *not* give it a chance. I'm not sorry for this second opportunity to be together, I'm only sorry I can't make it work . . . forever. As weird as it may seem, I think I am too young for the commitment you need. I'm not ready to stop working like this." I stopped for a breather.

He stood in silence and then spoke two words in disbelief.

"Too young?"

"Yes, but not numerically. It's because I'm still growing and changing inside, and I have no idea where I'm going to end up, like *no* idea. But I know the odds of me settling down in a Norman Rockwell-type farm home in a simple country town are slim to none. Maybe we are not destined to be together like we thought?" I stopped to gather my thoughts.

"We're different," I continued. "You . . . you know exactly where you are going to be ten years from now. Things might change a little here and there, but you'll live in Forestville, eat spaghetti at your mom's on Sundays, and still be working the same job or something very similar. Who knows, maybe you'll have inherited the company by then, but basically, you'll still be the same. Am I right?"

"What's wrong with that? You are right, except you've left out the part about YOU being with me and raising children together. I planned on spending the rest of my life with the girl I fell in love with back in high school."

God. And I thought I couldn't feel any worse.

"I wish I could say I felt the same way. And I'm not one-hundred-percent sure I'm making the right choice, but this is the right time. I might find out years from now that I made a bad choice by letting you go, and that will be on me. But if I don't do this now, I will spend the rest of my life wondering. It's not that I don't love you. It's just that I'm not sure I love you enough. I think there's something inside me that still needs to learn what part of me is missing. I need to learn how to love completely. Believe me, when a person chooses work over a great guy, there's something wrong with *that* person. Right now, that person is me, and I need to fix me."

"And you think you're gonna figure it out while managing a night club in Providence?" Luke asked.

"No. I don't think so. But I know I won't fix it living in the country, raising a child."

"I think you're wrong."

"I know you do, but I need to try."

Luke looked at me, said nothing, and walked out the door.

The apartment was completely silent again. I went to bed, turned the radio on low volume, and cried myself to sleep listening to "Unanswered Prayers" by Garth Brooks. The song reminded me of Luke because I knew that someday he would thank God for not answering the prayer to bring us back together forever. I drifted to sleep with that song in my head . . . .

She was the one that I'd wanted for all times.

And each night I'd spend prayin' that God would make her mine.

And if he'd only grant me this wish I wished back then,
I'd never ask for anything again.
Sometimes I thank God for unanswered prayers.
Remember when you're talkin' to the man upstairs
That just because he doesn't answer doesn't mean he don't care.
Some of God's greatest gifts are unanswered prayers.

Summer 1995 – thirty years old

Chapter 45

I stood over the second-floor railing, admiring the beautiful day, finally taking a breather from the afternoon rush. Narragansett Bay was wonderfully serene on weekend days when the tankers were gone and yachts and sailboats filled the marina. Working in an atmosphere overlooking the bay was a far cry from a fallout shelter of a strip joint full of G-strings and fake boobs.

"So, have you seen the sound guy today?" Jenna asked.

"No. Why? And stop with the instigating," I snapped.

Jenna, an energetic, redheaded young bartender, pretty and full of life, was a fantastic worker. She was one of the few bartenders who genuinely had an interest in the business and not just how much she made in tips. She was also my friend.

Jenna had become my closest female friend since Gabriella had married some Italian tough guy named Rocky. I still talked to Gabby a lot, but she was married, and we each led separate and busy lives. I'd grown close with a handful of employees, but most of all, I had become close friends with the owner, Nicky.

Nicky and I had become more like brother-and-sister besties. He was married with two small children, worked a full-time job at his recycling company, and still found time to spend far too many hours at the restaurant. Nicky was, as I was, a workaholic. We'd had our share of bad days and our share of knockdown fights, but when it came right down to it, he was always there for me. I'd found a quality in him that I hadn't known in anyone else. He was what I'd expected my uncle to be like, but where my uncle had eventually let me down, Nicky had not. Maybe it was because he had two terrific parents. I had always sensed that Nicky saw more of me, the *real* me, than others did. We had a unique bond that neither one of us ever mentioned, yet we were both aware of its existence.

"Yeah, where's the sound guy today?" Nicky chimed in as he snuck up behind Jenna.

"Chris, come on, the guy said if you agreed to go out with him, he'd chop off all that luscious hair for you. So, you have to go out with him!" Jenna demanded.

"Jenna, get real. We've both heard our share of ridiculous lines guys have used to get a date," I said.

"So, what!" Jenna said.

"She hasn't seen him, has she?" Nicky asked.

"Nope!" Jenna answered.

"Awww. I'll come back when this gets more interesting." He walked away, laughing.

"What the hell is he laughing at?" I asked.

I referred to this guy as "Sound Guy" because I could never remember his name. Sound Guy had a company that rented audio equipment to our venue for the bands we hired. It was much easier and made for a more consistent sound for the venue, and in all honesty, most musicians would rather spend their money trying to *look* like rock stars than invest in professional audio gear. I wasn't a big fan of musicians or sound guys, for that matter. As far as I was concerned, they were all the same. My years in the club world had taught me that most musicians sleep late, drink too much, take drugs, and have sex with women aside from their significant other, usually while their wives or girlfriends were out making money to support them. I was aware that my opinion was a bit of a generalization and there were exceptions, but Sound Guy looked like your typical band guy. And, if by some slim chance I turned out to be wrong about this particular guy, I wasn't ready to admit it yet.

"How come you won't just go out with him? When was the last time you went on a date?" Jenna asked.

"I've had dates!" I argued.

"Okay. When was the last time you had a date that really mattered to you?" Jenna asked. "And I don't count guys that you dated just to be nice or just because you were bored at the time. I know you. I know when you're serious, and so far, I've never seen you 'guy-serious.' "

"You mean real people? Real potential-serious-relationship kind of guys?" I asked.

"Yeah."

"The last serious guy I dated, I was engaged to, and that was almost three years ago. But there have been others, sort of. Besides, what does this have to do with that? I'm not looking for anything serious—ever! I like my life just the way it is."

And that was the truth. I did like my life just the way it was. My life was socially perfect. My friends were mostly co-workers, but I liked it that way, and I thoroughly enjoyed my job. I'd spent the past three years learning about me. I'd done things that the previous me would've never thought of doing, including getting wicked drunk a few times. Once with Gabriella, we'd even ended up at a motorcycle gang's clubhouse, playing pool with gang members till 4:00 a.m. Between the years at The Diamond Mine and now as manager of this club, I'd bonded with more walks of life than I'd ever imagined, good and bad.

I had grown to be a successful young woman in a respected position who had learned, out of survival, how to deal with humans of all kinds. I had the freedom to do what I wanted when I wanted, and for the first time in my life, I was finally *living* my life—for me! In fact, I was perfectly content.

Working hard came naturally to me. But the having-fun part was a new experience I'd learned from Nicky. Nicky worked hard every day, but when the work was done, it was time to put the work away and have fun.

"Well, maybe you should just get laid then. When was the last time that happened?" Jenna asked.

"Shut up!" I snapped back.

"Sound Guy doesn't seem like the rest of the band people, and he owns his own business, right? You're the one who makes sure he's here for every band date, so you know he's responsible. Sound Guy seems legit, and besides, he's hot. Why don't you just sleep with him?" Jenna asked, as if she had just come up with some bright idea.

"Okay, Einstein, that's enough. I know he's hot. And maybe he's not the same as other band guys . . . maybe. But Sound Guy is not my type, and long hair grosses me out."

"Yeah, but you didn't have to *tell* him that. I couldn't believe it!" Jenna said.

"Oh, come on, the guy wouldn't let up. He keeps saying he wants to marry me! Christ! I don't even know his friggin' name. And you heard me tell him that I would go out with him *once* if he cut that long hair. So, I offered a solution." I laughed.

"And if he walks in with short hair? What then?" Jenna asked, not letting up at all.

I stopped to think about it.

"Um, Sound Guy said he hasn't cut it since seventh grade. So, yeah, I'll take my chances, and *if* he does cut his hair, sure, I'll keep my word and go on the one date. Satisfied?" I asked.

"Yep. Oh, and here he comes . . . ," Jenna noted, and walked away.

I turned back to the opposite position of where we had been leaning and looked out onto the bay.

"Thank God. I thought she'd never leave," I whispered to myself. "Who the hell is she to talk? She doesn't have a—"

I stopped talking to myself, as someone tapped me on the shoulder.

Two words came out of my mouth, which I had no control of: "Oh, shit!"

His only reply was "What time do you get out of work tomorrow?"

It was the sound guy. And his long, thick, flowing black hair was *gone*!

Huh! What a difference! Okay, yeah—he was hot, like really hot. Contrary to what I had my friends believing, even with the long, icky hair, I had thought he was hot, and I had noticed he had melt-me brown eyes, but I'd never actually thought about dating him. I couldn't even begin to list the reasons why. Some had to do with him, but most had to do with me, as I was content in my safe and happy life.

I didn't want to even think about going through another relationship only to find myself sitting in the same place, reciting a similar version of why I wanted to work instead of settling down. If I'd learned anything about myself, it was that I was not very good at relationships.

But Jenna was right, I really hadn't dated anyone for years. And besides, one date due to losing a bet wasn't considered dating anyway.

There had been guys, but never a guy like this. Never a guy who'd made it a point to get my attention like this. This guy had been haunting—or more like hunting—me for weeks, maybe longer, though *I'd* just started noticing weeks ago. The rest of my friends said he'd been on my path for much longer, but I'd never said more than a simple hi, much less have an entire conversation. But lately, he'd been in my face often enough that I couldn't *not* notice!

Beyond the long, thick black hair down to his ass and the work clothes, Sound Guy was definitely nice looking, but so were half the guys in Rhode Island. There wasn't a shortage of nice-looking people in this state. Providence was like a small version of Hollywood with twice the vanity. Maybe that was it? This guy wasn't like Providence guys. This guy seemed real and down to earth, a rare quality in a person who worked in the music-and-club business.

And he wouldn't give up! He'd been selling himself to me as a one-of-a-kind product that I couldn't live without. Yet he'd managed to make that pitch without sounding obnoxious or egocentric in any way. While Sound Guy had attempted to sell me his down-to-earth and sincere demeanor, no matter what he said or how he said it, he'd managed to make me laugh. And I'd always turned him down for the same reasons: "I don't date guys with long hair, and I don't date guys that do drugs." I didn't really know if he did drugs, so I was admittedly just stereotyping, but he'd never denied it when I'd thrown that bait out there, so I didn't think I was wrong.

And each time, he'd walk away in defeat, and each time, my stomach was left with a warm, fuzzy feeling I hadn't felt in years.

Finally, after staring at his face as if I was trying to read a foreign language, I heard myself answer, "About six o'clock. Why?"

"Good. Then I'll meet you here, and we'll have our date," Sound Guy said.

Then he turned and strolled away as if our conversation had been as typical as talking about the weather.

"Hey, Sound Guy. Do you have a real name?" I asked.

"Yeah, it's not Sound Guy, it's Patrick," he answered, but kept walking.

I gazed at his back, amazed at what had just happened. When he turned down the stairs, I saw Jenna's head pop out of the hall.

She pointed at me and started laughing out loud.

I motioned for her to shut up and then turned back toward the bay, wondering what I'd just gotten myself into.

It was late August, and at almost midnight, it was still hot and humid. I sat with Patrick atop a tiny hill in a secluded Benefit Street park. We overlooked the beautiful and newly constructed Waterplace Park that ran along the Woonasquatucket River in Providence. Leaning against a rock on the ground, I thought this was by far the weirdest date I'd ever had.

Patrick hadn't stopped asking rapid-fire personal questions since our night had begun. I'd only known him for a few short hours . . . well, okay, we'd been work acquaintances for a few months now, but I'd only really started getting to know him a few hours ago. And in the few hours of this first date, I thought he'd learned more about me just from asking than all of my previous boyfriends combined. It had freaked me out at first, but after fielding question after question, it was clear that he had a genuine interest in who I was instead of the same old, mundane first-date favorite-color-hobbies-and-zodiac-sign bullshit.

Even though it was somewhat overwhelming, I was okay and comfortable opening up to this guy for whatever reason.

In return, I learned just as much about him because, with every question he asked, I felt obligated to counter-ask. Patrick wasn't without baggage. He'd had his share of drug issues and psychotic ex-girlfriends. He, too, had married for exactly the same reasons I had, because other people had wanted it more than him. He'd also gone through with a similarly elaborate wedding for the good of his wife and mother. But instead of burying himself in work, Patrick openly admitted that he'd self-medicated to escape reality, mostly with alcohol, and owned up to a laundry list of past indulgences like pot, cocaine, and some other hippie drugs I'd never heard of, but he said that cocaine had been his preferred escape over the past couple of years. I made it crystal clear that I would never be in a relationship with anyone that had those kinds of habits and was surprised at his response: "I know, you told me that a couple of weeks ago. That was when I stopped."

"What?"

"Well, you said you didn't date guys that did drugs, and I wanted to date you, so I decided to give that up. Besides, meeting you made me realize I didn't want to die by accident."

"You're kind of insane, you know." I laughed but continued to talk.

"So, you haven't taken any drugs since you started stalking me?" I wondered if I was getting myself into a situation I couldn't get out of.

"Nope."

"You do remember me telling you I have never done any drugs in my life, right? Including weed?"

"Yep. I remember everything you've ever said," he stated.

"And you're cool with never taking drugs ever again?"

"Yep."

"Why?"

"Because you finally went out with me."

"Oh. Thanks. I don't feel any pressure now."

"You shouldn't."

"Yeah. Okay. C'mon. I'm serious."

"I am too. I'm all done with that. I promise. And I won't break a promise to you."

Who the hell was this guy?

***

Patrick and I had seen each other every night for the last three weeks. So much for one date! Things seemed to be moving at the speed of light, and even though I had no complaints, it was far from my norm. Every day was a new adventure in conversation, and although I was consensually okay with the intense, nonstop inquisition, I did find that it left me raw at times. But even so, my gut said, "Just go with it." My heart, on the other hand, was very protective of itself and a bit apprehensive.

I had just finished working for the night and was sitting on the edge of the empty stage outside in the parking lot of the Pavilion under a tent we had rented for a John Cafferty and The Beaver Brown Band concert. Patrick was still working, breaking down sound equipment from the show that had ended less than an hour earlier. The tent was empty except for the two of us.

"Wanna go over to Wickenden Street for a late-night pizza?" Patrick asked.

"Sure. Sounds good to me."

He continued wrapping speaker cables and packing boxes while we talked.

"Can I ask you something personal?"

"Sure. Why ask permission now? You haven't stopped asking questions since Thursday," I said.

"This one's different," he said, still working.

"Okay. Shoot," I said, expecting some crazy sex question like "Have you ever done it in an elevator?" or something.

"Who abused you?" Patrick asked.

"What?" I asked quietly, wondering if I had actually heard what he had just said.

He walked closer to me and stopped.

"You were abused as a kid, right? I don't know if it was sexual or physical, but I am pretty sure it happened. I just want to know who did it and if you are okay. Or if you want to talk to someone about it?" he said, as if it wasn't any big deal at all.

"It was my dad, and I am okay, but talking about it would be cool," I answered, as if the question was as standard as he'd made it seem.

"Good. Let's go to your house tonight. Okay?"

"Sure."

I'd thought I played it cool, though my insides were a volcanic pit of molten lava, apprehensive excitement, and near panic-stricken fear, each fighting for a welcomed chance of escape after years of being stifled and secretly hidden.

Patrick learned, three hours and three shared bottles of wine later, literally everything I could remember about my childhood. I cried, and he held me. Patrick asked questions, and I answered.

He asked, "How often did it happen?"

I answered.

"Where were you the first time you had sex?" I asked.

"At summer camp," Patrick answered. "How old were you the first time you had sex?"

The subject was so absurd and horrible we turned toward sarcastic humor a few times to help make it through, as only those who felt as comfortable with each other as we did could use humor that way.

Maybe it was the multiple bottles of wine or perhaps it was the God-honest truth, but for the first time in my life, I could answer honestly.

"Four," I said, laughing hysterically at the horrific truth.

He hit me with a pillow but couldn't help but laugh too.

Our relationship continued just as fast and intensely as it had started, and by early fall, I had come to learn that Patrick was everyone I'd never dated. He moved at the speed of light, and I happily rode by his side. He was everything I had purposely kept myself away from for fear of finding myself.

Patrick wasn't afraid to ask questions. *Any* question! It had freaked me out at first, but that night filled with excessive wine and insane honesty allowed us to conquer hills I'd never been able to climb, so the fear of answering questions faded and was now a natural part of our relationship. In some ways, he was a bit like an innocent child. Children have no fear—or, at least, *most* children. A child would ask anything that came to mind just because that child wanted to know.

As adults, we stop asking things we want to know because society and our upbringings have built certain social constructs, walls even, to keep our behaviors within the boundaries of what is considered "acceptable" or "polite." And most adults get stuck within those walls, opting to never venture outside of them for fear that they'll offend or otherwise cross some boundary of social acceptability. Good or bad, Patrick had none of these boundaries.

Patrick had encouraged me to open a securely locked door leading to a virtual safe room full of secrets. But more than encouragement alone, Patrick had voluntarily walked into that terrifying safe room by my side. And together, we'd taken the first step and unlocked the door, a door that should've been unlocked years ago, and mentally released a room jam-packed with emotionally hoarded clutter.

It was an unusually pleasant late-November morning. I sat in the parking lot of the Pavilion employee garage, trying to come up with a respectful way to tell my boss, a guy who had become more of a family member to me than any member of my actual family, that it was time for me to move on.

I couldn't believe I was leaving Providence, a city I'd come to love, and moving to Connecticut to live with the sound guy. Even more unbelievable was that I'd made a conscious choice, with zero fear, to value my relationship over a job I loved, and I was unquestionably okay with that.

I thought about the path that had led me to make this obvious choice.

Children innately trust their parents from birth, and once conscience of parental attention, most young children place pleasing their parents at priority number one.

Adults are well aware of a child's mission to please and the power they hold because of that infinite goal. It's a parent's choice to use that power for good or evil, but those who use it to steal innocence from a child are heartless, vile monsters. A child abuse case is reported every nine minutes. But so many of us, for various reasons, walk the earth not reporting. Humans capable of acts like that shouldn't exist, but they do. I learned at a very young age that life can be terribly unfair.

We are born with zero life experience, yet we are immediately cast as decision makers. If I cry, will they hurt me? If I don't cry, will I starve? In reality, life is one big bucket of rapid-fire decisions, resulting in expected and unexpected outcomes.

Growing up, we are often forced-fed questions we're not experienced enough to answer correctly only to realize, years later, that our inexperienced decisions have left us with life-altering consequences.

I've learned that people can make poor choices out of greed or selfishness or to cut corners, and some, out of pure weakness. Me? I was weak, and life has slapped me with some serious reality checks along the way.

But the consequences of choices can linger, stain, and even scar. I think most of us keep our bad choices, whether intentional or not, stored away in emotional safety-deposit boxes, hoping never to have to face those choices or consequences again.

Is that healthy? Maybe. Maybe not. Some humans can justify things better than others.

It took thirty years on this planet to finally reach a point where I could recognize my mistakes and learn from them, allowing me to break the cycle of being doomed to repeat them. And that's no easy task for anyone.

The truth is, it took me far too long to learn that the saying "After all, they're the only family you've got" doesn't necessarily mean you need to always fall on your sword for them.

Today, I am very aware that only *I* have walked in these shoes, and no one will ever be able to pressure me into doing something I know is wrong again. I am entirely aware that guilt, when used persuasively, can be an overpowering weapon, and I've learned that sometimes it's okay to sidestep a bullet to avoid getting wounded.

All families are different. And families, whether good or bad, are not legally bound to be together solely out of sharing the same blood. The definition of "family" shouldn't be relegated to only those we are genetically linked to. Families are formed from the people that support, care, understand, and love you for who you are. Anyone can make their own family.

Still sitting in my truck, I asked myself, "Have I made some wrong choices in life?" Yes. Yes, I absolutely had.

But those choices, good and bad, have taught me many lessons. Lessons that I needed to learn. Life has taught me and vividly shown me that childhood sexual abuse, no matter how badly we feel the need to hide it, will brand you like a scarlet letter. I believe most abused children that have chosen to survive protect their awful secret. And others, *if* they survive, are sometimes forced to continue living with unhealable emotional scars. It took me over three decades to realize that I've managed to survive this against the odds and end up in comparatively better shape than many others like me. For that, I am immeasurably grateful.

Maybe someday I'll be strong enough to help others survive too.

Was I making the right choice now? I knew my gut was telling me that I was, and unlike many other choices I'd made, I was not going into this one knowingly regretting it before it began. Because, for the first time in my life, I was making a decision for the good of myself. And I felt with that choice, unlike others, I was going to emotionally succeed.

Would I live happily ever after? Christ! Who the hell really knew that?

But I did know one thing: I knew it was time to open a new door and toss that emotional safety-deposit box away.

It's almost implausible to think the two men that did me so wrong also gave me the strength to continue to grow. No child should ever experience one second of abuse, but that man I called Dad inadvertently gave me an innate inner strength to survive things that so easily bring others down. And from a man I once idolized, respected, and loved like the dad I never had, who chose to allow greed and power supersede his morals, ethics, and love, I, to this day, find myself unequivocally balanced for essential life lessons learned from him. He was right; my future is doing something on my own.

I had no idea where I'd be ten years from now or even two years from now, but I knew it was time to step out of that secure, comfortable shell. It finally didn't feel frightening, foreign, or wrong.

I opened the door of my truck, got out, and headed up to say good-bye to a place I'd likely never see again.

Surprisingly, previous problems seemed undoubtedly simple, like 70s-TV-*Brady Bunch* simple. And I find it ironic that I, of all people, have chosen to relate my life to not only a family but also one of pop culture's happiest families. I took my last trip up the Pavilion staircase, silently singing an aptly fitting song from a *Brady Bunch* episode:

"When it's time to change, you got to rearrange who you are and what you're gonna be. A little bit of living, a little bit of growing, all adds up to you."

End

Epilogue

We all know that our horrid memories will never really disappear. The best we can hope for is that they'll fade deep into the background as we learn to accept and come to terms with the fact that what happened to us was not our fault, while we try to put distance between ourselves and the situations that once controlled us.

Looking back, I'd tell my younger self to speak out. Especially now, since we've evolved into a society where children who never had a voice before now have the loudest voice they've ever had, with resources that did not exist when I was growing up.

The adults, the caregivers, these people that we helplessly trust and depend on should never abuse their positions of power by stripping us of our innocence and self-worth.

I had initially written my story twenty-plus years ago, mainly as an exercise in purging myself of the toxicity by putting it all on paper. I had this naïve notion that maybe this could help others suffering too. I quickly learned that it costs thousands of dollars to have a work professionally edited and prepped for publishing. I was in no financial position to spend that kind of money, yet I was determined to make it happen.

So, I created Monster Mini Golf, a fun indoor family entertainment concept, in hopes of working a simple, rewarding job while raising funds needed to edit the book.

Why monsters?

To me, building fun monsters was a therapeutic, ironic way to vent while hopefully creating a happy escape for others who maybe needed a little break from life now and then.

Twenty years and thirty Monster Mini Golf locations later, the business admittedly consumed me. And if you've just read my book then you know that it's kind of a pattern, but hey... some things never change. This pandemic has allowed me to take a step back, to breathe a little, refocus, and accomplish what I'd set out to do so many years ago.

It took me a while to understand that I didn't lose my inner strength. I'd just spent years allowing others to condition me into weakness. We are all born with an inner strength. I hope my story reminds others like me that they too can find the buried strength and perseverance needed to survive.

About the Author

Author, Christina Vitagliano and husband Patrick recently celebrated their 23rd anniversary and live together happily in Las Vegas with their two four-legged children (okay, Bulldogs) and a foul-mouthed, African gray rescue parrot.

Printed in Great Britain
by Amazon

83502752R00215